The ABC of Modern Biography

The ABC of Modern Biography

Nigel Hamilton and Hans Renders

AUP

Translation Hans Renders, thanks to Arthur Eaton, Madelon Franssen, Eric Palmen and Lodewijk Verduin.

Illustrations: Stichting AD & L
Cover picture: Nigel Hamilton and Hans Renders, Paris, November 2015

Cover design: Robbie Smits
Lay-out: Crius Group, Hulshout

ISBN   978 94 6298 871 2
e-ISBN   978 90 4854 102 7 (pdf)
e-ISBN   978 90 4854 103 4 (ePub)
NUR   680

© N. Hamilton, J.W. Renders / Amsterdam University Press B.V., Amsterdam 2018

All rights reserved. Without limiting the rights under copyright reserved above, no part of this book may be reproduced, stored in or introduced into a retrieval system, or transmitted, in any form or by any means (electronic, mechanical, photocopying, recording or otherwise) without the written permission of both the copyright owner and the author of the book.

Contents

Introduction	7
A is for Authorization	9
B is for Biography	16
C is for Composition	25
D is for Dictionaries of Biography	33
E is for Ethics	41
F is for Facts	51
G is for Group Biography	59
H is for History	68
I is for Identity	77
J is for Journalism	85
K is for Kings, or Rulers	93
L is for Life Writing	102
M is for Memoir, Memoirs and Autobiography	111
N is for Non-Fiction	120
O is for Obituary	129
P is for Psychology	139

Q is for Quotation	149
R is for Religion	158
S is for Sex	167
T is for Theory	176
U is for U-turn	186
V is for the Visual Arts	194
W is for War	202
X is for Xanadu	210
Y is for Youth	219
Z is for Zigzagging to the End	229
Bibliography	234
Index	241
About the authors	249

Introduction

Biography may be the world's second oldest profession, but it has recently undergone a tremendous transformation – and expansion. Technology has loosened the world's tongue, both in writing about the lives of real people, and people writing about their own real lives.

As more people produce biography and autobiography, however, there is a corresponding vagueness about what biography *is* today: what the word now implies, its modern rules – or lack of rules ('alternative facts') – and how the genre is changing shape, character and purpose across different platforms, from print to celluloid, and from digital pixels to hip-hop musicals.

No dictionary of biography today, unfortunately, provides an easily accessible map of modern biography. Such dictionaries still earnestly strive to list the names of worthy people who have been the subjects of biography, from President John Adams to General Jan Zizka; they are biographical *Who's Whos*, in other words.

This small book attempts to do something quite different. Written by two practising writers and teachers of biography, *The ABC of Modern Biography* seeks to describe, briefly and cogently, the new compass of modern biography via an ABC – from 'A for Authorization' to 'Z for Zigzagging to the End'. Our aim is not to be definitive – always a mistake for cartographers as well as biographers – but to provide the first simple overview of modern biography as it is understood and practised today, across different media and the globe, 2,000 years after Plutarch.

We hope *The ABC of Modern Biography* will amuse, entertain and inform the curious reader – and clear up a number of fallacies and misunderstandings as it does so. For example, it is extraordinary how many people still imagine a modern biographer needs 'authorization' (see 'A for Authorization') to write the biography of a prominent person, or consider it wrong for a biographer to 'kiss and tell' (see 'S for Sex').

Of all recent trends in our culture, modern biography – now often mislabelled life-writing (see 'L for Life Writing') – has become, almost overnight, the most elastic, vibrant, contested, controversial and popular genre, from blogs to biopics. It deserves our attention – and reflection.

In academia, there is new pressure at a number of universities to theorize biography, to help explain what is happening and why. In the meantime, this small work will hopefully pique the general reader's curiosity about the current (and yet so ancient) phenomenon we still call biography, in many of its contemporary guises, across the five oceans and seven continents of our modern world.

Enjoy – for at least now you'll have someone to argue with!

Nigel Hamilton
Hans Renders

 **is for Authorization**

What is a 'biography' and what does it mean, today, for a biography to be 'authorized'?

Simply put: a biography is a book written by a biographer about a specific individual. The biography is considered 'authorized' if the subject of the biography has read the text and declared the facts revealed therein to be correct. The same practice exists in journalism, where it is considered customary to allow interviewees to read passages in which they are quoted, prior to publication. The final responsibility for the interview, however, lies with the interviewer who created the interview.

Sometimes an interviewee attempts to stop publication, or the broadcast of an interview, after it has been concluded. Is this right? To help illustrate the answer to this question, let us turn to a well-known British television programme: *Traffic Abuse*.

Without exception, every episode of this reality programme shows at least one individual who becomes irate after being stopped by the police. The fines and tickets are not the cause of all this anger; it is the fact that the cameras are rolling. Nine times out of ten, the people in question make the same objection: 'you can't film me.' This, however, is a misunderstanding. Anyone who is out in public can be seen, filmed and commented on, whether we like it or not. Of course, there are standards regarding good taste and relevance to society, or other such concerns – such as the rise of the paparazzi and 'Gotcha' journalism: the cringe-worthy side of our right to gather news freely. But that is simply the price we pay for this core value: the right to be able to comment on and criticize what we encounter in public life. Art, science and political expression can thrive only in an environment where dissent is tolerated. Criticism sharpens the mind.

Anyone who has ever read police reports will immediately notice how the suspects' confessions are all remarkably similar. The illiterate petty thief uses the same language as the highly-educated fraudster. This is not really true, of course, but it is what happens once confessions are put into writing. A confession is the outcome of a negotiation. The suspect speaks, but the officer's written account uses official phrasing and terminology that can later be linked to legal texts known to the officer, but often not to the suspect. Should the petty thief sign the confession, it becomes canonical, so to speak, even though it is in someone else's words. The same phenomenon also occurs in biography: that is to say, with biographies of living people, or the recent dead, where there are relatives – widows, siblings, trustees of the estate – to deal with.

The biographer and the biographical subject (or legal representatives) negotiate over the business of access, as well as permission to quote material. In the case of 'authorized biographies,' however, this negotiation is always suspect. The parties involved may have spoken to each other only four times, or they might have spoken regularly over a period of years. In the end, the subjects declare with their imprimatur that they have not been misquoted or misunderstood. This, in theory, is modern 'authorization.' However, something else often creeps into these authorization agreements, namely the subject's belief that their imprimatur serves to indicate that they agree with what the biographer has written. Things become even more complicated when the subject of a biography demands in advance that the biography can only be published if the entire text has been 'authorized.' This is ludicrous: no serious biography is based solely on interviews, yet here we see the subject demanding the right to 'authorize' *all* quoted documents, letters and diaries, even when they were written by others.

Perhaps not everyone is clear about what a true biography is today; and that is the subject of this ABC. We live in a time of individual self-representation, and set ourselves the goal of gathering as many 'likes' as possible. We 'endorse' others on networking sites for their fabulous qualities and skills – in the hope that the gesture is reciprocated. This is not a terrible thing: everyone understands that we are selling something on Facebook and other social media sites, and that something is ourselves. This is the new Social Contract; which brings us to what a biography most certainly is *not*.

A good biography is not a book of praise, even though this misconception is perpetuated by the unending stream of so-called 'biographies' of stars, athletes, top chefs and other Famous People. These biographies are always 'authorized.' In reality, though, we are dealing with texts by ghost-writers hired by Famous People. In both the Netherlands and Britain there appears to be an endless deluge of these books; especially in England, where they are often called 'memoirs.' Like pulp fiction, they also exist in the United States. A recent example from early 2015 is the American actor Jon Cryer's *So That Happened: A Memoir;* in reality, a book of tall tales about his alleged experiences of sex and drugs during his time in the film industry. In a 'publisher's note', the publisher, Penguin, reveals that it is 'committed to publishing works of quality and integrity' – thereby washing its hands of the story – the experiences and words being 'the author's alone.' Not even the author's, as it turns out. Secreted in the Acknowledgements at the back of the book, Cryer admits that the book was written with a 'collaborator,' Robert Abele.

A typical example of so-called 'authorized biography' is that of *Game of Thrones* actress Carice van Houten, who openly admitted that she had negotiated with journalist Ab Zagt to have her 'biography' written. The announcement that the Dutch journalist Maarten Bax, who had previously written the authorized biography of the famous football siblings Frank and Ronald de Boer, would be writing the 'authorized biography' of the infamous kickboxer Badr Hari is another example. The press release announcing this book contained a revealing quote: 'This is the only authorized biography about me, Badr Hari. All others tell untruths, fairy tales. It is time to tell my story, and set the record straight. I have granted sports journalist Maarten Bax an insight into my life.' For his part, Louis van Gaal, the famous Manchester United coach, announced in a press release that his biography was 'the only biography written by himself'! Only too true! But such statements are a sad slur on the profession of serious biography.

Saddest of all is the reaction of self-serving stars and their fans when a biography is published that is not 'authorized.' Kitty Kelley, Oprah Winfrey's biographer, experienced this first-hand a few years ago. Kelley had also written a biography of Frank Sinatra. Would we have learned that Sinatra most certainly had ties with the mafia if that biography been 'authorized'? Kelley was the target of withering criticism and suffered many cold shoulders for *Oprah*, in which she showed how Oprah had embellished the story of her successful career and had even lied outright about the identity of her father. In response, Kelley published an article in *The American Scholar*, a quarterly magazine on literature, art, and science, which every biographer of a 'star' should read. Her essay, entitled 'Unauthorized, but Not Untrue,' is very revealing. She mentions how Oprah's management labelled her biography 'unauthorized,' almost as if this were a crime. Since the famed television celebrity had not been involved in the writing of the book, and had not given it her blessing, this was considered grounds for a boycott: potential readers felt they would be betraying their beloved heroine if they read the book. Well-known interviewer Larry King boycotted Kelley so as to avoid endangering his good relationship with Oprah. American talk-show host Barbara Walters proclaimed on the popular *Today* show that 'unauthorized' biographies were only written 'to dig dirt'. She held up a copy of *Oprah*. 'Who do you think knows best?' exclaimed Walters into her microphone, like a demagogue. 'Oprah herself or Kitty Kelley, the biographer?' You can guess the answer. None of the television stations carrying *The Oprah Winfrey Show* invited Kelley onto any of their news or entertainment programmes to talk about her biography…

Another fascinating case-study that is rife with misunderstandings concerns the biography of the world-famous Dutch composer Reinbert de Leeuw. Newspaper articles revealed how De Leeuw and his biographer, Thea Derks, had discussed in advance how the biography would be written; in fact, De Leeuw had initiated contact with the chosen publisher. Once she was appointed and given access to De Leeuw's archives, Derks got straight to work. Friction arose along the way, however, because Derks did not stick to De Leeuw's version, or vision, of himself. De Leeuw complained that Derks was writing too little about this and too much about that. She had overemphasized the story of his youth, and had made glaring omissions by barely writing about his friendship with the author Harry Mulisch, as well as a certain Piet Veenstra… From remarks made by both Derks and De Leeuw about the whole affair, it is that clear both of them fell victim to the misconception that is 'authorization.' The musician had promised, in a written agreement with the publisher, that he would not refuse authorization unless he considered the content 'unreasonable'. This clause effectively limited any criticism of De Leeuw in the biography, since the composer could dictate what was 'reasonable.' In retrospect, it seems incomprehensible that De Leeuw, Derks and the publisher all signed up to this ridiculous agreement. To add to the confusion, the contract stipulating 'authorization' as a condition for publication was written only *after* Derks had noticed De Leeuw was not giving her the freedom to do her professional job. However, in a three-way conflict in which each party had their own agenda, they did have one thing in common: they all authorized the perfect recipe for trouble!

Derks felt censored, even though she had unwisely signed the agreement. De Leeuw was troubled by the fact that his biographer had approached all sorts of people for their opinions and memories. He therefore withheld his 'authorization' of the final product, but was unable to explain fully in public the reasons why – understandably, because he obviously did not want to risk bringing even more attention to things he did not wish to see disclosed in his biography. 'For an authorized biography, this is unthinkable', De Leeuw said in an interview.

The conclusion of the affair was unsatisfactory for everyone. Derks published her book with a different publisher. Reviewers called it 'a wonderful monument,' with 'fitting praise and hallelujahs' – but also 'room for real humanity, thank god.'

Oprah could argue that she had not asked Kelley to write her biography, and that she felt pilloried. The same cannot be said of Reinbert de Leeuw and his 'authorization' of a project in which all parties had invested so much time. Why had he not simply written an autobiography or memoir, if he wanted it to be sanitized? The answer: because he knew that a 'biography' would have more status, precisely because it would not be a selfie.

In the United States, biographers are even taken to court for unjustly creating the impression that their work has been 'authorized'. This happened when the son of Audrey Hepburn and the executor of her estate filed a lawsuit against Diana Maychick, due to the latter's biography, published as *Audrey Hepburn: An Intimate Portrait*. According to the legal proceedings, it was not only the title that was at issue, but also the use of the phrase 'full cooperation' in promotional material and the language used on the jacket of the original hardcover. The publishers claimed that she had spent 'countless hours' with Hepburn, but in fact there were only a few phone calls. Maychick was thus creating the impression that her work was authorized – which would hurt the sales of Sean Hepburn Ferrer's *Audrey Hepburn, An Elegant Spirit: A Son Remembers*. Though Ferrer's book appeared more than ten years after Maychick's, the court found in his favour. Maychick was ordered to state, on the cover of a reprint of her biography, that the book was 'unauthorized'. Half of the world's literature has been written because parents and children refuse to understand one other, but the Hepburn case took this to new heights: Hepburn's son was allowed to claim his book was authorized, even though the book's subject had died before the idea for *Audrey Hepburn, An Elegant Spirit* was even conceived!

The simple truth is that a biography has to be independent, free from external influences and devoid of ideology. A biography does not exist to express the established view that the subject has of himself or herself: that is what autobiography or memoir is for.

Take it from us, then: no biographer should enter into an 'authorization' agreement lightly. Such an agreement will *always* involve giving up one's independence. The true biographer's only responsibility is that to his or her own sense of professionalism. Is the biography asking the right questions? Are the sources justified? Is the book well written? People can ultimately judge for themselves whether or not such aims have been accomplished. To those who have little faith in the professionalism of biographers, we therefore recommend that you write your own autobiography, rather than agree to a so-called 'authorized' one. The true biography will come after your death.

Sources: Kitty Kelley, 'Unauthorized, But Not Untrue. The real story of a biographer in a celebrity culture of public denials, media timidity, and legal threats', in: *The American Scholar,* December 1, 2010; Sean Hepburn Ferrer, *Audrey Hepburn, An Elegant Spirit: A Son Remembers* (New York: Atria Books, 2005); Diana Maychick, *Audrey Hepburn: An Intimate Portrait* (New York: Birch lane, 1993); Hans Renders, 'Biography is not a selfie: Authorisation as the creeping transition from autobiography to biography', in: Hans Renders and Binne de Haan (eds), *The Biographical Turn. Lives in History* (London: Routledge, 2017), 159-164; Carl Rollyson, 'Authorized biography', in: Carl Rollyson, *Biography; A User's Guide* (Chicago: Ivan R. Dee, 2008), 10-17.

 **is for Biography**

Biography is the study of the real individual. It is a generic term, covering the multitude of ways in which we record individual human lives, past and present. How we seek to make sense of them: the course of their life's journeys on this earth; their development as individuals; and what 'happened to them.'

Biography responds to this fundamental human curiosity in a way that helps define us as *homo sapiens*. Elephants have long memories and are known to mourn; only humans translate lamentation into memorials – memorials that have evolved over time into more and more sophisticated, artistic and searching reconstructions of an actual individual's life story.

Biography is a field of human interest ultimately dissatisfied by myth or fiction. It is one that seeks answers to our abiding curiosity about humankind by presenting and exploring examples of verifiable women and men who have lived and died, or will die. For death – real death – is the ultimate reality of biography, as opposed to fiction: the stone that Dr. Johnson famously kicked to demonstrate the reality of reality ('I refute it thus,' he dismissed Bishop Berkeley's theory of the non-existence of matter).

We may dress up 'life' for our entertainment, insight and enlightenment in fiction, but the reality is that every actual life eventually comes to a real end – and biography speaks to that awareness.

Biography is not 'a biography.' This misunderstanding has fooled a lot of people over the years; it may explain, indeed, why we study every conceivable aspect of modern culture from Sports History to Gender in our universities, yet rarely, if ever, biography – despite its interdisciplinarity, its popularity, its significance in our society. Biography, *tout court*, is something that is still *done* rather than examined.

This is sad, since biography not only has a long history deriving from ancient funeral rites – the 'commemorative instinct,' as Sir Sidney Lee called it – but today has a reach that extends into every medium and technology, from print to digital media, television to radio, film to art galleries.

Who could imagine a more stunning example of the biographical imperative, as we might call it, than the centenary exhibition of the life and work of Piet Mondrian that was held in The Hague in 2017? In room after room – in drawings, paintings, etchings, letters, photographs, film, hats, ephemera and the like – the extraordinary artistic and human development of one of the pioneers of *De Stijl* was presented, from his early dark Dutch landscapes to his ultimate geometric diamond painting, left tantalizingly unfinished upon his death in exile in New York in 1944.

Development is an important word for those interested in biography. Historians study the 'revolutions' of kingdoms and empires, as Samuel Johnson memorably noted, but biographers study the rise and fall of real *individuals* – and in that evolution, for good and ill, we secretly see reflected our own. It was for that reason that Dr. Johnson despised hagiography – he felt that it was fatuous to present only pure lives, when human beings are impure. In a biography, he urged, the 'most artful writer' is tasked with presenting both 'beautiful *and* base,' and embracing both 'vice *and* virtue.' As he told his biographer James Boswell, 'If a man is to write a *Panegyrick* he may keep vices out of sight, but if he professes to write a *Life* he must represent it really as it was.'

Thousands of biographical works, large and small, are produced every year across the world – yet still we neither teach it, nor examine it in our universities, save a brave few, such as Groningen, Hawaii, Norwich, Aix and Vienna. Why we produce biographies so prolifically, despite our lack of study of the genre, of biography, is the stuff of modern theory.* What we can say is that, like religion, biography is part and parcel of human civilization – but that, unlike religion, it is also closely tied to democratic society. First established as a genre of literature and history in the time of the Greeks and Romans (in the works of Xenephon, Plutarch, Suetonius and other authors), it took off. Since then it has remained an integral manifestation of the way we portray ourselves and our forebears: each generation researching, examining, recording and narrating the life stories of past and present real-life figures, great and small.

Why, we may well ask? Why is that pursuit still so important to us today, after more than 2,000 years?

One clue lies in the *symbolism* inherent in biography. In the same year that aficionados of modern art flocked to The Hague, a new national reckoning took place in the United States regarding memorials – sculptures, for the most part – dedicated during the post-Reconstruction period (i.e., post-1870) to the 'heroes' of the Confederacy: the treasonous, slave-owning southern States that had attempted to secede by force from the Union. The removal of these memorials from plinths and places of public honour in the South provoked a veritable storm of controversy and demonstrations, even fatalities.

Memorializing, in other words, is a political as well as a commemorative act. It can also be artistically controversial – as when a Vietnam National Memorial, destined for the capital of the United States, was chosen in 1981. The memorial was to honour US soldiers who had fallen in the Vietnam War, but its winning design was criticized by many people, including surviving veterans, as 'a black gash of shame.' The young designer, Maya Lin – a Chinese-American undergraduate at Yale University – had decided to use highly polished black granite, quarried in India, on which would be etched the names of each fallen individual, as in so many French village memorials to the fallen of World War I. Considered insufficiently symbolic of their courage and service, an 'anonymous' but figurative and symbolic memorial was therefore also designed, cast in bronze and placed alongside the Lin wall, near the Lincoln Memorial in the Mall, Washington DC, where it stands today.

Another example of this duality – the difference between naming and symbolizing – can be witnessed in Westerbork in northern Holland. There, where 107,000 individual human beings (including Anne Frank) were sent in train wagons from the railway transit camp to the extermination camps of Auschwitz, Sobibor, Bergen-Belsen and Theresiënstadt during World War II, a museum and a reconstructed hut, iron rails, wooden ties and a cattle-truck have been erected as a memorial, symbolizing the enormity of the crime against humanity. In a less well-known act of remembrance and atonement, however, local people and visitors line up and read aloud the full names and ages of every single individual transported to their deaths, once a year.

The memory of an individual life, *en bref*, can be both important in itself and symbolic of others, even millions of others. That is the *dialectic of biography*, we might say: the thing that gives biography both its substance and its reflection.

Given its 2,500-year-old history, where is biography going today? In 1988, a group of British academics and practising biographers asked the same question, entitling their deliberations *The Troubled Face of Biography*. It seemed to one of them, Professor Lord Skidelsky (biographer of the economist Lord Keynes), that too much time was being spent on the 'private lives' of modern biography's subjects, and too little, he cavilled, on their 'achievements.'

Doubtless this was so – but how could it have been otherwise, in the wake of the Sixties: of the Stonewall Riots, the Feminist Revolution, Woodstock, or the cries of Egalité, Liberté, Sexualité in Paris in May 1968?

Perhaps the biggest surprise was that biography, as a genre, largely evaded the predations of the deconstruction movement started by Jacques Derrida. Derrida had taken a playful but insidious wrecking ball to the relationship between text and meaning in a 1968 essay titled *Speech and Phenomena: And Other*

Essays on Husserl's Theory of Signs. It certainly proved a sign of things to come. Significant swaths of academia fell under the sway of linguists, philosophers, psychologists and literary critics – Chomsky, Derrida, Lacan and Barthes among them – to the point where almost no academic paper could pass peer scrutiny unless filled with the jargon of deconstruction.

Mercifully, biography appeared completely unaffected – mostly because 'biography' was not studied in academia! Thus, although the 'death of the author' had been proudly announced by literary critic and philosopher Roland Barthes, biographers merely continued writing regardless. *Le grand récit*, as exemplified in multi-volume biographies by writers such as Robert Caro, Edmund Morris, Blanche Wiesen Cook and Lyndall Gordon, proceeded unmolested. Deconstructionist writers and essayists, by contrast, failed to write a single biography that was readable, let alone informative or entertaining.

By eschewing deconstruction, biographers in fact did the opposite: they spread their wings, extending their work into every modern medium, from television to the Internet, in a massive popular expansion perhaps without parallel in cultural history. Moreover, this biographical proliferation was driven, in part, by the desire to extend the new life-cover, so to speak, being offered by the actuaries of biography. Life-cover was now accorded to large numbers of minority or hitherto marginalized individuals, from Australian aborigines to hermaphrodites: real individuals who had never before been represented, honoured or recorded, coming from every stratum of modern society.

Thus, rather than torturing their field into total incomprehensivity in fear of reading the wrong 'sign' or 'signifier,' biography blossomed. It even began borrowing from the latest tropes and narrative techniques of fiction, from flashbacks to inverted chronology – although those methods were applied to well-researched real lives. At one extreme, such works became even more scholarly than histories, exhibiting deeper, more forensic, more heavily-footnoted research skills than historians ('Biography as Corrective'); at another, they began chopping individuals' lives into smaller, more discrete periods ('Partial Biography'), to elicit a clearer picture of human agency or true turning points.

In investigation, in stylistic expression and in sheer compass, modern biography thus began to display vastly different features from a mere generation before. The quality of such work – as in every art and every science – was variable, to be sure, but no cultural sociologist could deny the burgeoning individual-symbolic dialectic. There seemed to be an ever-growing fascination in Western society with real lives – something not only evident in the public preoccupation with celebrity and fame, but a trend evinced by the increasing number of fiction writers who focused their novels on real individuals (so-called 'biofiction': e.g., Margaret Atwood's *Alias Grace* (1996), Julian Barnes' *Arthur and George*, (2005), T.C. Boyle's *The Women* (2009), Carlene Bauer's *Frances and Bernard* (2013) and Curtis Sittenfeld's *American Wife* (2008)).

Ironically, given biography's concern with the actual rather than fictional individual, the very *form*, trope or structure of modern biography even began to impress historians – especially historians of things. The title of *Cod: The Biography of the Fish That Changed the World*, published in 1997, may have borne an exaggerated claim, but the book certainly helped change the world of objects as objects of study. It became a harbinger of dozens of such works, even biographies of cities. Berlin, Paris, Vienna, Tel Aviv and Antwerp all attracted biographers, the writer Peter Ackroyd going so far as to envision England's capital city as a body with dreams and complexes in his *London: The Biography* (2000). Although biographers might smirk, imitation was indeed flattery.

The extension or crossing of one boundary, however, has come to cause practitioners of biography to feel a deep sense of anxiety: the matter of fact.

In fact, the growing war on fact.

This war crept up on biography and history, like a delayed and unintended time-bomb left by the long-departed deconstruction movement. In future decades, historians will seek to pin down the reasons. In terms of biography, however, it first became visible in a certain blurring of the borders between fiction and non-fiction – often referred to as 'faction', a sort of no-man's land.

Initially this was discernible in memoir, where authors sought to 'dramatize' real-life experiences by conflating individuals in their stories, in order to maintain a tight focus and increase the dramatic power. Thus, for example, Primo Levi's classic memoir* *If This Is a Man* (1947) – his harrowing account of surviving Auschwitz – harked back to the famous speech of Shylock, the Jew in Shakespeare's play *The Merchant of Venice*: 'Hath not a Jew eyes? If you prick us, do we not bleed?' Yet even Levi later acknowledged he had, either unintentionally or from false memory, simplified his account. The trend soon shifted into biography, however. For example, the biographer of the Dutch historian Jaap Meijer, Evelien Gans, found that she had no information about Meijer's life in the concentration camp Westerbork, where he had been incarcerated. She therefore took out a similar description from the biography from another Dutch Jewish historian, whose wartime experiences were similar, and inserted this description into the biography of Meijer. More famously, Truman Capote made the adjustment openly, in his biographical account of a brutal murder in America, *In Cold Blood* (1966), calling his account a non-fiction novel.

Narrative non-fiction* thus began to bridge fact and invention in the service of narrative art and the imagination. In doing so, however, it inadvertently contributed to the increasing sense of immunity to lies in civilized Western democratic society – and not always inadvertently. The growing popularity and commercial, even prize-winning, success of memoir led to some uncomfortable truths, as when the supposed authors of true-life memoirs turned out to be frauds – as convincingly described in Stefan Maechler's *The Wilkomirski Affair: A Study in Biographical Truth* (2001). Likewise, Enric Marco, another imposter, was only unmasked in 2005, years after he had published his invented Holocaust memoirs and won exalted Catalan government honours.

Along with their other tasks, in other words, biographers have had to become guardians of truth in 'non-fiction narrative' and memoir; not to spoil novelists' fun or display of imagination, but simply to ensure that we do not lose sight of what is, in literal fact, the truth.

Anyone who contests this need only consider the results of the 2016 presidential election, where a similar 'imposter' went largely unexposed by the media and a huge television audience that wished to be entertained rather than informed. Within two months of taking office, *The New York Times* was claiming that the 45th US President, the most powerful individual in the world, had said 'something untrue, in public, every day for the first 40 days of his presidency' – aided and abetted by a White House that dismissed all critical comment or analysis by the media as 'fake news,' and moreover asserted the right to broadcast 'alternative facts.'

Alternative facts? 'Facts' that were excused, ignored and forgiven by tens of millions of Americans? The threat was, and is, serious. In mid-2017, one cultural critic was led to wonder whether it was America's destiny 'to unravel in this way'? 'Or maybe,' he posited, 'we're just early adopters, the canaries in the gold mine, and Canada and Denmark and Japan and China and all the rest will eventually follow us,' *pace* Lewis Carroll, 'down our tunnel.' A tunnel, he wrote, in which the majority of Americans could no longer distinguish between 'true and untrue.' An Orwellian novel, *1984*, had come to life, 33 years after 1984.

Fact* *matters* in biography, as it also does in history.* And in politics, perhaps most of all – as twentieth-century dictatorships taught the world. It matters enormously. Without fact, or respect for fact, biography for its part morphs into something else, ranging from fiction to downright deceit and lies. Biographers beware! You are the guardians of a genre and a biographical imperative that go back 2,500 years and more.

Can biography survive the current war on fact? Time will tell. Biographers across the world hope that it will, and that truth will win: that in the hard and patient work of a biographer, in a great variety of media, there is not only artistic and intellectual personal fulfilment, but also a vital public good. That however controversial it may seem at times, biography makes us ponder myths and the life experience of real individuals, anchoring us to truth-telling about ourselves and about others – real others – rather than lies; without which anchor, as social beings, we cannot survive.

Sources: Eric Homberger and John Charmley (eds), *The Troubled Face of Biography* (New York: St Martin's, 1988); Hans Renders and Binne de Haan (eds), *The Biographical Turn* (London: Routledge, 2017); Nigel Hamilton, *Biography: A Brief History* (Cambridge, MA: Harvard University Press, 2007); Kurt Andersen: *Fantasyland: How America Went Haywire* (New York: Random House, 2017); Roland Barthes, 'The Death of the Author', in: *Aspen* (1967) 5-6; Carl Rollyson, *A Higher Form of Cannibalism? Adventures in the Art and Politics of Biography* (Chicago: Ivan R. Dee, 2005).

 **is for Composition**

Almost no review, newspaper article or interview with an author will ever tell you much about biographical composition. The world is primarily interested in the finished product alone: the life of the subject – a real person under scrutiny, whose essential data the writer seeks to pass on to an audience. The construction of the biography itself, as a work of craft – its shape, its framing, its narrative arc, the quality of its ingredients from archival discoveries to interviews, its style as prose or composition by the biographer – these are of scant interest to the reviewer or journalist. Whereas a novel, novella or short story, by contrast, is often picked to its marrow by literary critics.

This is no bad thing, in terms of simplicity: from the farm to the table. But it does make it difficult for the novice biographer to know where to start, literally and metaphorically, since the composition of biography is simply not taught, save for a handful of noble exceptions. The lack of guidance has led to some awful attempts at biography by would-be biographers, in fact. Virginia Woolf, having mocked 'plodding' biographers in her brilliant novel *Orlando*, later tried her hand at a genuine biography, writing the life of her late friend, the art critic and theorist Roger Fry. It became, as she complained in her diary, 'an appalling grind,' 'donkey work,' nothing but 'sober drudgery.' 'How can one cut loose from facts,' she asked herself, 'when there they are, contradicting my theories?' The result, *Roger Fry: A Biography* (1940), proved a commercial and literary disaster – causing Woolf to recognize she would never be a 'biographer,' for she had found herself, despite her attempts, unable to spark even 'a flick of life' in it. The same happened to Evelyn Waugh – arguably the finest comic novelist of the twentieth century – who tried his hand at writing the life of the friend who had helped him convert to Catholicism: *The Life of the Right Revered Ronald Knox*. This also proved an embarrassing mistake, argued the critic Angus Wilson, who damned it as 'dull, at times even empty.' Another felt it was addressed mainly to 'Old Etonians' rather than to normal readers. Moreover, it was so full of mistakes that the publisher had to bring out another impression instantly with 'a large corrigendum slip.' After failing to win a knighthood for his literary endeavours, Waugh – who had thought the book would be his 'magnum opus' – was devastated. For his part, Sigmund Freud not only imagined himself a biographer, but at one point thought biography, as the investigation of the minds of historical individuals, could be subsumed under the discipline of psychoanalysis, as he confided in a letter to his disciple C.G. Jung. His biographies of Moses and of Leonardo da Vinci ('the only beautiful thing I have ever written,' he later mourned) cast much psychological light on Freud himself as a revolutionary thinker and cultural agitator – but were utterly ridiculed as biographies.

Composing a biography, in other words, is much harder than it might first appear. Where, then, does the aspiring biographer start, in terms of composition – and how different is writing a biography from writing fiction?

In his *Midsummer Night's Dream,* Shakespeare's Theseus scorns 'antique fables' and 'fairy toys', mocking the 'lunatic, the lover and the poet' for their efforts:

> The poet's eye, in fine frenzy rolling,
> Doth glance from heaven to earth, from earth to heaven;
> And as imagination bodies forth
> The forms of things unknown, the poet's pen
> Turns them to shapes and gives to airy nothing
> A local habitation and a name.

Biography, by contrast, seeks not to invent but to discover *things known* about real people, and to interpret them intelligently and interestingly. To do this, the biographer must harness the skills of the journalist, scholar, historian, psychologist, portraitist, critic – *and* poet!

Since biography is neither taught nor its mechanics understood by most critics, let us briefly discuss seven of the many secrets behind biographical composition.

First, the biographer has to learn over time to whom he is addressing his account: his intended audience. And this is definitely not an audience of Old Etonians! Of course, he cannot necessarily know this in advance, since he begins his work as a simple collector: of information, of facts, of knowledge, of personal insights, of quotations, of detail during the long duration of the composition of a biography. It is not easy – as both Woolf and Waugh found. The work is often laborious, and it demands a certain humility and respect for sources – respect that does not come easily to the fabulist. Moreover, biography is quite different from other arts, too, where the artist seeks to impose a narrative structure upon an invented theme or idea. Like the historian, the biographer works *from the ground up*, not the other way around.

Yet here, too, the biographer's approach and intentions are distinctive. The biographer is no sociologist or social historian, attempting to find commonalities between the subject and other subjects in order to establish a statistical pattern or truth. Instead his aim is to capture what is truly distinctive about the individual in question – that which makes him or her *different* from others – before delivering his judgement. This inevitably becomes, in composition, a test of the author's honesty, intelligence, diligence, insight, even identification, with all the dangers that projection may involve – something that Freud, however poor a biographer, well understood. Constantly self-checking, the biographer wields a hidden scourge – self-flagellating in order to combat over-projection of the self. Despite this, though, he must also find a confident persona, as a narrator, that will attract and retain the reader's attention. It is, in effect, a 'two-way dialogue,' as the distinguished biographer and theorist Leon Edel put it:

for the biographer is anticipating the response of the reader as well as furnishing information or insight...

Next: the frame! Just as the portrait painter must consider the size, pose, and background of the subject, so the biographer, at some early point in his project and his research, must decide upon the *canvas* of his biography: whether it will encompass the whole of the subject's life, as in a full-length portrait, or just a part. He will also need to decide how large or small the canvas will be; i.e., a short, medium or large biography. This will not necessarily determine the level of detail, since biography – like fiction – *feeds* on detail, but it does determine volume, or mass. Many a biography has been rejected by the publisher for being too long, containing too much detail or explanatory prose; equally, some are faulted for brevity, and the author is encouraged to fill out the portrait by adding more detail, background or context. Once the frame is decided upon, this will shape the kind of portrait that is painted. *Truman*, a biography of Harry Truman, for example, weighed in at 1,117 pages, and covered the whole life of the 33rd US President's life – magnificently researched and recounted by David McCullough in 1992. A more recent biography, *The General vs. the President*, in 2016, focused just on Truman's famous firing of General Douglas MacArthur – yet still covered 439 pages. Both books represented choices the biographer had made in composing his life.

A third secret is the assembling of the contents: the research itself. To use the analogy of cuisine, biography is made in a cook's secluded kitchen, away from the restaurant. All manner of utensils are required to produce a meal – and in the case of the biographer these will range from the willingness and ability to make archival research trips, on the one hand, to the biographer's readiness and skill to go the literal extra mile. Nicholas Farrell, for example, spent five years in Predappio, the village where Mussolini was born, before he published his biography of the dictator in 2003. Robert Caro spent three years in the Pedernales area of Texas, conducting interviews with neighbours, friends – and enemies – of President Lyndon Johnson before starting his multi-volume biography (1982, 1990, 2002, and 2012).

The biographer has been to the market; he has more than enough ingredients; all he needs to do, then, is to cook!

A fourth secret, in composition, is selectivity: choosing the essential ingredients, i.e., those that are really germane to the task, as the task itself becomes clearer. For no biography is mapped out in advance, any more than the course of a human life is predictable. The story of a life that is told by a biographer only develops as the biographer recounts the tale, cutting and trimming, kneading and shaping as he proceeds. Selection becomes not only a matter of what to leave in and what to take out, but it also entails selecting the best method of sharing the material with the reader – where to begin the book or chapter, for example, and where to end it; what periods, what themes, what events, what people, what stories to include. Ever since the work of Thucydides, historical narrative has been a war between facts, perspectives, distancing, time, order, and context in the service of readable text. Every working (and thinking) day in the life of a practising biographer today is still marked by selection, selection, selection!

Fifth: within the chosen frame, by trial and error, the biographer must develop – to use another analogy – a technique of running. The narrative gait or pace adopted by the biographer is his style of discourse. It will be established, say, by the first forty pages or so of the first draft, or not at all! It is not a matrix of the book's overall design or eventual shape, for these may well shift in the process of composition and editing. Instead it is a kind of biographer's statement of authority over his material, and the reader's hopeful attention: Luther's 'Here I Stand!' A tone of narrative that will reflect – and ultimately define – the biographer's confidence and reliability in recounting his story.

A sixth secret returns us to the 'local habitation,' or literary persona, of the biographer *as narrator*. How does the narrator refer to himself in the text? In memoir* – the biography of the self – this is straightforward: the first person singular. (Not always, though; Julius Caesar's campaign history, *De Bello Gallico* (58-49 BC), was written in the third person; so was Henry Adams's *The Education of Henry Adams* (1907)). In the biography of someone else's life, however, the author himself or herself has to decide what role to play in the action. Whether to use the 'I' or 'We' on behalf of the reader. Or whether to be a hidden hand: recording, narrating, even judging – but only by implication. Between Marcus Aurelius's conversational *Meditations* (161-180 AD) and Richard Holmes's *Adventures of a Romantic Biographer* (1996) there are limitless permutations – and in postmodern writing, even the chosen narrative role can be a moveable feast, as Julian Barnes's spoof biography, *Flaubert's Parrot* (1984), showed.

Differing narrator voices have different aficionados – and deplorers. 'I' interposes a presence that can be more alienating than helpful, even though it is theoretically more 'honest.' 'We' can sound pious or presumptuous. Meanwhile the invisible narrator, narrating in the third person as an implicit presence, can leave the reader frustrated, wishing the author were more willing to express personal judgement or distaste – especially if the subject is contentious, or undeniably evil and abhorrent, as in the case of, say, Adolf Hitler, or members of his Nazi entourage. Whichever persona is chosen in the Dramatis Personae, or List of Characters – whether the biographer-narrator plays himself, or adopts the role of Greek Chorus, or the role of ghost, or simply stays hidden and embedded within the characters, actions and speeches – it is a vestment in which the biographer has to feel comfortable. For otherwise, the biography, as narrative, will lose readability and credibility. And credibility – trust – is important in biography! A biographer who admits to too much doubt, as in 'perhaps,' or 'possibly' or 'we can assume,' is on shifting, treacherous ground. The biographer will have started his research by conducting it without prejudice or bias; but, come the day, he must present his account in writing – and must by then have found his own persona. He is, after all, the intermediary between the information, as he has collected it, and the public. The biographer must negotiate that space, acting in a constant, tightrope-like role, trying not to fall. He is both prosecuting attorney and defender, tasked with truthfulness and objectivity, yet required to present his evidence and portrait in such a way that the reader can respect it and form his own judgement. Too hostile a brush and the reader may be put off; too defensive and the reader may become suspicious, or unconvinced. It is, in sum, a class act.

Which brings us, finally, to the biggest secret of all in biography. This is the pleasure, gratification, or sense of fulfilment its composition gives the biographer, rather than the reader! This may well explain biography's longevity, in fact, for biography has been an addictive drug for thousands of years – from Plutarch's many lives, and Suetonius's twelve Caesars, to the present day! Whether he writes ostensibly to earn money, or for kudos – the association with a famous subject – or for little or no return in order to satisfy a circle of readers with a particular interest in the biographee, there are very, very few biographers who do not, after writing a biography, go on to write another life of a different individual. Whether addressing successive literary lives (biographers such as Richard Holmes, Hermione Lee and Claire Tomalin), political lives (Edmund Morris, David McCullough and Robert Caro) or the lives of inventors (Walter Isaacson, Dava Sobel and James Gleick), biographers become addicted; an aspect or explanation of biography that is remarkable, and remarkably unexamined.

The process of composition must have something to do with it – a process that seems to meet psychological needs that are different for different biographers, yet is clearly habit-forming for them all. The new Biography Society (2016) may eventually help explain the pharmacology of the drug, but for the moment we must content ourselves with the fact that it is quite different from fiction, and substantially different from its sibling, memoir (which is seldom addictive). Its narcotic pull, if we are to hazard a preliminary guess, is that it permits the biographer to enter both into the public domain and the private story of another person's real life, for good or ill. Whether or not this is considered by the arbiters of taste and law to be too invasive, it comes to mean a great deal spiritually, intellectually, psychologically and artistically *to the biographer*. Armed with innocence and the simple weapons of data, footnotes, endnotes, sources and appendixes, the biographer, as narrator, walks onto the battlefield of a chosen person, like Sancho Panza – seeking to create 'the faithful portrait of a soul in its adventures through life,' as Edmund Gosse put it in the famous 11th edition of the *Encyclopaedia Britannica*. And Gosse had cause to know! He, too, was an addict – writing dozens of biographies of great writers, from Thomas Gray to John Donne, Ibsen to William Congreve, Thomas Browne to Robert Browning.

Gosse's own story, however, was perhaps the one he had secretly been seeking to tell all along. He had written a dutiful biography of his father, the distinguished English naturalist Philip Henry Gosse, in 1896, to satisfy his mother's wishes. But a decade later, in 1907, he decided to break the Oedipal taboo, albeit under the name 'Anonymous.' What he then composed was a new biography of his father, told as candidly as he could, yet without rancour: the account of a mad, anti-Darwinian religious bigot and yet determined scientist – and the effect he had on his wife and son: Gosse himself.

Gosse had not expected anyone to be interested; in fact, he feared he would be vilified. Instead, *Father and Son* became a bestseller. It was soon reprinted under Gosse's own name, and in time came to be considered a classic. Most of all, it enabled Gosse to come to terms with himself, after writing so many biographies and biographical sketches of others. Which may, in the end, tell us more about the pleasure, pain, challenges, defeats and yet sheer gratification of biographical composition than anything else.

Sources: Nigel Hamilton, *How To Do Biography: A Primer* (Cambridge, MA: Harvard University Press, 2008); Jeanne McCullough, interview with Leon Edel, 'The Art of Biography,' *Paris Review* 98, Winter 1985; John Batchelor (ed.), *The Art of Literary Biography* (Oxford: Oxford University Press, 1995); Mary Rhiel and David Suchoff (eds), *The Seductions of Biography* (London: Routledge, 1996); Julia Briggs, *Virginia Woolf: An Inner Life* (London: Allen Lane, 2005); Hans Renders and Binne de Haan, 'Roots of Biography. From Journalism to Pulp to Scholarly Based Non-Fiction', in: Hans Renders and Binne de Haan (eds), *Theoretical Discussions of Biography* (Leiden: Brill, 2014), 24-42.

is for Dictionaries of Biography

What's in a word? Well, history for a start.

Considering that the word 'dictionary' was first used in the fifteenth century by antiquarians who collected biographical facts and added them to their lists of English writers, it is striking to note that 'dictionary' only became a respected genre three centuries later in the seventeenth century, its new status won by Louis Moreri's *Le Grand Dictionnaire historique, ou, le mélange curieux de l'histoire sacrée et profane* of 1674. It was in the nineteenth century, though, that biography was separated from the *mélange*, when biographical dictionaries came to be widely published: first in France, then in various other European countries. People seemed to be more and more interested in other people – especially people they did not actually know.

Human curiosity – or curiosity about humans – was thus the mainspring of what became curiosity fever. At the end of the nineteenth century, 'a biography' in the popular mind could be anything from a feature in the newspaper to a mobile movie theatre in a tent, where the first films were shown. There were also, to be sure, two-, three- or even four-volume print biographies (entitled *Life and Letters of...*); but much more common was a 20- or 25-page portrait of someone considered interesting, often handed out as a pamphlet at fairs, exhibits or other such public events. Moreover, there was nothing intrinsically new in this. The phenomenon dated back to the eighteenth century, when biographies were sold at the market; especially during or directly after the execution of a criminal, it should be noted – adding to the notion of justice not only being witnessed in hangings, beheadings and guillotinings, say, but also in reports and biographical material, disseminated as a social deterrent.

This so-called 'crime biography' or, even more misleadingly, 'criminal biography', almost always had the features of a newspaper article – similar to those of other reports on individuals who were making waves in society. Often such portraits were sold as separate periodicals and, after ten or twenty editions, combined into a book and put on the market by the publisher at the end of the year, with the addition of an introduction, corrections and supplements, to bring them up to date. One example of such a series was *Mannen van Beteekenis in onze dagen* [Men of Significance in our time], published between 1870 and 1875 by the well-known Dutch publisher A.C. Kruseman. After 1875, the series was continued by Kruseman from 1895 to 1921 in collaboration with his fellow-townsman, the Haarlem-based publisher Tjeenk Willink, under the title *Mannen en Vrouwen van Beteekenis in onze dagen* [Men and Women of Significance in our time].

George Sand, a woman, had been featured in the first series as an exception. 'The mind knows no gender,' was the resourceful argument for including her, 'and for the mind alone is the pantheon accessible.' In that sense, the editors were following topical interest: women played no role of any consequence in public life. When the newspapers copied (mostly) foreign obituaries,* however, the editors of the fortnightly periodical *Mannen van beteekenis in onze dagen* did not want to be left behind.

The point here is this: *Mannen van Beteekenis* and other biographical dictionaries shed light on the original role and intended purpose of such texts, as well as the values and qualities that the selected subjects reflected and represented. They form a very significant resource for historians.

In terms of the development of such dictionaries and paradictionaries in the nineteenth century, we should also note the agency behind their proliferation; for it was precisely the more journalistic approach that enables us to define a watershed in the history of the biographical encyclopaedia. Biographies, after all, were already being written in the classical period, the best known among them being the collective and comparative biographies by Plutarch, and those of Pliny the Elder. In the fifteenth, sixteenth and seventeenth centuries, biographical encyclopaedias of martyrs, saints and royalty were published worldwide. Vasari's sixteenth-century *Lives of the Artists*, for example, was imitated throughout Europe. And in the eighteenth century, almost every country in the West had its own version of *Biographia Britannica: The Lives of the Most Eminent Persons Who Have Flourished in Great Britain and Ireland* (1747). Up until the nineteenth century, these biographical dictionaries can be classified in various categories: religious, nationalistic, didactic, historical, and so forth.

The most important thing these surveys have in common is that, though developing at a different pace in every country in the nineteenth century, they came to reflect current affairs and a new approach. The *Biographia Britannica*'s subtitle was: *From the earliest Ages, down to the present Times* – with journalists increasingly taking up the fascination with the 'present Times'. The selected Persons were still chosen on the basis of their elite status, but the entries themselves became increasingly independent and factual. This had major consequences for the language and style of the entries. Flowery, literary prose gave way to a more detached journalistic writing style, which became the norm, or rule. Biographical entries that had always been associated with commemorative literature and encomia, whether or not commissioned, now shifted into a new domain: a domain in which public opinion, a desire for learning, and verifiable facts* were increasing in significance; values no longer served by purple prose. Literature and biography thus parted company in the field of the biographical dictionary.

The nineteenth-century French journalist and novelist Jules Barbey d'Aurevilly was one of several individuals to draw attention to the disadvantages of this separation. Biographical research carried out by contemporary journalists was producing, in his opinion, useful information on topical matters, but the increased attention given to private lives also fed an undesirable phenomenon: the cult of personality. This now included people's looks; D'Aurevilly spoke of the new Siamese twins of vanity – biography and photography!

This appetite was certainly fed by popular curiosity, as it was by the camera, beginning with Daguerre's portrait of a man having his boots polished on a Paris street in 1839. As early as 1850, the American photographer and gallery-owner Matthew Brady published a book of photolithographs, in instalments, entitled *The Gallery of Illustrious Americans*. Publishers were soon tapping into public demand for illustrated portraits of famous people by producing books of photographs with titles such as *Men of mark: a gallery of contemporary portraits of men distinguished in the senate, the church, in science, literature and art, the army, navy, law, medicine etc.* (London 1876); *Galerie contemporaine, littéraire, artistique* (Paris 1876-1894); and in the Netherlands, *Onze hedendaagsche letterkundigen* (Amsterdam 1883-1887).

The portraits in these collective albums, which appeared in instalments, are sharp and unadorned. The object was to express the character and individuality of the person being portrayed, across a whole spectrum of human activities and trades. In these 'photo-galleries' we thus find, in addition to statesmen and scientists, famous writers like Victor Hugo and Jules Verne.

Thus, by the nineteenth century, the distinction between literary and documentary approaches to biography was nowhere more visible than in the arena of biographical collections or galleries. Novels were also becoming immensely popular – often serialized in newspapers, too – but the reader/viewer of biographies read these differently from the way in which they read novels. Why?

It is not only the factual nature of biographies that distinguishes them from fiction, but the *reliability* of the information being presented; a fact often emphasized by the author and publisher. Many of the biographies in *Mannen van Beteekenis* were written by experts: historians, journalists and biographers, but also well-known novelists who deliberately switched pens, as it were, to undertake the task. As a result, it is not possible to tell from the style of these biographical entries whether they were written by a 'literary' writer such as a novelist, or by a documentarian.

This was of profound importance for the development of biography and for the nature of biography's status as a professional 'trade' in society: *le biographe*. As biographical encyclopaedias took root in Germany, England, France and a number of other countries in the nineteenth century, the focal lens was trained on the named individual in history or society – but the aperture, so to speak, was much larger than that embracing a single individual. The generic prestige of biography and the biographer was thus predominantly that of a *collective* undertaking. True, sizeable biographies of individuals were written during the second half of the nineteenth century, but up until that point and beyond, the most popular form of biography remained the biographical encyclopaedia or collective, group biography.* Examples include *Lives of Distinguished Shoemakers* (1849), *Heroes of Industry* (1866), *Lives of the Electricians* (1887), *The New Calendar of Great Men: Biographies of the 558 Worthies of All Ages and Nations in the Positivist Calendar of Auguste Comte* (1892) and *Heroes of the Telegraph* (1891).

As collective biography gathered popular sway, so, too, did the notion of patriotic, formal, scholarly commemoration as a sort of collective national, even international memorial in biographical dictionary form. Between 1811 and 1828, Louis-Gabriel Michaud's 52-part *Biographie universelle ancienne et moderne* was published, the second edition of which became *Biographie universelle ancienne et moderne: histoire par ordre aphabétique de la vie publique et privée de tous les hommes*. It was a development that got under way somewhat later in England, on a strictly national basis, when Leslie Stephen (Virginia Woolf's father) and his successor, Sidney Lee, undertook the challenge of a 66-volume British *Dictionary of National Biography*, published from 1885 to 1901.

Stephen was considered an impressive theoretician of biography well into the twentieth century. He took pride in the fact that the *DNB*, as it was popularly known (it would later be renamed the *New Dictionary of Biography*), 'obliged contributors to seek information from first-hand authorities, and often from unpublished papers and records, making it an indispensable condition that writers should append to each article a full list of the sources whence their information was derived.' Numerous comments by Stephen and Lee testify to their insistence that the DNB should not only satisfy the 'commemorative instinct', but that it should also serve 'as a contrivance to guide burgeoning scholarship' in order to take full advantage of a new age in which so many new 'archives of printed books and manuscripts' were becoming available and accessible to scholars.

Stephen's influence was representative of his class in Victorian England, and it was substantial. The *New English Dictionary on Historical Principles*, produced after 1857 by Herbert Coleridge (grandson of the poet), among others, contained an extraordinary amount of biographical information from the very start. It was this tradition that caused Kruseman to launch his *Mannen van Beteekenis* in 1870. In 1875 in Germany, publication began of the *Allgemeine Deutsche Biographie*. By 1912, 56 volumes of this series had appeared. In the US, John Lauris Blake's *A General Biographical Dictionary, Comprising a Summary Account of the Most Distinguished Persons of All Ages, Nations and Professions, including more than one thousand articles of American Biography* (1835) led the way; by the twentieth century a vast array of biographical dictionaries had appeared in the US and were still being commissioned, such as the *Dictionary of American Biography* (1926-1937).

Biographical dictionaries were thus becoming universal. And in 2001, they achieved true universality: the advent of the World Wide Web and the Internet revolutionized many aspects of the ways in which people live and work. And among the stellar content-sites on the Internet is Wikipedia.

Wikipedia transformed the world of alphabetically-arranged biographical information. There had been commercially-produced digital encyclopaedias prior to Wikipedia, such as Microsoft's *Encarta* (hyperlinked) and *Encyclopaedia Britannica*, both in CD-ROM format. But the challenge of making it possible to produce such an encyclopaedia online for a world audience was triple: commercial, editorial and temporal.

Traditionally, it had taken decades to assemble and market encyclopaedias and dictionaries; indeed, the history of their genesis, such as the stories of the dictionaries created by Dr. Johnson and Denis Diderot, makes captivating reading today. Johnson earned himself fame and a doctorate for his labours on his great Dictionary – but it was time-consuming work that brought in little money. When Lord Chesterfield finally offered moral support – seven years too late – by writing positively about the venture in 1755, Johnson was irate. In a famous letter, he lamented that he had had to carry out his pioneering venture 'without one act of assistance, one word of encouragement, or one smile of favour. Is not a patron, my lord, one who looks with unconcern on a man struggling for life in the water,' he sneered, 'and when he has reached ground, encumbers him with help?'

The problem nowadays is little different. How to finance, produce, edit and update a vast new repository of factual information and interpretation, especially one that is biographical? Nupedia, an Internet encyclopaedia launched in 1999, had only produced twelve finished entries by the end of its first year, all contributed by volunteers but centrally edited. *Real Lives*, an Internet-based project developed by the British Institute of Biography (BIB) in London at the same time, had gone ahead with a pilot project to focus only on biographies, using several hundred students at London universities who would contribute illustrated entries for free in return for academic credits, in accordance with a template developed by the BIB's editorial team. This project, too, failed to attract sufficient funding before the dot-com collapse of that time.

It was at this point that the notion of an encyclopaedia, produced by volunteers with no central organization to edit content, was taken up by several entrepreneurs. The use of 'wikis' was the answer: websites providing a simple, open format in which content could be posted, corrected and developed *online* – for free! Google, the Internet navigational tool, sent users to the new site, Wikipedia – and the phenomenon took off and swiftly became global. By 2004, more than 50 per cent of the entries were in languages other than English, with more than a million articles in over 100 languages. Moreover, the site, owned by the non-profit Wikipedia Foundation, was truly free in that it allowed no advertising and was accessible to all – save those countries that blocked it. Its by-laws still specify that its purpose is to collect and develop educational content, to be disseminated globally. Much of this content – perhaps the majority – is biographical, and the site has become a universal first port-of-call when seeking fact-based information about past and present real lives.

In other words, the world of the *biographie universelle* has come a long way since the seventeenth century. As any biographer knows, however, there is much more to lives than facts. In order to maintain its impartiality and objectivity, Wikipedia is unlikely ever to be more than a very basic, mostly factual biographical resource – moreover, one whose facts need careful checking! In time, however, we will surely see other, alternative web sites, exploring real lives in greater depth.

Sources: Nigel Hamilton, *Biography: A Brief History* (Cambridge, MA: Harvard University Press, 2007); Brian Harrison, 'A Slice of Their Lives: Editing the DNB, 1882-1999', in: *English Historical Review* 119 (2004) 484, 1179-1201; Ann Jefferson, *Biography and the Question of Literature in France* (Oxford: Oxford University Press, 2007); Lisa Kuitert, '"Reading the Body": Authors' Portraits and their Significance for the Nineteenth-Century Reading Public', in: J. Arianne Baggerman et al. (eds), *Controlling Time and Shaping the Self. Developments in Autobiographical Writing since the Sixteenth Century* (Leiden: Brill, 2011), 355-372; Sidney Lee, *Principles of Biography* (Cambridge: Cambridge University Press, 1911); Hans Renders, 'Contemporary values of life. Biographical Dictionaries', in: Hans Renders and Binne de Haan (eds), *Theoretical Discussions of Biography. Approaches from History, Microhistory, and Life Writing* (Leiden: Brill, 2014), 94-101; Simon Winchester, *The Meaning of Everything. The Story of the Oxford English Dictionary* (Oxford: Oxford University Press, 2004).

 **is for Ethics**

Biography is inherently controversial. How could it *not* be so? The biographer is, after all, affecting the reputations of real people, alive or dead: the 'immortal' part of oneself, as Shakespeare called it. (The remainder, the bard maintained, was merely 'bestial.')

Biography may be the most controversial of the arts. Suetonius, for example, was exiled from Rome for his infamous *Twelve Caesars*, whilst Sir Walter Raleigh was executed in part because of his biographical *History of the World*, including the history of princes, which offended the king.

To guard against such eventualities, biographers developed an unwritten but long-lasting code of ethics. It was a sort of Hippocratic Oath: a Plutarchian convention to protect biographers, they hoped, from possible blowback, lawsuits and incarceration if their work met with disfavour.

The first part of the unwritten ethical code was, and still is, to ensure that the biography is founded upon on *verifiable facts and sources*.

The second part of the code was, and is, to *be professional* – which is to say, to try to be impartial and avoid flattery, hero worship or ideology. Or deliberate vilification, for that matter – a part that has proved harder to maintain.

These two guidelines became the principal rules of the biographical genre for more than two millennia. They did not protect biographers from the law, but they did help in cases that went to law. In other words, they did not provide judicial protection against laws on libelling living individuals, nor could they ultimately resist the pressure brought to bear on the biographer of deceased subjects – such as by, say, a family's withholding of vital documents, or the imposition of copyright restrictions as a way of keeping biographers off the family reservation. However, they gave the profession some protection against the aggrieved subjects of biography who were still alive, or the relatives or aficionados of the dead. They also helped biographers to deal with those attempting to impose censorship on grounds of morality or secrecy, or to use authorization* to skew a work.

For the most part, biographers stuck to this ethical code of conduct with remarkable consistency. By the early twentieth century, however, biographers found themselves falling behind the cultural and artistic curve. In a sense, biographers had been *too* ethical, *too* virtuous – and thereby left out too much life in a real life! This had led to a moribund, predictable and largely drab genre. Located somewhere between journalism and history, by the early twentieth century biography had passed its sell-by date.

Lytton Strachey's *Eminent Victorians*, published in 1917, smashed down the gates of 'old-fashioned' biography and returned the genre to its Suetonian beginnings: beginnings in which sharp (though accurate and properly sourced) judgement had formed the third part of the biographical code. Channelling Suetonius, Strachey now challenged the reputations of four selected imperial forebears of the Victorian era, using facts and the appearance of objectivity or impartiality – but in truth, larding his essays with irony – to upset many, but delight many others.

For her part, his friend Virginia Woolf did the same when writing her spoof biography, *Orlando: A Biography*, in which the old-style biographer is pictured as tedious, plodding and blind.

Resurrecting Suetonius in the modern era – however amusingly it was done – was not likely to keep biographers safe from the law, though, or from opprobrium if they challenged public misconceptions about real people with real egos, real relatives and real wallets. And it did not. In a new century of political and cultural upheaval, biography inevitably became profoundly controversial again – in the law courts and in the press.

Woolf changed Orlando's gender half-way through her novel, but it was the taboo of sex* itself – revelations about sexual activity – that played havoc with biography's reputation in the post-Victorian world. Freud had already seen this coming in terms of biography – indeed, he outraged many people with his radical, sexually-explicit biography of Leonardo da Vinci in 1911. Emboldened by this, he even told his heir apparent, Carl Jung, that the genre of biography 'must become ours' – i.e., that it was ripe for colonization by psychoanalysts.

Mercifully, that ambition never came to pass. Biography, however, could not escape the demand for more critical treatment of the taboos and the reputations of real individuals, past and present. Biography was wading back into dark, Suetonian waters – and the blowback was inevitable in the modern world, code or no code.

Aristotle wisely proposed that in examining philosophy and ethics, we should proceed by example – i.e., we should look at how they play out in real life. In examining modern biography, let us look at some examples of ethical question-marks, and see what they tell us.

First off, the twentieth century illustrated how inimical dictatorship is to the practice of ethical, non-ideological biography; the Third Reich instantly burned books considered insufficiently laudatory of the Führer and his tribe. The same happened in the USSR – Alexander Solzhenitsyn, a veteran Russian artillery officer in WWII, was arrested and sent to the gulag for having been critical of Stalin in a letter home that was intercepted by the NKVD.

Democracy, however, is not necessarily a guarantee of free speech when it comes to biography. The law of libel, defending a man or woman's standing or reputation in society, ceases to apply when the subject dies. But only as a law; the *moral* or ethical question remains contested, post-mortem.

For her part, the Dutch biographer Elsbeth Etty has asserted the 'dead do not require privacy protection. Let us stop making excuses for concealing intimate facts of life.' Rather, she feels, it is important that biographers 'keep on searching for ways to track down these facts, and give them their indispensable place in life stories in responsible, reliable ways.' On the other hand,

Belgian historian Antoon De Baets disagrees: 'The position that the dead have no privacy or reputation is defensible on its own, and on strictly judicial grounds,' he concedes. 'Because the dead are not people, they do not possess human dignity, and therefore do not require rights such as privacy or reputation.' 'But,' he points out, 'because they are *former* people, they do possess *posthumous* dignity.'

Dignity has also become a contested term, the more so since the law of libel was itself largely abandoned for public figures (though not for private ones) in the US in 1964. Ruled unconstitutional by the US Supreme Court under the First Amendment, the American law of libel – a law that went back centuries in Europe – was stripped from the living as a legal defence against 'ethical' – i.e., non-malicious – criticism of their reputations. Malicious libel or spite, especially if untethered by verifiable facts, was not licensed in the process – and it can still land the biographer in court, with heavy fines levied for the so-called loss of 'reputation.'

Other countries were slow to follow suit. English libel law, for example, still lags 50 years behind America, with grave consequences for biographers. One English press baron, for example, was able to win a court case and significant punitive damages in the 1990s by claiming to have been libelled by a biographer who had inferred he was 'a snob'! This inference had damaged his reputation at his London club, which he visited on trips from tax-exile in France! More serious was the case of David Irving, a British-born writer, who sued the American historian Professor Deborah Lipstadt for libel in London's High Court. Irving claimed that the professor had materially impacted his 'reputation' by labelling him a 'holocaust denier,' and that this had reduced his royalties.

Irving was not as successful as the owner of the *Daily Mail*. By showing that Irving had no justifiable reputation to trash in relation to his writings about the Holocaust, Dr. Lipstadt's publishers (Penguin) were able to defend themselves effectively (though at vast cost, estimated at more than £20 million in legal fees). That case was quickly dubbed 'History on Trial' – but biography was, too.

The files of British and American law firms and literary agencies, if ever opened to researchers, will surely reveal the sheer profusion of cases where biographical works have had to be revised, rewritten or even withdrawn because the biographee objects to the biographical portrait – or even the idea of a portrait being written. The fiery feminist Germaine Greer, a journalist and professor of literature in England, was appalled, for example, when she found Christine Wallace, a fellow Australian, was researching Greer's past in Australia – memorably declaring Wallace (among other epithets) a 'dung beetle.'

With the gradual scrapping or diminution of the libel laws, however, family defenders increasingly turned to the law of copyright, both for living and past individuals. In 1994, for example, French historian Emmanuel Chadeau heard a judge decide that he had done a meticulous job in his biography of Antoine de Saint-Exupéry (1900-1944), even when he suggested the possibility that the author and pilot, who disappeared mysteriously, did not die during a night-flight accident, but had in fact committed suicide. During the court case, which was brought by Saint-Exupéry's grieving heirs, the judge did reprimand Chadeau, however, for illegally spreading unpublished material on Saint-Exupéry. Only the heirs could claim a moral and legal right to that material, according to the judge.

This area of the law (the so-called 'intellectual property' of the biographee) has become a minefield for biographers, since the boundary between public reputation and personal privacy can be truly daunting. The British poet Ian Hamilton came up against this when trying to write, in America, the biography of the novelist and short-story writer, J.D. Salinger. After *Catcher in the Rye*, Salinger had become a recluse living in New Hampshire. On hearing of the biography project, Salinger forbade any relatives or friends to talk to the author, nor would he permit any of his unpublished or even copyrighted work (beyond a handful of words) to be quoted – forcing, in a court decision, the disappointed (and admiring) biographer to back off. All Hamilton could then do was publish an account of why he had been unable to write the biography!

So burned was Hamilton by the incident that, in 1992, he even published a book entitled *Keepers of the Flame* – a doleful history of similar cases of quasi-censorship and wilful destruction of literary property by heirs, lest it fall into the 'wrong hands.' Sadly, Hamilton himself came to the conclusion (not held by many biographers today) that 'fifty years is not too long for us to wait for the "whole truth" about a private life.'

Invasions of privacy can certainly hurt individuals, though – if not always for reasons their biographers or outsiders can understand. There are countless examples of Jewish relatives of Holocaust victims, for example, who do not wish to hear their loved ones' names recited during public memorial services, or see their names in (digital) memorial archives. They have every right to feel like this, of course, but a biographer, in a free society, has a responsibility to his own professional ethics – and the truth.

Those ethics can always be judged in terms of the manner in which the biographer has handled his sources. But what of the sources he cannot, or is not permitted to handle? Take, for example, the biographers of the mid-twentieth-century American poet, Sylvia Plath. Her husband, the British poet Ted Hughes, had been in the act of divorcing her when, in a fit of depression, she gassed herself to death in 1963. Since she had made no will, Hughes inherited her estate – including her unpublished literary property and her copyrights. For the next 35 years, there was nothing to prevent him from destroying her irreplaceable journals and novels. He was also entitled to control the publication of her poetry and to ward off any biographer who came too close to the truth, using both the laws of libel (of his own reputation) and of copyright. Using his sister as his *consiglieri*, all biographies of Plath thereafter had to be vetted if the biographer proposed to use any of his or her copyrighted words. In a final snub to frustrated biographers, Hughes himself published, a few weeks before his death in 1998, his own pseudo-biography of their marriage: *Birthday Letters* – a touching volume of poetry, but hardly the truth, and certainly not a serious biography.

How can the biographer be expected to maintain, over the years that it takes to research and write a serious biography, a semblance of ethical self-regard, when his work may spark such passionate negative reactions?

As in the world of portraiture, the true value of a biographer's work will only come late in the day, or even post-mortem. Lady Churchill burned the portrait of her husband, Sir Winston Churchill, by the painter Graham Sutherland – a work of art much mourned today. Similarly, Robert Caro, the distinguished American biographer of Lyndon Baines Johnson, laboured for decades in the presidential archives in Austin, Texas – aware of Johnson's widow, Lady Bird Johnson, staring at him viciously every day he passed her office! Caro's multi-volume opus is today acknowledged to be a masterpiece of political biography. Similarly, the biographer of John F. Kennedy had his private mail opened and disseminated at the JFK Presidential Library in order to smear him in the early 1990s, only for the work, *JFK: Reckless Youth*, to be acknowledged as a classic biography of the young Kennedy decades later.

The truth is that biography can and often does cause pain – thus causing people to strike back. In the real world it is therefore insufficient for the biographer to protest that he is honourable and doing a professional job, according to a code of ethics dating back two millennia. A doctor may follow the Hippocratic Oath not to harm the life of a patient – but a serious biographer in the post-Victorian world *cannot fail* to hurt or disappoint *someone*, given the sensitivities of reputation and the expectations of a modern, curious public. This leaves the biographer having to steer a tricky course: attempting to honour the Plutarchian code of truth and relative objectivity, yet aware, as Virginia Woolf warned, that the modern biographer must present a life that is alive in its personality, its humanness, its individuality and its realness, if it is to be trusted, on the one hand; and yet compete with the extraordinary quasi-realist skills of fiction-writers on the other.

How do biographers thus manage? It would be interesting to find out not only about the trials – metaphorical and real – that modern biographers have undergone to produce and publish their works, but how they see their task morally and ethically, in a world where they will, *inevitably*, be called bad names.

Henry James was but one of the many writers and egoists who abhorred biographers for their intrusive curiosity about real lives, leading to 'unethical' behaviour. James's novella *The Aspern Papers* (1888) portrayed a biographer willing even to seduce the sister of a famous poet's lover to gain access to secret love letters. A century later, critics were *still* following James's precedent. Intrigued by the seeming immortality of Sylvia Plath and the struggles of biographers to get at the truth behind her marriage to Ted Hughes, Janet Malcolm, an American essayist, damned them all as perverts in 1994. 'The transgressive nature of biography is rarely acknowledged,' Malcolm wrote,

> but it is the only explanation for biography's status as a popular genre. The reader's amazing tolerance (which he would extend to no novel written half as badly as most biographies) makes sense only when seen as a kind of collusion between him and the biographer in an excitingly forbidden undertaking: tiptoeing down the corridor together to stand in front of the bedroom door and try to peep through the keyhole.

Malcolm had come to worship Hughes, despite never meeting him when writing her articles. Time did not change her mind. Even eighteen years after Hughes's death, when his extraordinary louche and predatory private life had become public knowledge, Malcolm still upheld Hughes' posthumous right to privacy. Jonathan Bate's new biography of Hughes rendered her almost apoplectic, she claimed, on behalf of Hughes's surviving third (actually second) wife Carol, who had rightly, in Malcolm's view, refused posthumous copyright permission for Professor Bate to use Plath's or Hughes' writings (even laundry bills) for his biography. Beyond Professor Bate's tastelessness, she wrote in an essay in 2016 in the *New York Review of Books*, 'there is Bate's cluelessness about what you can and cannot do if you want to be regarded as an honest and serious writer' – a self-respect that should, she felt, exclude any mention of the suicides of Hughes's partners, his love of deliberate adultery right up to his death, and his liking, she wrote, for 'rough,' 'sadistic' sex.

The moral? Writing biography has, in our litigious world, become an increasingly contested ethical undertaking, with hurt inflicted on every side. Malcolm herself was sued for almost ten years for supposedly fabricating quotations from an interview; the popular American biographer Doris Kearns Goodwin was sued and found to have unwittingly plagiarized significant passages from another biographer, ruining her reputation.

Whether or not he lands in court, our own view is thus that every biographer must live with his own conscience; as must every artist. In 1996, for example, after a long search, the biographer of the famous Dutch poet Jan Hanlo found Mary Bateman, a British lady who had been the poet's girlfriend sixty years previously. Mary was an important source for the biography of the homosexual Hanlo, since she had been the only woman in his life with whom he had had sexual relations. She never understood why their amorous contact had never developed into an actual love relationship – Hanlo not having had the courage to be open about his homosexuality. Mary, who lived far from the Netherlands and Dutch literary culture, and had spent her whole life after Hanlo in Henley-on-Thames, had to hear this news from the biographer. There had been more incidents in her life that she had preferred to keep secret; this was why she distanced herself from her past as best as she could. She had changed her name, no longer spoke to or saw her children, and initially lied in person to the biographer, claiming she had never met Hanlo. Three years after the biography's publication in 1998, however, the biographer was approached by an English-speaking lady from Spain. It had come to her attention that he had spoken to her mother. This knowledge greatly saddened her, for she had not seen her mother for over twenty years! She had not even known whether she was still alive. She asked the biographer to share her mother's address and telephone number.

This question presented the biographer with an ethical dilemma. Mary Bateman obviously did not want to be confronted by anyone from her past, not even her daughter. The biographer had not approached Mary Bateman under false pretences (unlike the fictional storyteller from *The Aspern Papers*) – he had merely wanted information that only she could give him. Mary Bateman had had every right, for her part, to refuse to cooperate with him, but had, in the end, done so. To each his own. But did this mean that it was now the biographer's duty to help her daughter?

He wrote a letter to Mary Bateman in Henley-on-Thames, enclosing the contact details of her daughter, in Spain. If the latter was ever approached by her mother is something we do not know.

Sources: Christine Wiesenthal, 'Ethics and the Biographical Artifact: Doing Biography in the Academy Today', in: ESC: *English Studies in Canada* 32 (2006) 2-3, 63-81; Elsbeth Etty, 'Doden hebben geen privacy. Het persoonlijke in de politieke biografie', in: Hans Renders and Gerrit Voerman (eds), *Privé in de politieke biografie* (Amsterdam: Boom, 2007), 97-107; Antoon De Baets, 'Postume Privacy en reputatie', in: Hans Renders and Gerrit Voerman, *Privé in de politieke biografie* (Amsterdam: Boom, 2007), 108-123; Benito Bisso Schmidt, 'When the historian peeks through the keyhole: biography and ethics', in: *História* 33 (2014) 1, 107-126; Nigel Hamilton, *Biography: A Brief History* (Cambridge MA: Harvard University Press, 2007).

 is for Facts

Without facts, there is no biography. Only fiction.

This is no joke. Living in an era of dictatorships, George Orwell (1903-1950, né Eric Blair – a fact!) saw the threat first-hand. In *Nineteen Eighty-Four* and *Animal Farm,* he used allegorical stories to reveal what happens to a society that no longer respects facts. Thus, the current fact that, in the United States – which is not even a dictatorship – a senior member of the administration could describe uncomfortable truths as 'alternative facts' and 'fake news' is deeply troubling for citizens who value democracy – and biography.

What are 'facts,' though, and when did they become acknowledged as such?

The word 'fact' derives from the Latin, *factum*, a deed, and *factere*, to do. By the early sixteenth century, increasing numbers of writers, jurists and scientists were employing the word to describe verifiable information – and to counter untruths, myths and unsubstantiated claims. Philip Massinger's 1632 biographical play, *Emperor of East*, to take but one example, was based on the life of the Byzantine Emperor Theodisius II and his wife Theodocia, whose rumoured infidelity with a courtier, Paulinus, was the fulcrum of the dramatized version. 'Great Julius would not Rest satisfied,' the printed version of the play ran, 'that his wife was free from fact, But only, for suspicion of a crime, Sued for divorce.'

Fact as a verifiable deed (often an evil deed) led to fact as encompassing more than deed: things such as events, and evidence itself. It was never an absolute. It did not mean that facts could not be disproven by better, more verifiable evidence or proof. Indeed, in this sense the matter of fact is, in its way, much like biography itself. For biography, like history, is a constantly moving, generational genre: a process of careful research and interpretation of facts – interpretations that necessarily speak to the changing concerns of successive generations – and new, or more verifiable, facts; including facts that are found to be false.

In this respect, too, biography is different from fiction. When you are in a library and have to choose between a sixty-year-old biography of Tolstoy and a recent one, you will generally pick the latter – but no one ever argues we should rewrite *War and Peace*!

Every biography, then, has a use-by date, even though this is something that biographers themselves do not like to hear. What concerns us here are the different kinds and qualities of facts used in biography; for when examined close-up, they are more complex than they might initially seem.

First, facts in themselves have little biographical significance; this is something they gain from the manner in which they are employed. Biography, we might say, is never the accumulation of facts, but the relations of them – and between them. A so-called 'factual biography' is a euphemism for a bad biography, sometimes described as the 'beaver versus butterfly' method of writing biography. The beaver 'collects' facts and arranges them in the same way an accountant would; the butterfly respects the facts, but eventually considers their importance and transforms fact into action by working them into a convincing narrative.

Facts do, however, have an intrinsic character, which is something a biographer grows to understand. They range from 'plain facts' to more colourful ones – something that in part goes back to biography's close connection with journalism. In sixteenth- and seventeenth-century England, for example, facts were associated with 'observable truth.' The wonderful travel accounts of exotic countries, written with scientific pretensions, were specimens from the borderland between history and journalism. Claims that people on Terra Australis had tails, and that black people in Africa sported eyes in their souls (in their chests), were taken to be true for a long time. In order to promote these kinds of stories, emphasis was added to the unusual, the weird and the wonderful – preferably in a manner that elevated the unusual, the weird and the wonderful above verifiable facts.

Newsgathering in the seventeenth century was designed to add something to a news story: it commented on the obtained facts. But as C.P. Scott would later argue – 'Comment is free, but facts are sacred' – commenting on something is no excuse for covering up, or even manipulating, facts. 'Discourse of fact' legitimized the possibility of comparing opinions and facts from diverse sources. This increased the importance of facts as *observed events* – i.e., the point of view of the actual observer. In this way, testimony and reportage became part and parcel of fact. The significance of the account of one person's story grew, not because he was a king or a general or an authority, but because he was an eyewitness – something that would become of increasing importance in biography, in terms of evidence.

The more serious periodical press combatted readers' suspicions regarding the more fantastic stories they printed by mentioning the exact time and place of events more often – larding their assumed veracity. Some articles not only featured quotes by eyewitnesses, but added their names as well. At the end of the seventeenth century, some English newspapers even went as far as to publish the names of coffee houses where readers could consult eyewitnesses of a miraculous event, or where readers could find documentation proving the factuality of a described occurrence. The first-person singular was used more and more in such reportage when describing accounts of these happenings: 'I saw this and that'. In his political report on the Netherlands entitled *Observations upon the United Provinces* (1673), Sir William Temple included a 'Map of their State and Government,' suggesting at the very least that his eyewitness account should be read as being purely factual. Of course, such inclusions were not hard evidence for whatever was claimed, but they did create the impression that the facts were *verifiable*.

Through such journalism, the notion of 'fact' became a challenge to biographers. Newspaper reports were increasingly accepted as reliable and factual sources – and therefore useable in biographies. A news report in an English newspaper of the birth of a monstrous child in Holland recorded that this fact was confirmed by 'persons of quality.' As long as they could find witnesses who were perceived as being trustworthy, journalists and scientists would concern themselves well into the seventeenth century with the monstrous, the curious and the wonderful. The story about a man-fish hybrid sighted in the river Thames, sporting a political petition in his hand (or fin), was taken to be true because six sailors had spoken to the politically-conscious amphibian, and all their names were featured in the report. These kinds of eyewitnesses were later used in biography in order to authorize the most wonderful events.

Newspapers would also write about criminals who were found guilty for a fact. This meant that judicial fact became a fact in news – which, in turn, led to biographical fact by its documentation in the then-popular genre of Crime Biography. The broader meaning of 'fact', as a debatable event or an idea with a common interest, thus expanded; the wilful gullibility of the audience becoming part of the biographical equation, or inherent dialogue between biographer and the credulousness of his readers. High-brow biography and low-brow biography, as in the press, tended to pivot on the credibility of the facts and their interpretation.

There were also embarrassing facts – i.e., those facts that some people did not wish to become known. These could range from state secrets to scandalous facts. Since the eighteenth century, these kinds of facts have, arguably, increasingly become the subliminal attraction of reading or viewing biographies. Just as we read who-dunnits in fictional literature, so in biography we have come necessarily to ask the author: who was this person – and were they all that they were cracked up to be, for good or ill? We want to be granted access to deeper, possibly more scandalous information and an understanding of the real subject, via the facts.

Via the facts. For it is the gathering, the arrangement and the interpretation of the facts that makes biography today so potentially contentious, given the 'fact' that there will inevitably be people and even institutions that do not wish such facts to be disseminated or interpreted – leading, as often as not, to judicial outcomes, since it is often a judge or jury who must decide. And not on the intrinsic verifiable veracity of the fact or facts, but their *use*.

One example – which stands for many – is the case of Dutch film-maker Louis van Gasteren, who managed to keep a certain painful fact known within his family circle out of his biography, only for it to be replaced by a judicially ruled fact that everyone knew to be untrue. In 2003, an Amsterdam district court accepted that 'established facts' demonstrated that Louis' sister, the actress Joséphine van Gasteren, 'was rumoured to have [had] an intimate relationship with W.L., boss of the *Sicherheitsdienst* (SD) in Amsterdam as SS-Sturmbahnführer, and, from 1941, supervisor of the *Zentralstelle für jüdische Auswanderung*' – the central office for Jewish 'emigration,' i.e., mass murder. Because the High Council had ruled fifty years earlier that Joséphine had had intimate relations with another SD member, at a time when the true name could not be made public, the High Council ruled again, by precedent, that it could not be made public this time either.

Facts may therefore be colourful and contain truth – but, as argued by Daniel Boorstin, not necessarily palatable truth.

Time and again, biographers stumble across facts that they know will not be appreciated by certain readers, defenders of reputations, or those with political reasons not to welcome them. The biographer of President William J. Clinton, for example, when interviewing the hospital nurse who was on duty when Clinton's mother gave birth to him in Hope, Arkansas, in August 1946, found that the future president had been born full term, weighing over 13 lbs – only eight months after his supposed father had returned from military service in Italy. No factual evidence has yet been found for his real parentage.

Does it matter? Since biographers deal with the lives and deaths of real individuals, it matters to them – but they can at least take comfort in the fact that one day, through DNA analysis, the truth will emerge and will be incorporated in Clinton's life story. After all, it took many years for Annette Gordon-Reed, the biographer of President Jefferson and his family, writing in 2008, to get the Hemings family of Monticello to accept the fact that the deceased president had had a sexual relationship and numerous children by his black slave Sarah, or Sally – a truth finally proven by DNA analysis; or, moreover, that many of these family members had been sold at auction six months after Thomas Jefferson's death in 1826. It was at last a verifiable fact laid bare by a biographer – but it proved a tough fact to accept in a world beset by political, racial and social problems, not only on the part of the two black-and-white branches of the Hemings family, but also on the part of the wider public.

Whether or not 'the facts' can be made public – or how welcome they will be if they are – is one of the greatest challenges facing the dedicated modern biographer. But that, at least, is an honourable challenge, involving freedom of speech, the arcane labyrinth of our systems of justice, the power of the press, and the vicissitudes of a marketplace in a democratic society that tolerates much – arguably too much – of what biographers (especially autobiographers or memoirists) have to offer today.

What is of greater concern to us, increasingly, is the fact that we now live in an age where truth, expressed through verifiable fact, may be trumped so openly, and at such a high political level, by lies – whether these are lies of wilful ignorance or deliberate lies.

Fact, in this respect, is having a hard time; ironically, after having had such a good time! As early as 2005, the satirist Stephen Colbert could mock the leader of the free world, the-then President of the US, George W. Bush, as someone uninterested in, even opposed to, facts – dismissing them and proven data as 'just another opinion.' 'I'm no fan of dictionaries or reference books: they're elitist,' he lampooned the president – coining the word 'truthiness' and inventing this (non-factual) quote: 'I don't trust books. They're all fact, no heart. And that's exactly what's pulling our country apart today.'

Not even Colbert imagined his imaginative lampoon would become established fact a decade later, in a United States where fact-free thinking is *la règle du jeu* in parts of the media and on the hustings – and fact-checking is considered unnecessary, since it might contain an 'inconvenient truth.'

Which is not to claim that fact – verifiable fact – is easy to determine. 'Truth is rarely pure,' wrote Oscar Wilde in *The Importance of Being Earnest*, 'and never simple.' But if biographers will not, or are not permitted, to seek it, there will be no such thing as biography – only hagiography or fiction.

This is an increasingly complex field of study for literary scholars and historians, given the fascination that writers of fiction have shown in modern times, and in view of the market for such work. Julian Barnes wrote a pioneering biographical novel, *Flaubert's Parrot*, in 1984 – half tongue-in-cheek, half playing on French Deconstruction. Nevertheless, he, like most novelists since Virginia Woolf's *Orlando*, was content to call his book a work of fiction. Not all writers are so honest.

The fact is – to use a cliché that often means the very opposite – we live in an age and a culture where traditional boundaries are being elided in the pursuit of greater entertainment, dramatic power, storytelling skill and (*pour vrai dire*) money. Audiences of the 2015 rap-dance-theatrical *Hamilton: An American Musical* – created by Lin-Manuel Miranda – can at least read the biography on which it is based, researched and written by historian Ron Chernow. But what of current memoir,* or Life Writing,* where authors are urged in community colleges and university classes to tell the unverifiable 'facts' of their upbringing, their travails, their supposed experiences (often the worse, the better)? Should these works be classified under autobiography?

However the boundaries may shift in the years ahead, we must hope that fact, at least, remains fact; something that was, sadly, not understood by Margaret Seltzer (pseudonym of Margaret B. Jones) when she published *Love and Consequences* (2008) as a work of non-fiction. She framed the book as the memoir of a girl, part white and part Native American, growing up in South-Central

Los Angeles as a foster child in a world of drug dealers and gang members. During interviews, she would speak with an African American vernacular dialect. The book was praised as 'humane and deeply affecting' by *The New York Times* before being fact-checked. It then turned out that she was white, and that the work was completely fabricated.

Sources: Leon Edel, *Literary Biography* (London: Rupert Hart-Davis, 1957); Leon Edel, *Writing Lives: Principia Biographia* (New York/London: W.W. Norton & Company, 1984); Barbara J. Shapiro, *A Culture of Fact. England, 1550-1720* (Ithaca/London: Cornell University Press, 2000); Daniel Boorstin, *Image: A Guide to Pseudo-Events in America* (New York: Harper, 1961); Jill Lepore, 'After the Fact. In the history of truth, a new chapter begins', in: *The New Yorker,* March 21, 2016; Ray Monk, 'Life without Theory: Biography as an Exemplar of Philosophical Understanding', in: *Poetics Today* 28 (2007) 3, 528–570; Richard Allen and Malcolm Turvey, 'Introduction', in: Ludwig Wittgenstein, *Philosophical Investigations* (Oxford: Basil Blackwell, 1967); Ira Bruce Nadel, 'Fingerprint or Photograph?', in: *Cercle* (2015) 35; Jacqueline Rose, *The Case of Peter Pan or The Impossibility of Children's Fiction* (London/Basingstoke: Macmillan, 1984).

 **is for Group Biography**

Biography is not to be confused with prosopography – a term invented for historians by Lawrence Stone in 1971. Prosopography is the attempt to picture and understand past societies where there is very little biographical evidence to go on – as in the case of, say, Neanderthal society. Its collective portraiture, operating like a blurry school photo and based upon multifaceted evidence ranging from food in surviving prehistoric stomachs to cancerous bones, can be of great help to the historian. It is pretty useful to biographers, too. Every biography of an individual has to examine that selected person within a socio-historical context in order to avoid false historicism. Nevertheless, prosopography is not biography.*

So where does this leave *group* biography: the study of two or more individuals? And how many more, in this respect, is 'more'?

This is not a facetious question. In fact, it goes to the heart of biography – which is, of course, never about a single life alone, but inevitably covers, however imperfectly, a multitude of lives – from family and friends to colleagues and enemies. Whereas a photographic portrait or a painted portrait can be restricted to a single person in a studio, biography can never pull the frame in that far. A biography may certainly shine the spotlight on a single character – but it also needs a cast, or *dramatis personae*, to make it true-to-life: real life, in which, from the moment of our birth, we are never entirely alone.

Spotlights on groups, rather than single individuals, first became popular with Plutarch, whose *Parallel Lives* paired Greek and Roman subjects, the better to contrast and compare them – thereby creating a literary pantheon that has never really been surpassed. His overarching purpose was to explore the ethical aspects of his subjects' life journeys, without losing sight of their individuality. Another biographer of the time, Suetonius, was more interested in succession *within* a group: comparing successive Caesars against those who had preceded them, the better to define and distinguish their individual life courses. His work, *The Twelve Caesars*, also became a lasting literary achievement; it is still read today, thousands of years later.

Over subsequent centuries, interest in the biography of groups never really died, whether in recording and comparing the lives of saints, or kings* and queens, or artists, or military figures; or, later, engineers. A reader who is interested in one individual, after all, might well be interested in more of them – with authors willing to oblige in what the biography-essayist Craig Howes has called 'collective lives.' Such groupings, however, remained largely those of category or profession, and it was not until biography itself changed in the early twentieth century that the nature of the group biography may be said to have changed – something that is worth examining more closely.

In *Eminent Victorians* (1918), Lytton Strachey led the swing back to the Plutarchian fascination with ethical rather than collective biography. But where Plutarch had been concerned with locating human virtue, Strachey was determined to expose the opposite: namely, the mythic or phony nature of nineteenth-century 'virtuous' heroes. From the first line of the book he made clear that he was declaring war on history, as practised by Victorian historians. 'For ignorance,' he thundered, 'is the first requisite of the historian' – men who had admittedly assembled a 'vast quantity of information,' but to little purpose other than to conceal the truth about the age. Spotlighting the lives of 'an ecclesiastic' (Cardinal Manning), an 'educational authority' (Dr. Arnold), a 'woman of action' (Florence Nightingale) and a 'man of adventure' (General Gordon), Strachey skewered their noble reputations with deft, mocking accounts of their real underlying characters in order to 'illustrate rather than explain' how misrepresented they had been, especially by long-winded historical biographers. 'Those two fat volumes, with which it is our custom to commemorate the dead – who does not know them,' he asked, 'with their ill-digested masses of material, their slipshod style, their tone of tedious panegyric, their lamentable lack of selection, of detachment, of design?'

The response from the reading public both in England and America was ecstatic, thanks to the desire to lampoon an older generation that had led the world not to peace, but into world war. In part, however, *Eminent Victorians* was admired because Strachey was finally standing in shoes as big as those of Plutarch and Suetonius in his willingness to be an author, not simply a scribe.

Eminent Victorians thus set a twentieth-century literary example that inspired generations of biographers to undertake group biographies – works that not only helped record an age or dynasty, but *judged*, like Suetonius, its exemplary figures. Group biography, in other words, became an antidote to existing group-think or received opinion about past individuals: not only their public personas, but also their private ones, in a century where the *secrets d'alcoves* were no longer confined to the alcove.

It is this Stracheyian tension between group-revelation, on the one hand, and fascination with individuality on the other that has characterized the best of modern group biography. Humphrey Carpenter, for example, was the admiring biographer of writers such as J.R.R. Tolkien and W.H. Auden. He then found, though, he couldn't resist the desire to paint group portraits of such characters, such as the *Inklings* (portraying Tolkien, C.S. Lewis, Charles Williams and their friends) and *Geniuses Together: American Writers in Paris in the 1920s*. When it came to English interwar literature, however, he was more critical. He could not but recognize in Evelyn Waugh the dominant figure of the age. Waugh 'in his person and his writings,' as Carpenter explained, 'displayed the characteristics and conflicts of the group more intensely and dramatically, than any other member.' Modelling his group biography *Brideshead Generation* around Waugh, in 1989, Carpenter attempted a group portrait that would be read 'as a small piece of cultural history, an account of a certain strain in

English life and writing during this [twentieth] century': a warts-and-all parade of English class snobbery, of moneyed hedonism, and of post-World War I dystopia that no individual biography could so well convey. The numbers, in a word, counted – as they had in *Eminent Victorians*.

Other biographers took note, even where their critical antennae were less sharp than Strachey's – or Carpenter's, for that matter. Almost always they tried, at least, to revisit existing assumptions, myths, public ignorance or prejudices. Thomas Flemings' *The Intimate Lives of the Founding Fathers* (2009) thus sought not only to narrate the personal lives of America's revolutionary leaders, but to do so by including, for the first time, their wives and lovers in equal measure – thus removing the Founding Fathers from their pedestals and placing them in their bedrooms as everyday human beings. Fleming thereby prepared America for a revolution on the stage. When the hip-hop, immigrant-exotic musical *Hamilton* was performed on Broadway in 2016, based on Ron Chernow's 2004 biography, it was showered with laurels – though not by the anti-immigrant 45th US President, who tweeted that he had 'heard' it was 'overrated.'

Less personal but equally agenda-driven was *The Innovators: How a Group of Hackers, Geniuses, and Geeks Created the Digital Revolution* (2014) by Walter Isaacson. Isaacson had written an 'authorized' biography of Steve Jobs, the founding father of Apple. Moreover, earlier in his career as a biographer, in 1986, Isaacson had written a group biography of post-war high-level US Administration officials, *The Wise Men*. Inspired by his research for *Steve Jobs* in 2011, he now switched his attention to technology, not only to lace together the lives of men and women who had made a huge contribution to innovation, but to emphasize the element of creative *collaboration*: 'why their ability to work as teams made them even more creative,' as he wrote in the introduction to the book, since he aimed to show exactly how 'innovation actually happens in the real world.'

Group biography, in other words, was not abandoning the strong, scientifically-inspired curiosity that had marked its development (especially in collective biographical works) in the eighteenth and nineteenth centuries. It remained, at heart, *educative* – and it is perhaps this *Zwiespalt*, or tension, that distinguishes group biography from 'single' or monofocused biography. For the very act of choosing a group of individuals, rather than working outwards from one, implies a curiosity, at the very least, as to what, sociologically-speaking, *links* them.

Consider, for example, dynastic groups: the Twelve Caesars who ruled Rome after the fall of the Republic; the Tudors of England; the Hapsburgs of Europe; the Romanovs of Russia; the Bourbons of France; or the Kaisers of Germany. The group biographer of those families, although he is narrating the course of their lives and the power that they exercised in history, is fundamentally looking, like every good historian, for patterns – and anti-patterns, too, that may 'prove' the patterns. It is as though the group biographer were seeking a DNA that helps 'explain' their rise, survival and eventual fall, at least in dynamic relation to their times.

The same tension may be seen in the group biography of movements or 'isms' in history – such as impressionism, or expressionism, or existentialism. In telling the stories of the figures belonging to those movements, the group biographer is curious to see what common factors linked them, inspired them – or caused them to split away. That scrutiny, whether overt or implicit, is also the lure for the reader.

Take, for instance, Sarah Bakewell's *At the Existentialist Café* (2016). Bakewell, who had written *How to Live* in 2010, a highly-regarded life of the philosopher Montaigne, had first become interested in Jean-Paul Sartre at the age of sixteen. She had then studied for a PhD in philosophy, but had dropped out, and subsequently 'lost the knack of reading' the existentialist philosophers such as Heidegger, Sartre and Merleau-Ponty. It was only decades later, while researching Montaigne, that she became aware of how far the world had moved on from existentialism. She became intrigued as to what exactly the existentialist movement had been, and why – as well as how it held up in comparison with the fads and favourites of two decades later. She also became fascinated, in a new way, by the individuals who had been in the movement: what bonded them and what divided them. Taking her cue from the English existentialist philosopher-novelist Iris Murdoch – who had written a full-length book on Sartre – she became intrigued by the notion of 'inhabited philosophy,' or the *personal* stories of the people who collectively created and developed the existential movement. 'We should be able to look in through the windows of a philosophy, as it were, and see how people occupy it,' Bakewell wrote, 'how they move about and how they conduct themselves.'

A generation earlier, such an approach might well have been mocked – for whether in the study of art or science, or mathematics or philosophy or literature, biography was largely considered a distraction from 'pure' appreciation of the work produced. Ending her group biography of the existentialists, Bakewell put this very well. 'When I first read Sartre and Heidegger,' she wrote,

> I didn't think the details of a philosopher's personality or biography were important. This was the orthodox belief in the field at the time, but it also came from my being too young myself to have much of a sense of history. I intoxicated myself with concepts, without taking account of their relationship to events and to all the odd data of their inventors' lives. Never mind lives; ideas were the thing.

'Thirty years later,' she confessed, 'I have come to the opposite conclusion. Ideas are interesting, but people are vastly more so.' It was in this way that Bakewell, reviewing 'all the fury and vivacity of the existentialist cafés,' was finally able to understand and come to terms with her hero Jean-Paul Sartre's extended subservience to the doctrine of Soviet infallibility.

Group biography, then, has returned to its original ethical and political agenda, as in the time of Plutarch and Suetonius: biographers seeking to understand patterns and movements in history, yet mercifully open to the uniqueness of the individual human being, just as in a 'normal' modern 'single' biography.

That said, group biographies are almost necessarily superficial, from the 'single' biographer's perspective. How could it be otherwise? Single biography is tough work; it takes a minimum of three years' research and composition to publish a serious life based on original sources. Multiple lives, if addressed in the same way, would take decades. Group biographies therefore tend to be 'based' on the work of 'single' biographers, and thus inevitably come across as second-hand, borrowed, even plagiarized. With some exceptions, they are not generally written by biographers who have already undertaken the biography of a single member of the chosen group: a distinction that tells us more than any theorizing of the difference between single and group biography. A single biographer *cares* about his portrait of the individual, and will go to great lengths to get it right, down to the tiniest details – details which, as Plutarch noted, are vital not only in conveying the individual personality of the subject, but also in persuading the reader to trust a biographer willing to go to such lengths. This cannot be said of group biography. In fact, as readers we often find we *don't* really trust the portraits contained in the group. What we are more interested in are the connections – direct, implicit or merely comparative – between characters that an intelligent group biographer reveals and highlights. At least, such would have seemed the case even a decade ago. Yet in our twenty-first century, we can also see a new dynamic that is favouring group biography, one that is driven by two trends.

The first is the global phenomenon that has come to be known as 'the social network' – indeed, the phrase began as a biographical film called *The Social Network*, in 2010, telling the story of the group of billionaires who invented Facebook. Facebook, Instagram, Tumblr, Twitter... In an era of radical technological development linking people across hitherto-daunting social, economic and global distances, the ties of interpersonal relations have made the very science of *group* observation more trendy than individual dissection – though it often wallows in the sheer diversity of character and performance across such groups. Whether it be family, such Mary Lovell's *The Sisters: The Saga of the Mitford Family* (2001), friendship (such as Dennis Rasmussen's *The Infidel and the Professor*, 2017) or profession (such Denise Kiernan's *The Girls of Atomic City*, 2013), the public's curiosity about *group* dynamics shows no sign of abating.

The second new phenomenon is due to science rather than technology: the Human Genome Project. The story of the discovery of DNA in 1952 was memorably told in a history written by Dr. James Watson, *The Double Helix* (1968) – a sort of group memoir, but so human and honest in its record of sexism and connivance that its first publisher, Harvard University Press, declined to bring it out. Watson himself, having won the Nobel Prize in 1962 for the discovery, was in 1990 named the Project Head of what became the National Human Genome Research Institute, with the target of identifying and mapping the entire human genetic code. Expected to take fifteen years, in the event the project was declared complete in 2003. Its sequencing had vast implications not only for medicine and the study of evolution, but also group biography. 'Six degrees of separation' had been a joking reference (first made in 1929) to the overt and hidden connectedness between all humans. Now, suddenly, science was able to show this was in fact the truth – indeed, there was potentially less genetic difference between a white person and a black person than between two black people. This, in turn, has caused the world to revisit a thousand assumptions, prejudices and misperceptions, as shown by Annette Gordon's *The Hemings of Monticello* (2008); and has caused an exponential spike in interest in family biography and genealogy.

The result? Rightly or wrongly, double/treble/multiple group biographies have grown enormously in popularity, and we anticipate that they will continue to do so. Just as one of the important tasks of biography in a free society is to correct historiography – especially superficial history – a new and major task of 'pure' or 'single' biography will be, we expect, to provide trustworthy data and correction to group biography: the wave of the future.

Sources: Nigel Hamilton, *Biography: A Brief History* (Cambridge MA, Harvard, 2007); Craig Howes, 'Collective Biography,' in: *Encyclopedia of Life Writing*, ed. Margaretta Jolly (London: Fitzroy Dearborn, 2001); Sarah Bakewell, *At the Existentialist Café* (New York: Other Press, 2016); Adam Rutherford, *A Brief History of Everyone Who Ever Lived* (New York: Experiment, 2017); Plutarch, *Vitae parallellae*, numerous editions; Lawrence Stone, 'Prosopography,' *Daedalus*, Winter 1971, 46-9; Lytton Strachey, *Eminent Victorians* (New York: Modern World Library, 1918).

 **is for History**

In February 2018, the parliament of Poland – a state that belongs to the European Union – passed a law forbidding the use of the phrase 'Polish death camps,' and made it a crime to accuse the 'Polish nation' of complicity in the Holocaust, punishable by a fine or up to three years in prison. 'Scholars fear a new initiative could whitewash history,' *The New York Times* reported.

History had once again joined its sibling, biography, in falling foul of criminal law – and for indicting national honour, just as biography had so often questioned the reputation of an individual.

Standing in society's dock for impugning honour is, of course, not the only connection between history and biography. Since Greek and Roman times, the two genres have followed many of the same paths and observed many of the same disciplines or methods, especially in the field of data-gathering and examination. Moreover, in its quest to chronicle times past, history has provided the crucial context for biography, while biography has provided information and insight into the individuals who 'make' history.

Inasmuch as biography may be said to be the history of an individual, historians have always supplied the very lifeblood of biography. A shared desire to discover and reveal facts, to expose myths and establish a verifiable, credible idea of the truth about our human – even non-human – antecedents has always been what unites historians and biographers, even if the ultimate goals of their genres are different. What threatened to split them apart in the nineteenth century was the rise of History in German universities as a learned profession, a pseudo-science, followed by British and American colleges; while biography was assigned no place, let alone a capital 'B'.

As the historian Richard J. Evans has pointed out, the 'science' of history was in fact a linguistic misnomer rather than an accurate definition. *Wissenschaft* in *Geschichtswissenschaft* – the German word for history – merely means learning and knowledge. The term 'science,' however, gave the discipline of history an added cachet in English. In time, historians began to believe it themselves. Leopold von Ranke coined the memorable phrase, *wie es eigentlich gewesen ist* – i.e., the search to discover the past 'as it really was' – and thus, before the nineteenth century was out, the American historian Herbert Baxter Adams could claim history had 'evolved from a nursery dogma into a laboratory of scientific truth.' By 1903, the Regius Professor of History at Cambridge University, J.B. Bury, was claiming 'History is a science, no less and no more.'

Such an ambitious assertion was bound to produce a backlash. Even Ranke had been criticized for being insufficiently nationalistic, like certain contemporary German historians such as Heinrich von Treitschke. After all, History, in pursuing knowledge of the past, had always contributed to the sense of cultural and national identity in a country; in other words, whether as the stuff of Shakespeare's plays or the analysis of economic capitalism, it was always political – and often politicized as a source of political, social and economic lessons for the society of today and tomorrow. How, then, could it be likened to an objective science? Undeterred, historians loved the notion. In 1918, for example, the historian Oswald Spengler published *The Decline of the West*, followed year later by *Prussianism and Socialism*, predicting a future of Caesarian socialism: society becoming a 'totality' in which 'the happy citizen receives orders and obeys them' – under a dictator.

Like many thousands of others, Adolf Hitler became an avid reader of Spengler; he particularly approved of Spengler's dismissal of Marx as a Jewish historian with a religious hatred of physical labour that went against the long ethos of Prussian history. 'In history as it really is, there can be no conciliations,' Spengler wrote, updating Ranke. Whoever thought there could be compromise was plainly deluded, or attempting to avoid his fear of 'the absurd ways in which events do occur,' by thinking he could 'control them by means of treaties. There is but one end to all the conflict, and that is death' – by which Spengler meant the 'death of individuals, of peoples, of cultures.' In their place would arise an 'imperialism,' a 'domination of Faustian civilization, i.e. of the whole earth, by a single formative principle, not by appeasement or compromise but by conquest and annihilation.'

This was heady stuff from an historian – and sounded all the more so as Hitler's Wehrmacht attacked France, Holland and Belgium in 1940, and the Soviet Union in 1941. Clearly there was an enormous difference between the historian as chronicler or antiquarian, and the historian as interpreter, even speculator.

As the world adjusted to the subsequent defeat of Hitler and the Axis powers and sought – in the West, at least – to remove rampant ideology from the study of history, literary critics and linguists pointed out that even language itself is ideological, and claimed that historians, working and writing in their various languages, were thus living in a bubble of their own making; moreover, they were not even aware of the bubble. Structuralism became post-structuralism and deconstruction, together making for postmodernism. It became a movement across many fields, including anthropology and literary studies. It was particularly threatening to the study of history, however, since the very undertaking of history itself was under attack. History, historians such as Hayden White argued, was not only unconsciously ideological, but its methodology and tools were exposed as fraudulent – tainted by philosophical ignorance, racism, sexism, colonialism, patriarchism, and other isms.

By the early 1990s, many 'traditional' historians had had enough of such attacks. The German-born British historian Sir Geoffrey Elton, a specialist in the Tudor period and Regius Professor of History at Cambridge, spoke for the majority of his colleagues in the profession, denouncing postmodernist ideas about history as 'menacing' and 'absurd.' Postmodernists, Elton claimed, had committed the 'ultimate heresy' – introducing into the academy a 'frivolous nihilism' that was poisoning young gullible historians, especially in the United States, where anything new had automatic credibility. 'In battling against people who would subject historical studies to the dictates of literary critics,' as well as linguistics professors such as Ferdinand de Saussure and Jacques Derrida, 'we historians are, in a way, fighting for our lives. Certainly we are fighting for the lives of innocent young people beset by devilish tempters who claim to offer higher forms of thought and deeper truths and insights – the intellectual equivalent of crack.'

For such historians, what hurt the most was the postmodernist assault on truth as being nothing more than a fiction. Lawrence Stone, Dodge Professor of History at Princeton, publicly denounced the 'attack from extreme relativists from Hayden White to Derrida' on the 'hard won professional expertise in the study of evidence that was worked out in the late nineteenth century.' The notion that 'truth is unknowable' was anathema to Stone – not because he believed in *the* definitive truth, but because he felt the *search* for it, and the disproof of fiction, myth, lies or misapprehension, was an essential part of the historian's role. For his part, the labour historian Raphael Samuel denounced the 'deconstructive turn' in modern intellectual discourse; he pleaded for a return to the notion of history as a 'record of the past, more or less faithful to the facts,' rather than sneering at facts as 'an invention, or fiction, of historians themselves.'

Certainly, such devoted historians had a right to feel besieged, for, in a way, they were: they were sitting ducks, and the perfect enemy for critics unable or unwilling to do real research work, or write readable narrative history themselves. In the view of critics, the historians in their sights tended to be successful authors and educators: established figures in their profession, and clearly too comfortable by far in their assumptions. 'By the 1980s,' Richard Evans wrote, 'the long search for a scientific method of history had failed to yield any definitive results,' and the 'argument that history is, or should be, a science, in principle not different from quantum mechanics or crystallography, began to come under sustained attack, more radical than ever before.'

The new assault – like D-Day – was made on five beaches. First, there was the language being used by historians, whose employers were derided by Derrida for their lack of linguistic reflection; the 'text' per se. Then there was the *use* of texts by historians as evidence – again, without self-critical linguistic reflection. Third, there was the 'literary' nature of history – its storytelling essence, closer to fiction than science. Fourth, there was the arrogance of the historian: his or her assumption that the past could ever be reconstructed 'as it really was,' when this was impossible: the observer, as in the analogy of Schrödinger's cat, inevitably influencing the result of the experiment or project. And finally, there was the problem of relativity: that there could be no pure 'facts' or accepted truths, for everything was relative, mere figments of the imagination in the eyes and mind of the beholder.

Simultaneously with this linguistic assault, however, came those who felt history, as *le grand récit*, was wanting in another respect: namely, that it had left out too many aspects and people in the past, from colonial citizens to women to blacks to transgendered individuals. History thus sustained a major attack on two fronts at the same time – in its language and its chosen subjects of examination.

As postmodern observers such as Professor Alun Munslow noted with embarrassment, this was ironic: history was under 'sustained attack' for being an impossible undertaking, one that was no more than fiction, while *also* being indicted for not including enough history in its purview by telling the history of women – 'herstory' – and other excluded or forgotten subjects.

The once-proud – over-proud – discipline of History, as a result, retreated into a postmodern tapestry of minor fragments, exemplified in the *Annales* school of history, whereby those historians still willing to brave deconstructionist critics and put their work out for public view would do so only in tiny doses, with modest, tentative aspirations. Even the titles of their journal papers were required to include ironic or opposite terms, to indicate to the reader the author's unwillingness to be seen to be advancing any kind of actual rather than tentative interpretation of (non-) events....

History, in other words, became a big mess – with many a student or would-be practitioner wishing historians had never masqueraded as scientists.

For biographers, this saga, stretching across several decades from the 1970s, was a sight to behold. Many biographers had studied history at university; was it then possible that the whole historical enterprise was now being trashed as fiction – mutton dressed up as lamb? Moreover, how would the 'sustained attack' affect biography, they wondered? Would biographers have to retreat to the benches and content themselves, like unwanted baseball players, with practice nets? The only journal devoted exclusively to the genre, *Biography*, had been started in Hawaii by Leon Edel, the distinguished multi-volume biographer of Henry James. Soon Edel, too, was cast as a villain, his journal swamped by linguists and literary postmodernists warring against *le grand récit*, and in love with brackets.

Fortunately, on the mainland of America and across Europe, non-academic biographers – that is to say, writers devoted to storytelling and the record of real, as opposed to fictional, lives – were unimpressed by *Biography*, even where they knew of the journal's existence. In the postmodern assault on history, they saw in fact a great opportunity. Instead of cowering behind barricades or in dugouts, they set about making biography the *grand récit du jour*: an unashamed, unfettered, unselfconscious attempt to explore and reconstruct past (and even present) real lives. What had become tainted in the hands of historians was now part and parcel of a fresh multi-pronged approach to non-fiction storytelling, employing techniques derived from journalism, filmmaking, television, design, the arts, psychology, criminology, literary studies and other professions – yet benefitting most of all, ironically, from the practice of history before its fall from grace.

The 'biographical turn,' as it was later called, thus became a golden age of biography, almost 2,000 years after Plutarch, as historian after historian now turned to biography, rather than to history, in order to recount man's (and woman's) past, by focusing on selected real lives. Because biography had never been taught at university, or been subjected to theorizing – indeed, had been ignored as amateur – it was free of deconstruction and what was called 'deconstructive consciousness,' better understood as self-consciousness. For as every child knows, effective storytelling must maintain the interest and curiosity of the reader, viewer or listener – and too much self-consciousness, or tentativeness, was death to storytelling.

Historian after historian thus joined the growing cohort of un-deconstructed biographers – Doris Kearns Goodwin, Alison Weir, Blanche Wiesen Cook, Ian Kershaw, Robert Dallek, Andrew Roberts, Martin Gilbert, H. W. Brands, Martin Sherwin, David Nasaw, Annette Gordon-Reed, Ben Pimlott, Niall Ferguson… In doing so, such historians joined with fellow-authors representing every realm of the humanities in the modern (rather than 'postmodern') biographical enterprise: authors who welcomed them, since they had always looked to historians for reliable historical context for their own work, and to maintain the guiding principles of good research. The latter included respect for facts and truth, as well as a serious, well-founded *moral* engagement in exploring the past: the very aspects most under attack by deconstructionists of history.

Even historians writing history took courage from this biographical, non-deconstructionist wave, and began reverting to *grands récits* history, complete with footnotes and without brackets. However, to their horror, the cultural and political damage done – whether inadvertently or deliberately – by deconstructionists had gone much deeper than they realized, in fact had reached the internal or vital organs of state. Russians had always had an ambivalent regard for the truth. But in 2016, with the rise of an outsider-businessman as president of the United States, the Western world also experienced the public trashing of traditional concepts of 'facts,' 'truth' and 'verifiable' news and sources. What empirical, traditional historians had always feared – and warned against – now came to pass as modern cybertechnology and social media were cynically employed to deconstruct, ridicule and avoid the critical apparatus which historians, among others, had spent centuries developing in order to separate fact from fiction, and truth from propaganda. Too late, it was found that Russian trolls had subverted the US presidential election campaign by using invented web names and addresses, hacked emails and widely-spread disinformation – sadly undetected by a press and a public weakened by decades of deconstructionist notions of relativity and the supposedly impossible nature of truth, and the collecting of factual evidence.

Watching this tragedy unfold, biographers were as troubled as the historians. For the most part, however, they felt less guilty at having surrendered their high ground to poststructuralists and postmodernists, with such disastrous real-life – i.e., not theoretical – results. Biographers had never subscribed to the view that their work was scientific, or a model for present or future society. Their focus had always been on *individuals*: their portraits unashamedly moral in that the author, too, was an individual, advancing a personal opinion – but one based on hard work. For *work* was what separated, in their view, the theorist and the historian. With the exception, perhaps, of Michel Foucault (author of *The History of Sexuality*), no theorist had ever produced a serious, readable and useful work of history, biographers had noted with fascination.

Work, in short, was the ultimate *sine qua non* of historical discourse – and of the exhumation of past individuals, too. Spending years researching and interpreting a real life gave the biographer the right not only to re-tell that person's life story, but to offer, as a result, personal judgement. Practice – the practice of biography – might not make perfect, but it did demonstrate real work, real thought, real evaluation, and real presentation or narrative, which anyone was at liberty to contest *if they also did the requisite research and work*. Ignorance was no excuse for 'alternative' views.

In a Western society in which the market for real-life stories was constantly expanding, and in divergent media, biography became a continuously self-correcting field, as history had once been.

And what a lot of work biographers *did* put in! A fusion of traditionalist, empirical historianship and the unashamed, personal narrative of real lives, modern biography offered – and still offers – the historian safe passage beyond the ruins of deconstructed history. Retiring in 2014 from his Regius Professorship of History at Cambridge University, Richard Evans – doyen of historians of Nazi Germany – decided to write a biography, on which he is now working.

Appropriately, it records the life of a fellow historian.

Sources: Marc Santora, 'Holocaust Law in Poland Chips at Shared Pain,' *The New York Times*, February 7, 2018; Richard J. Evans, *In Defence of History* (New York: Norton, 1999); Joyce Appleby, Lynn Hunt and Margaret Jacob *Telling the Truth about History* (New York: Norton, 1994); Alun Munslow, *Deconstructing History* (London: Routledge, 1997); John Tosh, *The Pursuit of History* (New York: Longman, 1995); John Lewis Gaddis, *The Landscape of History* (Oxford: Oxford University Press, 2002); Gordon S. Wood, *The Purpose of the Past* (New York: Penguin, 2008).

 # is for Identity

In a volume of essays funded by his friends in 1841, Ralph Waldo Emerson was at pains to point out the subjectivity of history, especially biography. 'We are always coming up with the emphatic facts of history in our private experience,' he wrote, 'and verifying them' in our own life stories. 'All history becomes subjective,' he mused; 'in other words, there is properly no history; only biography'.

That statement became a sort of shibboleth, scorned by historians who ignored his essential point. As a poet, Emerson wished readers to *feel* about the figures whose real lives and experiences they were reading:

> Every revolution was first a thought in one man's mind, and when the same thought occurs to another man, it is the key to that era. Every reform was once a private opinion, and when it shall be a private opinion again, it will solve the problem of the age. The fact narrated must correspond to something in me to be credible or intelligible. We as we read must become Greeks, Romans, Turks, priest and king, martyr and executioner, must fasten these images to some reality in our secret experience, or we shall learn nothing rightly. What befell Asdrubal or Caesar Borgia is as much an illustration of the mind's powers and depravations as what has befallen us. Each new law and political movement has meaning for you. Stand before each of its tablets and say, 'Under this mask did my Proteus nature hide itself.' This remedies the defect of our too great nearness to ourselves. This throws our actions into perspective: and as crabs, goats, scorpions, the balance, and the waterpot lose their meanness when hung as signs in the zodiac, so I can see my own vices without heat in the distant persons of Solomon, Alcibiades, and Catiline.

Identity and identification thus went hand in hand for Emerson. For his part, Thomas Carlyle, the Scottish philosopher, historian and biographer, felt the 'distant persons' should be confined to 'great men of history', as he wrote at the same time as Emerson, in 1840.

> We cannot look, however imperfectly, upon a great man, without gaining something by him. He is the living light-fountain, which it is good and pleasant to be near. The light which enlightens, which has enlightened the darkness of the world; and this not as a kindled lamp only, but rather as a natural luminary shining by the gift of Heaven; a flowing light-fountain, as I say, of native original insight, of manhood and heroic nobleness; — in whose radiance all souls feel that it is well with them.... No nobler feeling than this of admiration for one higher than himself dwells in the breast of man.

And with that – deploring the 'dilettantism, the curse of these ages, a curse which will not last forever' – he delivered his famous dictum: 'The History of the world is but the Biography of great men.'

Mmm. Fast-forward a hundred years, to a time when the world was consumed by world war. The notion of great men as a light-fountain for admiration had become somewhat tarnished, and the notion of great men as the basis of history more contested. Carlyle had claimed that 'the Hero has been worshipped' in 'all times and places. It will ever be so. We all love great men; love, venerate and bow down submissive before great men: nay can we honestly bow down to anything else? Ah, does not every true man feel that he is himself made higher by doing reverence to what is really above him?'

Hitler, Mussolini, Hirohito, Stalin? It did not seem such a great idea in the 1940s. In reality, Carlyle had cautioned against reverence for false 'figures,' though, in his 'Lectures on Heroes', and had gone on to plead for conscientious, serious biography as the way to examine supposedly great men more thoughtfully, and to recognize where their feet were made of clay. Only a 'superficial unbelieving generation', he wrote, 'with no eye but for the surfaces and semblances of things, could form such notions of Great Men.'

In any event, a century later, following the most violent war in human history, there was an understandable move away from 'Great Man' biography, and a demonstrable swing towards Emerson's alternative: the subjective view of history and biography. In the post-war, existentialist world of the 1940s and 1950s, subjectivity was expressed in proliferating biographies, autobiographies and memoirs of people who would never have been thought worthy of a life-chronicle in earlier times, but whose suffering identities now connected with the subjective experience of readers, just as Emerson had suggested. People of colour, for a start. Women. Homosexuals ... Identity itself became a new fulcrum of interest, replacing old heroes. 'Only connect', Margaret Wilcox had exhorted in E.M. Forster's *Howard's End*, in 1910. Half a century after publication of the novel, the biographee was connected with the reader in a multiplicity of identities – rich and poor, and of every stripe. It was as though an anthropologist had spread magic powder over the post-World War II world, energizing literature, history, biography and science. Social scientists like Alfred Kinsey, for example, proceeded to amass statistical evidence of complex modern sexuality and behaviour, while the universe of biography experienced a similar big bang, exploding in every direction in lives with whom readers could subjectively identify. Black suffering, feminist reportage, Holocaust victimization, transgendering ... Their biographical accounts – whether portraits or self-portraits – probably came to constitute the largest archive of human individual identity and experience ever assembled – a treasure trove for future generations or extra-terrestrials interested in who we once were...

Within this biographical expansion, it was the autobiographical memoir* which most exploited this trend – a fact that university literature and language departments were quick to exploit. The close study of Cervantes' or Corneille's texts elicited far less responsiveness among students than the chance to study and to practice, *themselves*, memoir and what became known as 'creative non-fiction' – later called blogs. If identity was subjective – namely the construct that a person creates of himself – then there were many who found themselves dissatisfied by their existing identities. The search for a new, alternative, or deeper, personal identity now underwrote – figuratively and literally – myriad autobiographical personal outpourings, while in the public arena Identity Politics became a marketplace for claims of oppression. In 1988, the distinguished biographer Robert Skidelsky had protested in vain that the study of achievement, in biography, was giving way to an almost exclusive focus on the 'life itself, not what the life enabled a person to achieve. Or more precisely,' he lamented, 'the life *is* the achievement.'

Skidelsky's complaint was prescient. The lure of subjective, Emersonian identification with other people's identities became so strong, in fact, that faux-memoir became inevitable, as more and more memoirists sought to climb on the commercial and public bandwagon, inventing stories of their travails under the Nazis, or racist oppression, sexual abuse or drug addiction. James Frey's memoir of incarceration and drug affliction, *A Million Little Pieces* (2003), became a huge bestseller, lauded and promoted by Oprah Winfrey on her TV book club show in 2005 – until exposed as a fraud. In 2008, Margaret B. Jones's *Love and Consequences*, about growing up as an American Indian foster child, also became a bestseller before being exposed as a fraud; while Misha Defonseca's *Misha: A Memoire of the Holocaust years* – in which she claimed her parents had been executed as members of the Belgian resistance – took eleven years to expose as fraudulent, in 2008. 'Ever since I can remember,' as the author defended herself, 'I felt Jewish'.

Biographers, mercifully, proved less gullible – possibly because less money was involved. Their routines and their increasingly professional, forensic investigation techniques made them less prone to fantasy and the lure of big sales. But not always. Hugh Trevor-Roper, the distinguished British historian and biographer of the figures around Hitler (immortalized as quasi-operatic figures in his book *The Last Days of Hitler*) was paid by newspaper publisher Rupert Murdoch to authenticate and promote Hitler's 'lost' diaries in 1983. There were 60 volumes, which Murdoch's newspapers were intent upon serializing. When the so-called diaries – written on post-war paper – were exposed as fraudulent, Trevor-Roper's reputation was ruined, and the men responsible for the forgery were sentenced to four-and-a-half years in prison. Clearly, identity theft was not only a banking problem.

The rise of Identity Politics – demanding greater attention for past suffering at the hands of abusers – is having a major impact on modern Western society in the twenty-first century. Apologies and even reparations are increasingly being demanded. *Harper's Magazine*, for example, estimated that $100 trillion was, in theory, due to descendants of black slaves who had done an estimated 222,505,049 hours of forced labour – and the first step, a resolution passed by the US House of Representatives, was taken in 2008. Meanwhile, lawsuits against banking, insurance, textile, railway and tobacco companies were filed – though exactly who would qualify in terms of aggrieved identity and be eligible for restitution was less clear.

As much as Identity Politicians have sought to trumpet their causes and identities, however, so they have tended to exclude or diminish others in theirs. Black Lives Matter became a *cause célèbre* in America in 2016, but it almost inevitably inflamed a counter-sense of grievance among white citizens – one which, in part, led to the election of a deeply anti-immigrant white man as the 45th US President, having claimed his black predecessor was not by birth an American, and therefore ineligible to be president, while his female rival was a criminal. With battle lines being drawn – literally – and deaths resulting over issues such as the removal of Civil War monuments, as well as fierce opposition to immigrants growing across the world, cultural identity has become a tinderbox: a minefield for writers. In a sort of misappropriation of Cultural Appropriation – originally a non-judgemental term in sociology and anthropology, describing the adoption of elements of a society by another society

– identity politics now proscribed the right of writers to write about certain identities – women, say, or gays, LGBT persons, transgendered individuals – unless the author 'identified' with the individual of that caste. No books about blacks by whites; no books about women by men; no books about trangenders save by fellow transgenders... For the biographer as well as for the would-be memoirist, such twenty-first century victimology poses a veritable minefield. 'Whose feelings of identity must I be wary of offending?', the biographer asks himself when reconstructing and judging a real life. Am I 'entitled' to address an individual whose identity is different from my own? Emerson's philosophical reflection had become fact.

These days, in short, identity is toxic. That said, however, the matter is not wholly negative. The tension between society and the individual has always been the stuff of biographies – and of great importance, in turn, to the historian and the historical sociologist as well as political scientists and jurists. In preparing legal arguments for same-sex marriage before the US Supreme Court, for instance, it was found important to cull examples of quasi-marital relations between people of the same gender, in what were called 'Boston Marriages' for example, to demonstrate their stability, longevity and lack of threat to the fabric of society. Sibling and familial, even filial, identity is also of perennial interest to psychologists, criminologists and sociobiologists – and those identities are most often accessible via biographies. One scholar famously examined 10,000 biographies to draw up statistical evidence for his theory that the first-born male child will tend to be successful in establishment roles in society, while the second-born will tend to be rebellious or artistic. A swath of scientific, or quasi-scientific, works on the 'pecking order' in families, as well as father-son, mother-daughter psychological dynamics, has appeared in recent years, based on biographical data. In other words, identity in biographies and autobiographies – whether garnered from interviews or published works – becomes the seedbed for myriad disciplines and scientific theories.

The biographer himself, by contrast, works in the reverse direction; for the very notion of an individual being the statistical product of a statistically-demonstrable identity is deeply antithetical. Yet for all that, the biographer is dependent on group identity to contrast and fashion his individual, distinctive portrait. The biographer thus rarely, if ever, starts with a tabula rasa, but sets out, rather, to test, overhaul, contest or deepen our understanding of given identity. In this sense, biography is not only a corrective to history – one of biography's primary functions in culture, it has been argued – but is a corrective to scientific theories relating to human and group identity; a constant, interactive relationship that has gone on for several thousand years.

Take, for example, the biography of Adolf Hitler, Führer of the Third Reich, who identified as quintessential German, though born in Austria. Why did so many Germans follow such a self-identification, even to their own deaths, in their millions? In the wake of World War II, political scientists turned to sociologists, sociologists turned to historians, historians turned to psychologists. And in the end, all turned to biographers.

Warily, following the defeat of Germany, biographers attempted to contrast and compare competing theories of modern messianic leadership and social submission. Theories of his childhood, Hitler's failure as an art student, his combat experience in WWI, his anti-Semitism, his reading of nineteenth-century philosophers, his sensitivity to music and to Wagner, his mental and physical health... Biographer after biographer, from Alan Bullock to Joachim Fest, was expected to place Hitler's metaphorical corpse under X-ray-like examination, as art historians do to paintings. Or detectives in a murder investigation. 'I had never thought, until a few years ago, that I would write a biography of Hitler,' Ian Kershaw prefaced his book, *Hitler, 1889-1936: Hubris* in 1998. Biography 'had never figured in my intellectual plans as something I might want to write,' he confessed. Yet Kershaw ended up writing two 800-page volumes, the second of which was entitled *Hitler, 1936-1945: Nemesis* (2000). In submitting to the lure of biography, he saw his biography as an attempt to bind together the personal with the impersonal elements in the shaping of some of the most vitally important passages in the whole of human history. What has continued in the writing of the book to interest me more than the strange character of the man who held Germany's fate in his hands between 1933 and 1945 is the question of how Hitler was possible: not just how this initially most unlikely pretender to high state office could gain power; but how he was able to extend that power until it became absolute, until field marshals were prepared to obey without question the orders of a former corporal…

The notion that most human beings may spend their lives searching for, and trying to establish, their individual and social identity: this provides part of the 'plot' for any modern biography. Whether in addressing a hero or just an 'ordinary' person, it is the *interaction* of the chosen individual with his environment and life experience that is the object of biographical curiosity and fascination. That relationship between the personal and the impersonal, the individual personality and the community, drew Kershaw, like so many thousands of biographers in their quest to establish the unique and true identity of their subject: not to establish a statistic, but to contribute to a personal *and* a more general understanding.

Sources: Jens Brockmeier, 'Identity,' in: Margaretta Jolly (ed.), *Encyclopedia of Life Writing* (London: Fitzroy Dearborn, 2001); James Young, *Cultural Appropriation and the Arts* (Oxford: Blackwell, 2015); K. Woodward, *Questioning Identity: Gender, Class, Ethnicity* (London: Routledge, 2004); Leslie Stephen, 'Emerson,' in: *Studies of a Biographer* (London: Duckworth, 1902); D.J. Trela, 'Carlyle', in: Margaretta Jolly (ed.), *Encyclopedia of Life Writing* (London: Fitzroy Dearborn, 2001); Nigel Hamilton, *Biography: A Brief History* (Cambridge, MA: Harvard, 2007); Nigel Hamilton, 'Biography as corrective,' in: Hans Renders et al. (eds), *The Biographical Turn: Lives in History* (London: Routledge, 2017).

 # is for Journalism

The development of biography over the past several centuries is, in many ways, analogous to the development of journalism. Not just analogous, but interconnected, and mutually reinforcing.

Interpretive biography evolved in the periodical press in response to current events and popular interest; thus, in turn, it played a role in the formation of public opinion – and to an extent, that is still true today, where newspapers still (though in diminishing numbers) publish reviews of serious new biographies, and carry interviews with biographers, while biographers tackle lives of current interest to readers of newspapers and journals. In other words, there is a tradition of synergy between the two professions: many biographers writing journalism, and many journalists writing biography. This does not mean their purposes or practices are necessarily the same, however!

In England, France and the Netherlands, countless numbers of biographical magazines were published in the course of the eighteenth and nineteenth centuries. Little scholarly research has been conducted to establish the extent to which journalism, literature and current affairs determined the content of these magazines.

Samuel Johnson's writings on current affairs and biography are often seen as heralding the modern biographical genre. His 'twopenny' periodical, *The Rambler*, was published between 1750 and 1752. Johnson drew on a wide variety of sources for his biographical works – not only conventional published sources, but also private correspondence, diaries and information derived from interviews. (He memorably remarked in the *Rambler* that most biographers of his time paid 'so little regard' to the 'manners or behaviour of their heroes' that 'more knowledge may be gained of a man's real character by a short conversation with one of his servants, than from a formal and studied narrative, begun with his pedigree and ended with his funeral'!) Using his own preferred methods of research, Johnson undertook to write a biography of the young actor and poet Richard Savage, which was published in 1744, shortly after Savage's death. The result was a deliberate, almost exclusive focus on Savage's life rather than his work – especially the sordid or salacious details that illuminated Savage's moral failings. Savage's poetry, which any reader was at liberty to study for himself, was hardly mentioned.

Journalism, in other words, was primarily written to satisfy human *curiosity*, rather than provide in-depth intellectual analysis. James Boswell certainly fell under the journalistic spell of the 'Great Doctor.' His famous biography of Johnson, reprising Johnson's focus on journalistic research to build a complete understanding of the activities of the biographical subject, was very much *à la Johnson*. Indeed, Boswell did not hesitate to include 'even journalistic, gossipy detail and colour' when writing about Johnson's life – a life and work that would be a catalyst and model for the many biographically-inspired periodicals that would appear in later years.

A distinctive biographical interest also flourished in the French press. The nineteenth-century journalist Jules Barbey d'Aurevilly published articles about chosen people under titles such as '*Les Blagueurs en literature*' and '*Les Chroniqueurs*', first in newspapers and magazines, then as pamphlets. He later compiled them in book form. D'Aurevilly was self-critical – or cynical – enough,to put his own journalistic practices under the proverbial microscope, however. Journalism and biography were alike, he wrote: they form a conspiracy against history. They are but temporary products: dangerous if historians then come to rely upon them, as though they encompassed eternal truths – for they do not, he claimed. Biographers are predators in need of prey; if there is no prey, they invent one, or base one on malicious rumours. Biographers exploit their subjects for publicity, just as is said of journalists…

However outspoken, D'Aurevilly's allegation that biography has more to do with journalism than with literature or history is probably right: biography is a means, after all, to popularize lives. This was a trend that had developed in eighteenth-century newspapers, fed by the rise of a press aimed at mass appeal; and once begun, it never ceased. By the mid-nineteenth century, Anthony Trollope could write (in *Doctor Thorne*) that, 'In these days a man is nobody unless his biography is kept so far posted up,' in his imminent obituary,* 'that it may be ready for the national breakfast-table on the morning after his demise.'

Mass appeal, however, was double-sided – with the upper and conservative middle-classes always nervous about the power of a press that could swing between hero-worship and excoriation at the flip of a coin. A coin controlled by newspaper barons, such as Joseph Pulitzer, who thereby wielded huge political power. The American journalist Mary Abigail Dodge (who wrote under the pseudonym 'Gail Hamilton') was particularly caustic about her fellow newspaper journalists – decrying their slack, hurried and even poisonous biographical work. In 'The New School of Journalism,' an article published in her *Skirmishes and Sketches* in 1865, she blamed the curiosity, impatience and lack of respect for dignity and privacy shown by newspaper editors and their reporters. Her dying friend Rachel, she lamented, would 'soon be given over to the worms and the biographers' – a fate even worse than mere death. Moreover, one that was increasingly being inflicted *pre*mortem – to the distress of Rachel's family, friends and admirers.

> It is the unhappy fate of her survivors to have reached a day in which biographers have grown impatient of the decorous delay which their lowly coadjutors demand. They can no longer wait for the hungering soul to yield up its title-deeds before they enter in and take possession; but, fired with an evil energy, they outstrip the worms and torment us before the time.

It was, at heart, a sin that beset all human beings. 'Dear to the heart of man,' she noted, 'has ever been his neighbour's business.' Curiosity, gossip and envy were the immortal drivers. 'Precious in the eyes of woman is the linen-closet of that neighbour's wife.' As Dodge complained,

> the law awards to a man the right to his own possessions through life; and the personal facts and circumstances of his life have usually been considered among his closest, most inalienable possessions. Alas that the times are changed, and we all be dead men as far as concerns immunity from publication. The sole safety is to lie flat on the earth along with one's generation. The moment an audacious head is lifted one inch above the general level, pop! Goes the unerring rifle of some biographical sharp-shooter, and it is all over with the unhappy owner.

Class played a major role here; popular journalism seen by aristocrats and intellectuals as catering to the vulgar needs and the nastiest traits of the general public. The penny newspaper was meant for the common people, whereas a book was for the civilized citizen. In other words, the journalist did not serve a higher purpose. And behind that snobbery lay a deeper fear: public opinion was a sleeping monster that could awaken at any moment, and bring turmoil into the streets – including a potential revolution that would make the linen-closets of private property *public*!

'Pure' artists compounded the snobbery – in fact, they were often companions-in-arms to conservatives in denouncing popular journalism. Current affairs and news were, according to these critics, phenomena that should be absent from the lives of a refined 'arts-for-art's sake' elite. Thomas Mann became a poster-boy for such attitudes, writing a vast tome, *Betrachtungen eines Unpolitishen*, in 1917 that won him an honorary doctorate – but which he later disavowed, once Hitler took power and it became clear that artists, like ordinary people, could only ignore politics at their peril. Even in the autumn of 1927, the magazine *Margins* devoted three special issues to '*Les maladies actuelles de la littérature*' – one of which was the over-popularization, and interest in current affairs, of media. There had been a tremendous growth in literacy, but mass culture and public opinion were, in the eyes of many, still distinctly dubious phenomena.

Short of dictatorship and censorship of media (propaganda), the growth and popularity of media were impossible to reverse, however. As Dodge wrote, the American Civil War had impelled the 'New School of Biography' to furnish the newspaper-reading public with information about prominent figures, from the President to generals, governors and senators – and half a century later, journalism became even more central in society during World War I. Moreover, over time, the journalism itself evolved. In her study analysing the interaction between journalism and literature in the interbellum, or interwar years, the French researcher Myriam Boucharenc describes the *reporter-écrivain* as the stepbrother of the *écrivain-reporter*. The interwar *écrivain-reporter* prompted a new, influential genre of non-fiction, penned by non-academic writers and read daily by tens of thousands. He wrote in a visual style, like a scriptwriter, and presented himself in his story – often as a tough explorer, or smart detective, with a passion for facts and truth. Such adventurers were free from the duty to report in the objective manner that had restricted traditional reportage. Such storytellers no longer had to follow the compelling laws of topicality and public opinion so rigorously; they just had to ensure that they entertained or surprised the readers of *Le Parisien* or *Le Matin*. One rule, though, could not be questioned: each story could be unbelievable in its surprise or originality, but – in those days – it had to be true. That rule was the professional code that separated them from authors who wrote plausible but false stories. Once they had met this condition, nearly everything was permitted.

The nineteenth-century New School of Biography – impelled by public curiosity into invading people's once-sanctified privacy

– had been revitalized, in short, by a New School of Journalism fuelled by world war and its aftermath. As rules of privacy were further challenged and discarded, biographers began tentatively to follow suit; the New Journalism increasingly powering – and even authoring – what Virginia Woolf called, in *The New York Herald Tribune* in 1927, 'the New Biography.'

Thanks to their training in current affairs, resumé-writing, interviewing and research, such journalist-biographers were no longer intimidated when tackling prominent figures, past and present. Moreover, they were seasoned *writers* – trained and able to *interest* a readership. Following World War II, 'the New Biography' became a largely journalistically-impelled genre. Although some journalists, such as Tom Wolfe, were turning to fiction, many turned instead to biography. The American journalist Robert Caro, for example, had trained at the *New Brunswick Daily Home News*, then worked for *Newsday* on Long Island for six years as an investigative reporter. Finally, in 1974, he published *The Power Broker: Robert Moses and the Fall of New York*, a pioneering biography of the unelected but deeply influential New York city planner; the precursor to his yet more pioneering, multi-volume biography of President Lyndon Johnson, beginning with *The Path to Power*, in 1982. Similarly, Walter Isaacson, another journalist, trained on the *New Orleans Times-Picayune*; his biographies of administration officials, scientists, technology entrepreneurs and inventors, beginning in 1986, would culminate in his *Leonardo da Vinci* in 2017.

Not all such journalistically-inspired work would be considered good or even well-written as biography – meriting the critic Janet Malcolm's famous rebuke of the 'amazing tolerance' shown by the reader of modern biography, 'which he would extend to no novel written half as badly as most biographies.' Her Dodge-style snobbery exaggerated the quality of most novels published in the 1980s, which could be considered equally badly written. Yet her stricture was in essence true; and for the simple reason that the reader of biography tended to be more interested in the *content* of the story than its storytelling qualities.

Behind the brickbats thrown at biographers, however, one thing was incontrovertible: namely, the revolutionary impact of post-war journalism on the research skills of most biographers, especially in the area of interviews.

At one level, this interview-mania could lead to tapestry-weaving rather than interpretive biography – as, say, *Salinger*, a reportage-style account of the famous hermit-author of *Catcher in the Rye* written by the duo David Shields and Shane Salerno. Salerno had been editor of his high school newspaper and spent ten years researching, writing, directing and producing the documentary film *Salinger*, released simultaneously with the book in 2013. Together with Shields, the two biographers had interviewed more than 200 people who knew Salinger, and had compiled a 'collage-style' life based on those conversations. Locating people who were close to Salinger but who had never spoken about the author in public before, the book (and documentary film) successfully breached Salinger's privacy-protecting edicts in New Hampshire to provide a fascinating human mosaic: a triumph of modern journalism, and a rebuke, in its way, to the less journalistically-driven poet and biographer Ian Hamilton, who had attempted to write a full-scale biography of Salinger in the 1986, only to baulk famously at Salinger's determination to hide from public view. The weakness of Shields and Salerno's biography, however, lay in the repetitiveness of the personal reports and its ultimate superficiality – leaving the reader as mystified as before.

At the more imaginative and literary end of the journalistic spectrum, however, the New Journalism of Wolfe, Hunter Thompson, Joan Didion and Gay Talese did serve to shake up and revivify even interpretive modern biographies and autobiographies. In 2009, Hermione Lee would note, in her *Biography: A Very Short Introduction,* that it was now a 'mixed, unstable genre, whose rules keep coming undone'; moreover, that there was no longer any 'such thing as a definitive biography.' No self-respecting modern biographer, for example, would now think to start with the subject's birth: an acknowledgement, in its way, of the manner in which post-war journalists such as Wolfe and others had transformed the 'lead' style with which newspaper journalists could report on people and events. In the 1960s, this type of journalism had created a new form of reportage, getting closer than ever to the skin of the person portrayed in the newspaper feature: so-called 'Gonzo Journalism.'

Gonzo journalism (a term from the porn industry to describe when the cameraman joins the filmed activity) launched a new style of journalism, deliberately written without claim to objectivity, often including the reporter taking part in the story via a first-person narrative. It was – and still is – memorably applied by journalists to portray political leaders in a very personal way, often by following on the coat-tails of a president or senator for years; the best-known example being that of Hunter S. Thompson, who gave a poignant picture of presidential candidate Governor Jimmy Carter in his *Fear and Loathing on the Campaign Trail '72*.

For good or ill, then, literary non-fiction* received a gigantic shot in the arm from journalism – as did biography. Like newspapermen, biographers were forced to have to be entertaining, as well as informative and insightful – but with truth sometimes taking a knocking.

An extra reason for biographers to sit in the front seat, not the back one.

Sources: J. Barbey d'Aurevilly, *Les Ridicules du temps* (Paris: Éd. Rouveyre et G. Blond, 1883); Myriam Boucharenc, *L'Écrivain-reporter au coeur des années trente* (Villeneuve d'asq Cédex: Presses Universitaires du Septentrion, 2004); Nigel Hamilton. *Biography: A Brief History* (Cambridge, MA: Harvard University Press, 2007); Samuel Johnson, *Life of Savage*, ed. Clarence Tracy (Oxford: The Clarendon Press, 1971, original 1744); Stephen Lee Myers, *The New Tsar: the Rise and Reign of Vladimir Putin* (New York: Alfred A. Knopf, 2015); Hans Renders, 'Roots of Biography. From Journalism to Pulp to Scholarly Based Non-Fiction', in: Hans Renders and Binne de Haan, *Theoretical Discussions of Biography. Approaches from History, Microhistory, and Life Writing* (Leiden-Boston: Brill, 2014), 24-42; E.W. Johnson and Tom Wolfe (eds), *The New Journalism* (New York: Harper & Row, 1973); Beverley Southgate, *History Meets Fiction* (Harlow: Longman, 2009); Hunter S. Thompson, *Fear and Loathing on the Campaign Trail '72* (New York: Simon & Schuster, 1971); Kurt Andersen, *Fantasyland: How America Went Haywire: A 500-Year History* (New York: Random House, 2017).

# is for Kings, or Rulers

Since the dawn of civilization, royal biography has been a major component not only of history, but also of biography. And, today, of drama – with plays and films of former, even current, monarchs abounding.

'Why is that so?', we may well ask. Monarchies no longer exist in the majority of nations, and where they do, they are mostly ceremonial: a fall-back institution for moments when there are political crises that need arbitration...

Biographers have no special explanation for this, but their modern focus may offer a clue.

In the beginning was not only the word, but also power. Historians of the ancient world, whether in the Middle East or the Far East, recorded the reigns of rulers: from Assyrian kings and Egyptian pharaohs to emperors in Peking. Biographers thus became the guardians, the scribes, of these rulers' records, reputations and legacies.

It was Plutarch who first sought to break away from this uncritical or merely commemorative stance, in order not only to distinguish individual monarchs from each other in personality, but also to tie personality to performance; i.e., to judge kings and rulers from a personal, *moral* point of view, within the context of the times in which they ruled. This was the foundation stone of what much later, in the seventeenth century, was formally called 'biography' (a term first coined in English in 1661), but which had its origin in the Greek word βίος, or lives. From Plutarch onwards, βίος were narrated by writers telling the stories of real lives in every field of human endeavour – but with the biographies of rulers occupying a central place in the biographer's canon, at the core of man's commemorative pyramid, so to speak. (Biographies rather than autobiographies, it should be noted; very few kings or rulers wrote their autobiographies, lest this diminish their special aura or mystique, even demi-divinity. Roman emperors such as Julius Caesar and Marcus Aurelius were exceptions, but even they declined to use the first person singular.)

During the Renaissance, there was renewed interest in the classics, with a special fascination for the biographical works of Plutarch and Suetonius. Such 'royal' biographies could shed fresh light, it was recognized, on the ethical and political challenges of leadership in the emerging post-medieval world. William Shakespeare, for his part, could not resist using their stories as allegorical frameworks for his staged dramas. Coriolanus, Julius Caesar, Anthony and Cleopatra: such rulers fascinated the Bard of Avon, and they set a standard for new, thespian βίος of which Plutarch and Suetonius would have been proud.

The closer the subjects of Shakespeare's history plays (more biography plays than history plays, in fact) got to Elizabethan times, however, the more potentially contentious, even dangerous, his plays became. Shakespeare's contemporary, the poet, privateer and adventurer Sir Walter Raleigh, put the matter very well in his *Historie of the World*, published in 1614, when explaining why he was not bringing his account up to the present time: 'To this I answere that who-so-euer in writing a modern Historie, shall follow truth too neare the heeles, it may happily strike out his teethe.'

Raleigh's concern was prescient; in 1618, he was beheaded for having been, among other sins, too cocky towards princes in his work – excoriating fellow biographers, for example, who merely 'flatter the world, between the bed and the grave.' (He himself remained a brave and courageous knight to the end. To the sheriff charged with his execution, Raleigh remarked of the axe, 'this is a sharpe medicine but it is a physician that will cure all diseases.')

Between flattery and criticism stretched a fissure that, in recounting 'royal' lives, came to reflect the very dualism of biography itself as an endeavour – a dualism, moreover, that distinguished biography from its sister genre, history. Absorbed in narrating the patterns of the past, historians had neither the necessary intimate knowledge, nor the interest in individual personality, to spend time questioning the myths and accretions attached to past people rather than events. Their human characterizations were thus inevitably superficial, tied always to deeds rather than persona – and largely inoffensive, for the most part, to the powerful.

Biographers and biographical dramatists trod a different path, the one profession impacting the other. Shakespeare based his Roman history plays on Plutarch's *Lives of the Noble Grecians and Romans*, as translated by Sir Thomas North in 1579, and his English history (or biography) plays on the second, censored edition of Raphael Holinshed's *Chronicles of England, Scotland and Ireland*, published in 1587 – as did Shakespeare's contemporary, Christopher Marlowe. It was Shakespeare's handling of political issues – such as when it is right to rebel against a corrupt or evil king – that exercised historians, but it was Shakespeare's evocation of the personalities and minds of his kings that held biographers to account. The Bard might be – and was – mistaken in many of his characterizations, but what characterizations they were! Richard II's haunting introspection, Richard III's malice: these were astonishingly intimate reconstructions, made the more lifelike by the fact that they were acted live, presenting an abiding challenge to Raleigh's 'flatterers' of monarchs. Serious biographers, in the aftermath, were thus faced with a treble task in Western culture: first, to move past flattery as far as was possible (or safe); then to correct historians (and dramatists like Shakespeare) in assembling a more accurate account of past kings; and finally, to match the psychological depth that Shakespeare had mined in his stage portraits.

Those challenges pretty much defined serious 'royal' biography for 300 years after Shakespeare's death. Then came, however, the Russian Revolution in 1917, the resignation of the Tsar – followed later by his execution – and the abdication of the German Kaiser. The title of Richard Watt's *The Kings Depart* (1968) captured this historical transformation, or royal demise, in a neat phrase. Yet for all this, the allure of kings for biographers and the reading public did not diminish – in fact, arguably it only increased. Emasculated politically where they were not chased out or murdered, royal families attracted fresh interest largely because it was now possible for biographers to do their real job: telling the truth about lives seen up-close; lives that had so often been kept from public view in closed royal archives, denied autobiographies, and held secret behind pursed lips in the face of requested interviews. From the 1960s onwards, a veritable flood of new royal biographies appeared, such as Robert Massie's *Nicholas and Alexandra* (1968), Antonia Fraser's *Mary Queen of Scots*, and Frances Donaldson's *King Edward VIII: The Road to Abdication* (1974).

Adding to this revived interest in kings and queens as a dwindling and endangered species was the celebrity culture burgeoning across the US and Europe: an epoch that now considered Hollywood to be its epicentre,, not decaying royal palaces. Fairy tales had always relied upon popular children's fantasies of marrying princes (or princesses); now, in an age of proliferating divorce and actual marriage between royals and commoners (since royal marriage was now inconsequential with regard to power), there was no reason for adult biographers and their readers to hold back. In other words, the *romance* of 'royal' biography made it a favourite stage on which to portray not power, but make-believe and anti-make believe.

Romance could only stretch popular gullibility so far. After his abdication, having chosen the title 'the Duke of Windsor', the former Edward VIII had called his book, the first English royal autobiography of a royal, *A King's Story* (1947). Two days after his death in 1972 (and thus the death of the reach of libel lawyers in Britain), a television documentary by Ludovik Kennedy, *The Uncrowned King: Edward VIII*, began the process of chipping away the foundations of Edward's posthumous reputation, however. *Edward and Mrs Simpson*, a drama series based on Frances Donaldson's 1974 book, followed in 1978. In print, the distinguished British biographer Philip Ziegler attempted to hold back the proverbial gates in 1990 with his 'royally-approved'

King Edward VIII: The Official Biography, using the royal archives at Windsor Castle. It was a losing battle, however. In 1995, after British and German files were opened, a multipart television documentary, *Edward VIII: The Traitor King*, was released; and in 2009 came a further television dramatization, *Edward VIII: The Nazi King*, based on newly declassified FBI files. By 2017 the global bookseller Amazon could recommend that readers buy Kitty Kelley's *The Royals* (banned, though, in Britain) as the 'perfect' accompaniment to a new television multi-part, multi-season drama series about Edward's niece, Queen Elizabeth II, *The Crown*. 'They are the most chronicled family on the face of the globe,' Amazon's website declared, with some justification.

Family and the female gender had also played into this evergrowing twenty-first century biographical 'romance' phenomenon. The six wives of Henry VIII came in for special attention: in print, on the stage, in the cinema and on television (both documentary and dramatized). *Wolf Hall*, Hilary Mantel's 2009 novel based on life of King Henry VIII, seen through the eyes of his chief minister Thomas Cromwell, was soon dramatized not only for television but also for the stage, together with a slew of books and programmes devoted to Henry's multiple consorts. *Versailles*, a French three-season multipart television drama based on the court of King Louis XIV, soon followed in 2016. Which only left the vicar to the King of Kings, the Pope, to be 'biographized' – and in the autumn of 2016 a fictional drama, *The Young Pope*, was premiered: a Franco-Spanish television series to be followed by *The New Pope* – spawning fresh biographical interest in the real popes of Rome (and Avignon)...

What was clear was that the lines between real lives and romanticized, fantasy lives, in the royal or ruler-arena at least, were becoming ever more blurred.

For serious biographers, this phenomenon presented a growing problem, for royal fantasy was now becoming symbolic, or representative, of the fantasy games and amusement spilling into every facet of modern American life; and from American culture, inevitably, to other Western cultures, even some non-Western ones.

In this postmodern scenario – which the cultural critic Kurt Andersen would term, in his book *Fantasyland: How America Went Haywire* (2017), describing a 'Kids-R-Us culture' – the blurring could only have dire consequences. 'American adults, like no adults before them – but like all who followed – began playing video games and fantasy sports,' Andersen chronicled. They were also, 'dressing like kids, grooming themselves and even getting surgery to look more like kids.' The result was, increasingly, a narcissistic culture in which everyman became king, or queen, and queens became kings and vice versa: a 'Me Decade,' a world in which the border between fantasy and reality was no longer recognized – and the difference between opinion and fact became more and more degraded. Until, by the 2010s, the trend was – like gold being exchanged for paper currency – finally turned into a political reality few people had ever really believed possible: a quasi-monarchical, clownish, narcissistic American President, elected in November 2016.

By then, the US President had become more powerful than any king had ever been in the history of the world: by virtue of the US Constitution commander-in-chief of a military two times more powerful than that of the next two most powerful nations combined. Yet a man considered by the majority of psychiatrists and mental health professionals in America to be suffering from a form of 'malignant narcissism' in which 'grandiose fantasy trumps reality' – with the gravest consequences not only for Americans but also for the rest of the world, as they argued in their petition-like protest, *The Dangerous Case of Donald Trump* (2017).

Which brings us to *presidential* biography – or the biography of presidents as quasi-kings, now that kings are passé.

Ironically, the Founding Fathers, when devising the US Constitution in the late eighteenth century, sought to avoid what they saw as the perils of monarchy – namely, tyranny and the abuse of royal power, especially over colonies. The US President would therefore be elected, or re-elected, to office every four years, whether in times of peace or war. However, Alexander Hamilton argued in *The Federalist*, in order to be an effective chief executive of the new American republic, the president would need to be able to focus his energy on the security of the nation by being constitutionally empowered to show 'decision, activity, secrecy and dispatch,' as well as being protected against legislative encroachments on the efficient use of his power. And this was how the American experiment begin in 1789 – arguably vesting the president with more power than the monarch in Britain, the very nation that had been forced to grant its American colony independence. Britain was thus left, historians have noted, without an effective monarchy, while the US became a monarchy, so to speak, without kings.

In terms of biography, the experiment has probably given rise to more presidential biographies – in print, in drama, and on the screen, large and small – than any monarchy has ever evinced, including the British royal family. From George Washington to Abraham Lincoln, Theodore Roosevelt, Franklin Roosevelt and beyond, the lives of the US presidents have been recorded, lauded, excoriated, judged, ranked and rued, alive or dead, with a unique lack of legal recourse (i.e. libel or other forms of biographical protection) by a national ruler anywhere in the world. Royal mystique played no part in presidential power, endowed every four years. Such biographies, right from the experiment's start, thus became models of critical thinking, of political perspective, and huge public curiosity. Biography came to *mean* something in American society from 1789, because the role, performance and lessons of the presidency affected every man, woman and child in America – with biographers becoming the viziers of the public, charged with telling the life-stories of the nation's chief executive, unencumbered by concerns of *lèse majesté*.

This aspect of biography's history has been insufficiently examined by scholars, yet it is a central feature of biography's development in America since the late eighteenth century – and one that was electrified in the 1960s with the first assassination of a US president since President McKinley was shot in 1901, when on 22 November 1963, President John F. Kennedy was murdered in public in Dallas, Texas, and his wife 'stole' his body (which by law required an autopsy before it could be removed from the state). Fanned by political mayhem over civil rights and the Vietnam war, the public fascination with the role, performance and personality of the reigning president culminated, on 9 August 1974, in the first-ever forced resignation of a president, Richard Nixon, under threat of impeachment – broadcast live from the White House.

Shakespeare would have been hard-pressed to produce a more dramatic play. In the aftermath, more and more biographers turned their forensic lenses on 1600 Pennsylvania Avenue, aiming to focus more tightly on the person of the president and to hone their own deepening research skills – propelled by an insatiable public appetite for information, insight, scandal and access to the truth. The Watergate conspiracy was exposed by journalists using a secret FBI source (known only by the name 'Deep Throat'), but the refusal to be fobbed off by Nixon's band of mafia-like 'plumbers' and White House acolytes became a kind of badge of honour for the new Biographical Inquisition, as it might be termed: biographers crusading on the backs of investigative journalists to provide the public with the unvarnished truth about their elected ruler. From Garry Wills's *Nixon Agonistes: The Crisis of the Self-Made Man* (1969) to Roger Morris's *Richard Milhous Nixon: The Rise of an American Politician* (1990), the unfortunate 37th US President was biographized literally to the death (he died in 1994), and beyond. Undeterred, the former president meantime wrote autobiographical volume after volume in his effort to exculpate himself. His lies and obfuscations were unconvincing, however. Not considered honest enough to be allowed to keep his autobiographical tapes, recorded in the White House during his presidency, neither he nor his family were granted the privilege of a federally-funded Presidential Library until 2007.

In this way Richard Nixon's 'royal' biography, like those of all 45 US presidents (and counting), would thus come to be seen as the quintessential realm, the symbolic media melting-pot, in the depiction of real lives today – biography no longer viewed as an art, but as modern man's multi-faceted attempt to address the often difficult truths of a major, powerful real-life individual, impacting – as well as being impacted by – the real world.

In this sense, presidential and ruler-biography – despite an abiding unwillingness within academia to teach or promote the study of βίος – continues to represent the very core of what has allowed the study of other people's real lives to continue and develop over the past two millennia: a public-driven field of human enquiry that has gone on since the time of Plutarch and Suetonius, and that shows no sign of abating.

Sources: Nigel Hamilton, *Biography: A Brief History* (Cambridge, MA: Harvard University Press, 2007); Jordan Lancaster, 'Royal Biography,' in: Margaretta Jolly (ed.), *Encyclopedia of Life Writing: Autobiographical and Biographical Forms* (London: Fitzroy Dearborn, 2001); Kitty Kelley, *The Royals* (New York: Grand Central, 1997); Kurt Andersen, *Fantasyland: How America Went Haywire: A 500-Year History* (New York: Random House, 2017); Ta-Nehisi Coates, 'The First White President,' *The Atlantic*, October 2017.

 **is for Life Writing**

'Life Writing' is really a misnomer. The term was invented to inaugurate a new field in academia; one that would be based primarily on the long-standing study of autobiography, a genre that was to be forcibly separated or spun off from its now elderly uncle, biography.

How 'Life Writing' will fare in the academy is anyone's guess, given that a growing number of 'Centres of Life Writing' have sprung up in the past several years – much as 'psychobiography' journals and conferences sprang up in the last century, only to wither in the course of time. (Few if any 'pyschobiographers' succeeded in writing psychobiographies of any merit. 'Life Writers,' if such a designation is ever sought by authors writing what used to be called autobiographical works, face a similar uphill battle.)

How, the historian of cultural change may ask, though, did 'Life Writing' courses begin? What was the matter with the practice of autobiography over the past two millennia, or its study in journals such as *Auto/Biography Studies* (1987-), and its traditional inclusion in English Language Arts at university level?

It is perhaps too early to say, but a number of reasons can be discerned, beginning with the burgeoning rise of individualism in the West after World War II: the notion that the interests and rights of the individual in society are paramount. And that serving those interests, in turn, is the best way for a democratic society to avoid the perils of communism and stultifying collectivism.

While that trend had political and international ramifications that defined the Reagan era, the fall of the Berlin Wall and the end of Soviet communism, it also had a profound influence on education in the West. Tom Wolfe was quick to describe the 'Me Decade' in 1976, describing a post-war generation of 'baby boomers' – the most self-absorbed and spoiled in history, he judged. The once 'common man' had become interested 'in this business of "realizing his potential as a human being,"' Wolfe sneered. Moreover, things did not, in Wolfe's view, get any better in the decades that followed. Alongside the digital revolution in communications towards the end of the twentieth century, attention spans became ever shorter in the field of learning, while the numbers of students attending college or university increased exponentially – from 3.4 per cent of young people in 1950 in the UK, for example, to more that 50 per cent by 2010, and rising. Not only were the majority of such students unwilling to work as hard to expand their knowledge as earlier had been the case, but their personal, individualist expectations became ever more fabulous – in both senses of the word. Students would no longer read long or demanding texts; physical libraries showed declining numbers of books borrowed, while the 'great works' of literature increasingly went unread. They were simply too long in an age moving inexorably towards the maximum of 140 characters of a 'Tweet' on Twitter, an Internet service created in 2006. (One hundred and forty was an arbitrary maximum that was doubled to 280 in November 2017). Meanwhile, teachers of Literature and Language were compelled to assign shorter and shorter texts for their classes – and to bend to the will of the majority in focusing on literary memoir,* given that students wished to hone their *own* linguistic skills, especially in social networking and self-expression, as transmitted in Blogs – a term first used in 1999 to describe an online diary.

'Autobiography' was seen as an old-fashioned, elitist word, and 'memoir,' as a focus of university study, was considered too narrow for a phenomenon that was having an enormous cultural impact, and 'egodocument' (coined in 1958 by the Dutch historian Jacques Presser) was too recherché. The more populist term 'Life Writing' was therefore invented, beginning with the

'Centre for Life Writing Research' established in 2007 at King's College, London. The centre was dedicated to the 'theory, history and practice of life-writing' – a field that would cover, in the college's view, the whole gamut of modern human, individual self-expression, from 'social media, blogs, audio and video,' and would draw upon 'experts in psychology, languages, education, culture, comparative literature, media and creative industries, history, music, neuroscience' and more. The ultimate aim, especially through a new Master of Arts programme, was to encourage and promote all 'forms and practices of self-presentation,' presumably by 'Life Writers.'

Since memoir – a writing lens trained primarily on the self, rather than the other – had traditionally been seen as a branch of biography, 'Life Writing' could thus be seen as a venerable, distant cousin of biography, but one that was wearing new clothes. Except, however, that it seemed to accrue the same sort of neo-liberal agendas that had earlier fuelled 'cultural studies.' As the distinguished British biographer Michael Holroyd wrote in *The Guardian* on 6 November 2009: 'While biography is merging with history in the general marketplace, in academe it is being reinvented as "life writing" and subsumed into sociology." Biography was passé. "The very word biography strikes some academics as "elitist," as does its focus in the past on single remarkable or merely fashionably well-known people. Life Writing has a different agenda,' Holroyd noted, for it 'concentrates principally on people who belong to and represent categories or classes of people who have been victimized in the past. It offers retrospective justice.' The study of autobiographical work was being used not to understand it better, Sir Michael felt, but to promote causes – a path that he, a lifelong biographer who had been educated to respect objectivity, considered deeply disturbing.

Concern with the victimized, distressed and dispossessed was nothing new, to be sure, and had been expressed long before 'Life Writing' courses were invented. Engraved on the Statue of Liberty in New York Harbor in 1903 was a sonnet written by Emma Lazarus, dedicated to the 'mother of exiles':

'Keep ancient lands, your storied pomp!' cries she
With silent lips. 'Give me your tired, your poor,
our huddles masses yearning to breathe free,
The wretched refuse of your teeming shore.
Send these, the homeless, tempest-tost to me,
I lift my lamp beside the golden door.'

As Tom Wolfe noted seventy years later, however, the post-war, baby-boomer 'Me Decade, had not turned out to be what 'utopian socialists of the nineteenth century – such as Saint-Simon, Owen, Fourier, and Marx,' had anticipated, nor what their 'Yale and Harvard' successors had planned in the early 1950s: men in 'Hudson Bay shirts, tweed jackets, flannel trousers, briarwood pipes, good books, sandals and simplicity'; moreover, men who were expected to be living, say, in a Worker Housing project designed by Walter Gropius and Mies van der Rohe (also exiles). Not only did the 'new man' decamp, instead, to the suburbs – 'the *suburbs!*' – and park '25-foot-long cars out front and Evinrude cruisers up on tow trailers in the carport,' determined to 'do-it-himself,' but he was joined, as time went on, by semi-literate men and women, brought up on trash television, who saw in the new technologies of communication the means to voice a new 'primal scream.' Self-expression not only gave voice to the victimized, in other words, but it went with an outpouring of uncensored bile, exemplified by personal radio talk show hosts such as the baby-boomer Rush Limbaugh, whose sheer white-male rancour and biliousness, first on air in 1984, was initially considered 'entertainment.'

Limbaugh's radio programme gradually garnered an audience of 20 million listeners per week, though, and was joined, on television, by the Fox News cable channel in 1996, run by Roger Ailes, a media consultant to Presidents Richard Nixon, Ronald Reagan and George W. Bush. *You are the message: Secrets of the*

Master Communicators had been Ailes' autobiographical *apologia pro vita mea* in 1988. It became his special contribution to modern American culture, backed by the Australian media mogul Rupert Murdoch. After openly calling a competitor, David Zaslav, a 'little fucking Jewish prick,' Ailes the Master Communicator was investigated by NBC, but the invective was but the tip of his race- and character-baiting iceberg. Gabriel Sherman's biography, *The Loudest Voice in the Room: How the Brilliant, Bombastic Roger Ailes Built Fox News – And Divided a Country,* duly exposed Ailes' hate-riddled agenda and the danger he posed to America, given that almost 100 million American households received Fox News. It did not dent the winning formula, however – for the medium and its audience now made the message arguably more powerful than religion. (Ailes himself would eventually fall personal victim to years of his own sexual harassment of Fox employees; he was forced to retire from Fox News, but died in 2017 before he could be successfully indicted.)

Backed by 'big money,' unbridled and untrammelled 'self-expression,' *en bref*, was having a powerful influence on the development of American culture – and political attitudes. The election of a neophyte billionaire realtor and TV personality as the 45th President of the United States in 2016 – a man who had honed his skills in insults and deceitful self-expression in nightly Tweets – seemed finally to cap the trend that Wolfe had captured so well 43 years before. Meanwhile, new 'Life Writing' centres had been established, such as the 'Oxford Centre for Life-Writing' at Wolfson College, Oxford University, in 2010, ostensibly designed to 'support those who write auto/biography.' But whose kind of autobiography, and with what purpose – or reward?

Rush Limbaugh was reported to be earning $79 million per year by 2014, making him the 11th highest paid media personality in the world. Were 'Life-Writing' centres willing to address the social, cultural and political fall-out from the 'Me Decades,' and the real-life political, economic and social consequences of such unrestricted autobiographical self-expression? Or did the new centres have a different agenda, as Holroyd suspected: namely to promote their own (or their students') ideological agendas, by choosing to review those texts that suited their political and social views?

The problem, as biographers like Holroyd saw it, was that the term 'Life Writing' had been coined to sound like 'Life Science' – but there was no science to be seen in such writing, and very little in its study! There was certainly no one who would or could without embarrassment call himself or herself a 'Life Writer' – just bloggers, journalists, tweeters, essayists and memoirists. And academics.

What exactly was the *purpose* of Life Writing, then, in academia? Was it a new contribution to literary studies, or to sociology, or to political science? As the self-improvement/self-expression field of communications remorselessly expanded, thanks to burgeoning new technologies in the 2010s, no one in academia appeared to be monitoring or analysing critically the actual *effect* of such self-expression on the polity or culture of the society being exposed to this autobiographical tsunami. Instead, more and more people were, often remotely (i.e., without ever meeting), merely 'crowd-sourcing' the popular trend – especially those who were feeling marginalized either by their limited access to education or to public self-expression, or, as Holroyd noted, who were driven to pursue a distinct 'agenda' – ranging from victimized women to conspiracy theorists, and from transgendered persons to white supremacists.

In such a climate, as noted elsewhere in this ABC, modern autobiographical self-expression was going unanalysed and unexposed to objective, critical thinking – the very standards that universities were supposed to apply. Contrary to what microhistorians and biographers do, no distinction was thus made in the 'Life Writing' centres between published and unpublished letters and diaries, for example. The border between fact and fiction was meanwhile becoming less and less clear, thanks in part to the lack of restraint or caution in the new mediums of self-expression – yet this was a trend that the Oxford Centre for Life-Writing openly considered of no consequence, since the centre's mission was, in the view of its founders, to encompass 'everything from complete life to the day-in-the-life, from the fictional to the factional.'

Even the distinction between fiction and non-fiction *within* sources was not considered important – for ideological concerns, in promoting self-expression, trumped scholarship.

Biography, however, like history, is built on fact.* For biographers, whose profession has existed for 2,000 years, such wilful blindness both to scholarship and to the larger questions of how ego-texts arise – how authentic they are, what their agenda is, with what social consequences, and what our agenda may be in using them – is a matter of understandable concern. Without respect for fact, but only uncritical support for self-expression in all its proliferating modes, Life Writing centres have served to valorize the articulation of identity regardless of whether the authors of autobiographical materials were, or are, telling the truth or not. The consequences of such uncritical laxity have been sad – such as a US President choosing to communicate with the public entirely by means of shameless, unverified, deceit-filled and often insult-laden Tweets, put out as forms of Life-Writing!

Small wonder, then, that serious biographers such as Holroyd had difficulty being inspired by the advent of so-called Life Writing centres.

For serious biographers, who had traditionally used autobiographies, letters and diaries for their research,, the new, alternative Life Writing courses and conferences seemed strangely selective in the texts they chose to discuss. These appeared to be impelled by ideological agendas, spotlighting and interpreting ego-documents that featured major themes of current interest to certain social groups, such as discrimination, gender, race and sexual orientation.

Such blind focus on self-expression as "Life Writing" was alarming, since Life Writing centres were calling for a discussion about marginalized groups of people by quoting their autobiographical texts – but all too often without critical evaluation of those sources, or examining the dangers of unbridled autobiographical outpourings in our society. Thus, a diary of a disabled person or a gay person, according to Life Writing proponents, was extolled as a window on all people suffering disabilities and all homosexuals, regardless of their historical context – and often regardless of whether the 'ego-document' was authentic. As Kevin Young, director of the Schomburg Center for Research in Black Culture, noted in his *Bunk: The Rise of Hoaxes, Humbug, Plagiarists, Phonies, Post-Facts, and Fake News* (2017), faux memoir in the late twentieth century was not only an insult to genuine autobiographical work – 'Fake memoirists plagiarize another's pain,' as Young put it – but raised profoundly serious questions about the *readers* of such fake documents. James Frey's book *A Million Little Pieces* was found to be completely invented autobiography – yet for millions of people, this no longer mattered! As the venerable newspaper editor David Shribman lamented in the pages of *The New York Times*: 'The larger question remains: Do people still care?' Young felt similarly concerned. 'Legions of readers,' he pointed out, 'knowing that Frey falsified his memoir, still persist in saying the book is truthful' – and the same held true for Tim Barrus's *The Blood Runs Like a River Through My Dreams*, published in 2000 under the faux name Nasdijj, and for Margaret Seltzer's faux autobiography, *Love and Consequences: A Memoir of Hope and Survival* (2008). 'Truthiness' became more important than fact or truth – and facts of no importance in comparison with 'alterative facts,' in the words of Kellyanne Conway, White House counsellor to the President of the United States.

In Young's view, 'our age's reliance on memoir is also an over-reliance on "memory," rather than history, on the imminently subjective rather than the immanent or verifiable.' By contrast, 'We are drawn in biographies most to those figures who help explain our times ([such as] past presidents), or those rarities for whom our times shed light on theirs,' he noted – genuine light rather than faux facts, since biography conforms to the changing *context* within which the biographee lived, moreover seeks to chronicle the changes in an individual's life story, and allows for the biographer's changing assessment of that context over time.

Change, rather than identity, is what biography is all about – something "Life Writing" does not appear to be interested in. And even if it was, why then limit the focus to "Writing"? What happened to several thousand years of depiction of an individual's life in different *media*: something biography – from the Greek βίος, for life and γράφω, for depict – has ceaselessly addressed, as this ABC shows?

'Life Writing'? *Caveat emptor*! Not to be confused with Biography, or Biography Studies!

Sources: Hans Renders and Binne de Haan (eds), *Theoretical Discussions of Biography. Approaches from History, Microhistory, and Life Writing* (Leiden-Boston: Brill, 2014); Susanna Fellman and Marjatta Rahikainen (eds), *Historical Knowledge In Quest of Theory, Method and Evidence* (Cambridge: Cambridge Scholars Publishing, 2012); David Shribman, 'Yes, the Truth Still Matters,' *New York Times*, December 12, 2017; Nigel Hamilton, *How To Do Biography: A Primer* (Cambridge, MA: Harvard University Press, 2008); Kevin Young, *Bunk: The Rise of Hoaxes, Humbug, Plagiarists, Phonies, Post-Facts, and Fake News* (Minneapolis: Graywolf Press, 2017); Kurt Andersen, *Fantasyland: How America Went Haywire: A 500-Year History* (New York: Random House, 2017).

# is for Memoir, Memoirs and Autobiography

Memoir is the bad boy (or girl) of modern literature. It is a genre invented in the late twentieth century in ten parts: four parts entertainment, four parts narcissism, two parts self-help. It has nothing to do with biography. It cannot be quoted by biographers, save in assessing the self-image of the author, since it is unverifiable. Often it is not even written by the author, but constructed with the help of a ghost-writer. Its purpose, in any case, is not to be read as historical evidence – a matter best left to memoir's two distinguished birth-mothers, autobiography and memoirs (plural).

Nevertheless, memoir does represent a fascinating case of modern literary mutation. It became almost instantly the darling of professors of English who despaired of students' unwillingness to read or discuss 'long' novels by Dickens, George Eliot, Thomas Hardy or Joseph Conrad. It even helped spawn a new teaching module, 'Creative Non-Fiction,' in which students could themselves try their hand, and for which they would need professorial guidance, credits – perhaps even counselling, if the memoir went too deep. For memoir (singular) is both autobiographical-porn and autobiographical-pain…

If this seems harsh, it is. Memoir should never be confused with biography, and its inclusion in the would-be new academic fields of 'Life Studies' and 'Life Writing'* is at best unfortunate. In an age threatened by 'alternative facts,' 'fake news,' bogus blogs and website mendacity, memoir is radioactive material.

Seen dispassionately, however, memoir is a fascinating phenomenon: one that is interesting both to analyse on its own literary merits and to compare with other literary modes of expression, from the fictional novella to the narrative of dreams. In an era of ever-expanding individualism in the West it has inspired some fine writing, and – like film – often been revelatory in terms of human experience: highlighting harrowing supposed *secrets d'alcove*, *pace* Charcot, that were long hidden, from child rape to child soldiers. Good or bad, works of memoir have offered contributions to modern writing – to narrative structuring and to expressive, sometimes impressive linguistic skills. They are also contributions to our understanding of modern culture and mores, and of the psyche. They are not, however, contributions to biography; whereas autobiographies and traditional memoirs are.

Autobiography, by contrast, has a venerable history, though the word 'autobiography' was not invented until the late seventeenth century – and then amid much argument. S*elbst-biografie*, or self-biography, seemed more self-explanatory, but also perhaps too self-laudatory. As one reviewer wrote in 1796, criticizing *Some Observations on Diaries, Self-biography and Self-characters*: 'We are doubtful whether the latter word be legitimate. It is not very usual in English to employ hybrid words partly Saxon and partly Greek [such as self-biography]: yet autobiography would have seemed pedantic.'

Pedantic or not, 'autobiography' gradually became the accepted neologism in English for a historical, descriptive and reflective account of the author's own life – though *Selbstbiographie* lived on for many years in Germany, in preference. Whether as autobiographies or S*elbstbiografien*, however, all were modelled on biographies – using the narrative archetype that biographers had created over the course of many centuries.

There was something else that autobiography shared with its paradigm, beyond the second word, however: namely its literary and social *purpose*. Autobiography was intended to be useful, even if it lacked literary stature as art. Like biography, it offered valuable information that could help readers better understand national, regional, local and social history, customs, etc. It offered moral lessons, too, that could be drawn from the course of whole, real lives – i.e., not fantasy or fictional ones. It could not, however, provide readers with the one thing that made biography itself so compelling: the death scene.

Autobiographers, then, largely followed a path beaten for them by biographers, who had invented the word biography more than a century earlier. The autobiography-path had the same cultural borders as biography: rules where meadow-grass or forest began, bearing the warning 'Keep Off!' What could be included in the work, and what not, were thus the same in both genres – in fact the rules for autobiographers were perhaps even more constricting. Biographers since the Gospel-writers of the New Testament could indulge in a certain degree of hero-worship, whereas an autobiographer was advised to be more restrained in self-glorification. Magnifying the status of the self, for example, was *verboten* in the Muslim world as an affront to God.

There had been one major exception to this rule: the first truly great literary autobiography (before the word's coinage): St Augustine's *Confessions* (426 AD). Augustine had had, however, the good sense to couch his *Selbstbiografie* as a religious dialogue with God, if recorded on one side only. Moreover, the dialogue itself suggested a purpose that would become unique to autobiography, namely the overt examination of one's own life and existence as an *apologia pro vita mea*.

This moral dimension – one that tended to be muted in biographies, where the author was unwilling to pass judgement without extensive, objective research and an examination of the facts – was central to autobiography; but it was also its chief problem. For whereas a biographer could make a real life so objectively interesting that the reader could ignore or glide over the biographer's side-judgements, the autobiographer had a far harder task. Somehow, if he wished to record his own life he had overcome the reader's presumed aversion to vanity, and make his self-reflection fascinating. Few authors rose to the challenge, save for writers like Montaigne – whose work, in any case, comprised *Essais* rather than the history of a whole life subjected to self-examination.

The result of this very high, indeed impossibly high, bar was *mémoires*: a genre known in the Anglo-Saxon world as 'memoirs,' a plural English word borrowed from the French. These were life-chronicles, in the form of memories, that did not purport to be self-examinatory but were only self-descriptive, without self-judgement. As biographies, for their part, began to grow in popularity, such *mémoires* grew in tandem, such as those of Philippe de Communes (1447-1511); the duc de Rochefoucauld (1613-1680); the duc de Saint-Simon (1675-1755); and De Chateaubriand (1768-1848). What threatened to throw a spanner, so to speak, into the genre of such *mémoires*, was a new version of St Augustine's *Confessions*, this time written by Jean-Jacques Rousseau (1712-1778): a masterpiece of radical self-chronicling and self-examination.

Rousseau's deliberate aim was to be as honest as St Augustine had been in recounting his childhood and later memories – but to address his text not only to God, but also openly to potential readers after his death. For students of literature this would mark a turning point in self-portraiture. 'I have entered upon a performance which is without example,' Rousseau began his *Confessions*,

> whose accomplishment will have no imitator. I mean to present my fellow-mortals with a man in all the integrity of nature. Whenever the last trumpet shall sound, I will present myself before the sovereign judge with this book in my hand, and loudly proclaim: thus have I acted; these were my thoughts; such was I. With equal freedom and veracity have I related what was laudable or wicked, I have concealed no crimes, added no virtues; and if I have sometimes introduced superfluous ornament, it was merely to occupy a void occasioned by defect of memory.

As he cautioned: 'I may have supposed that certain, which I only knew to be probable,' but, he defended himself, he had

> never asserted as truth, a conscious falsehood. Such as I was, I have declared myself; sometimes vile and despicable, at others,

virtuous, generous and sublime! Even as thou hast read my innermost soul: Power eternal! Assemble round my throne an innumerable throng of my fellow-mortals, let them listen to my confessions, let them blush at my depravity, let them tremble at my sufferings; let each in his turn expose with equal sincerity the failings, the wanderings of his heart, and, if he dare, aver, I was better than that man.

Biographers could only marvel – for if all men were willing to chronicle their own lives with such honesty and respect for veracity, the task of the biographer would be greatly simplified. Not all men were, however. Also, the very intent – to reveal oneself, naked, to the world's eyes – was not universally lauded; indeed, it skirted on the borders of self-pornography. The philosopher Friedrich Schlegel (1772-1829), for example, declared in 1798 that such 'autobiographies are written either by neurotics who are fascinated by their own ego, as in Rousseau's case; or by authors of a robust artistic or adventurous self-love, such as Benvenuto Cellini.' Or, he added, certain 'women who also coquette with posterity.'

In short, Schlegel, a Prussian, felt the business of autobiography to be impossible and unseemly; even traditional authors of *mémoires* were, in his view, 'pedantic minds who want to bring even the most minute things in order before they die and cannot let themselves leave the world without commentaries.' Such authors were little better than advocates, setting '*plaidoyers* before the public,' not to speak of those writers who were 'autopseusts,' or self-deceivers.

Fortunately, no-one listened to such strictures, at least insofar as they concerned *mémoires*, or memoirs – even those dressed up as autobiographies. Such works served a useful informational, commemorative purpose, especially when printed by widows or descendants – and could be highly remunerative, such as the *Personal Memoirs of Ulysses S. Grant*, published in 1885. Running in parallel with biographies, and using biographies as their models, these autobiographical works ranged from Casanova's

Histoire de ma vie (published first in German in 1822) to Stendhal's *Souvenirs d'égotisme*, or *Memoirs of an Egoist,* and those of a host of luminaries in the nineteenth century, such as Benjamin Franklin's *Autobiography*; *Narrative of the Life of Frederick Douglass, an American Slave*; or *The Life of P.T. Barnum, Written by Himself.* Collectively they formed a fund of factual, generally truthful, sometimes (but not overly) introspective ,works written – like biographies – to be accessible by general readers.

Biographers cherished (and still cherish) them as rich source material; in fact, Virginia Woolf's father, the professional biographer Sir Leslie Stephen, declared autobiography to be so interesting he had 'frequently thought' that 'it should be considered as a duty [to be written] by all eminent men; and indeed, by men not so eminent.' Their accounts might not be completely reliable, but biographers would take that into account. Besides, they conformed to a reliable Victorian archetype, biography – which flattered biographers.

Until, that is, the early twentieth century, when Lytton Strachey and Virginia Woolf put a metaphorical bomb under both genres: an explosive charge that that did not revolutionize biography overnight, but certainly put it on notice. Not only did biography – and in consequence autobiography – need to be more critical, but it needed to brush up its literary style; to be, in short, more dynamic, more entertaining to the modern mind. Like fiction.

Novelists in the nineteenth century had evaded (for the most part) the problems of candour (and libel) when dealing with real lives by fictionalizing them. Often such novels, too, mimicked the archetypes of biographies and autobiographies – as, say, Alexandre Dumas' *Count of Monte Christo*, Thackeray's *Vanity Fair*, Hardy's *Tess of D'Urbevilles*, Dickens's *Oliver Twist*, *David Copperfield*, *Great Expectations*, or Charlotte Brontë's *Jane Eyre* and Emily Brontë's *Wuthering Heights*. The loosening of social and legal mores in the West in the twentieth century, however, finally permitted biographers and autobiographers to catch up with novelists – if they dared, or could get away with more critical examination and self-examination.

Perhaps Henry Miller put the challenge most vividly in his quasi- and semi-autobiographical novel *Tropic of Cancer*, written in the early 1930s and published in France by the Obelisk Press in 1934: 'This is not a book. This is a libel, slander, defamation of character... This is a prolonged insult, a gob of spit in the face of Art, a kick in the pants to God, Man, Destiny, Time, Love, Beauty.'

It was the delayed publication of Miller's book in America by the Grove press in 1961 which led finally to a Supreme Court trial. Their decision was that Miller's work was not obscene, since it was art – fortunately, in view of Miller's view of Art! Inevitably, autobiographers took note, and courage. Little by little, in outliers, their work began to incorporate something of the spirit of Rousseau's *Confessions* as well as the sexual narcissism of Henry Miller. However, there was a limit to which sexual self-examination across a whole life could be expected, or made, to interest the average reader, compared to the traditional, if less artistic, rewards of 'plain' autobiographies by eminent, celebrated people. The kick in the proverbial pants was thus put on hold until, in the late 1990s, when the more adventurous among autobiographers recognized in new biographies a new trend they could imitate: Slice of Life.

In their determination to ignore poststructuralism and deconstruction, biographers had assumed the mantle cast off by fearful historians. In a cascade of new biographies, they had applied deep forensic historical methods, borrowing from microhistory to correct and X-ray received ideas and myths of the past in relation to real individuals. To do this successfully, such biographers had begun to focus more and more on a specific event or turning-point in the subject's life – and in this innovation autobiographers and academics saw a fresh archetype that could be turned to gold. The once-venerable book trade in conventional autobiographies and memoirs – the self-biographies of World War II generals such as Douglas MacArthur, Mark Clark, Field Bernard Montgomery and Erich Manstein, or politicians such as Charles de Gaulle, Winston Churchill and Konrad Adenauer – was now hit by a tsunami: *memoir.*

Autobiographers had never employed footnotes or given verifiable sources for their chronological accounts, for it was understood that they respected facts and truth. As Rousseau had written, he had never 'asserted as truth a conscious falsehood.' Now, however, with English departments overtaken by deconstructionists and postmodernists, the very concepts of truth and falsehood were declared pliable, if not passés. There was no need to place memoir – the narcissistic telling of the story of a moment in one's own life – in the rich, twelve-volume opus of one's autobiography across a lifetime, as Rousseau had done. By taking its archetype no longer from biography, memoir (singular) could, instead, use the fictional novella as its literary format – indeed, *could aspire to the status enjoyed by literary fiction*. Where biography was not taught at any mainland university in America and only a handful in Europe, memoir could be: offered as classes within language and literature departments whose professors were shamelessly uninterested in history, in facts, in verifiable truth or the social consequences of licensed mendacity. All that was required was that it should be entertaining, artistic and emotionally compelling. Truth could go to hell.

Modern 'Memoir' was thus born and, together with its stepsister, 'faux-memoir,' it enjoyed sterling literary and commercial success, garnering prizes and proceeds for its authors. By 1998, however, even memoir-writers themselves were having second thoughts. In a collection of essays, *Inventing the Truth,* the new genre's chief teacher, William Zinsser, confessed to being shocked by growing American schlock: a 'national appetite for true confession,' which had

> loosed a torrent of memoirs that are little more than therapy, the authors bashing their parents and wallowing in the lurid details of their tussle with drink, drug addiction, rape, sexual abuse, incest, anorexia, obesity, co-dependency, depression, attempted suicide, and other fashionable talk-show syndromes. These chronicles of shame and victimhood are the dark side of the personal narrative boom, giving the form a bad name.

'If memoir has become mere self-indulgence and reprisal,' Zinsser warned, it was bad news; it would become a 'degraded genre.'

Zinnser's warnings came too late – the genre having taken hold of a new generation, prey to even more self-indulgent and self-deceiving entertainment. 'That which is fully known cannot be falsified but with reluctance of understanding, and alarm of conscience,' Dr. Johnson had noted in 1759 – a warning that holds good today. Memoir thus has nothing to do with biography – or with *mémoires*, memoirs (plural) or autobiography. It will therefore be interesting to see whether the genre, in the inevitable countersurge against mendacity, will eventually fade, ceding its place to the serious, historical-centric archetypes where it began.

Sources: James Goodwin, *Autobiography: The Self Made Text* (New York: Twayne Publishers, 1993); Robert Folkenflik (ed.), *The Culture of Autobiography: Constructions of Self-Representation* (Stanford, CA: Stanford University Press, 1993); Tristine Rainer, *Your Life as Story: Discovering the 'New Autobiography' and Writing Memoir as Literature* (New York: Putnam, 1997); William Zinsser (ed.), *Inventing the Truth: The Art and Craft of Memoir* (Boston: Houghton Mifflin, 1998).

# is for Non-Fiction

Storytelling is still the heart-pump of modern fiction and non-fiction: the mode by which the author communicates with the reader.

Oral storytelling goes back to the beginnings of civilization. When incised on clay tablets, word-of-mouth stories inevitably found their way into the otherwise mundane recording of accounts and inventories, as rulers commemorated (via their scribes) their exploits and achievements. Among the several million cuneiform 'documents,' baked in clay, that have survived from Sumerian and Assyrian times, pride of place probably goes to the *Epic of Gilgamesh*, the greatest epic poem before Homer's *Iliad*.

The story of King Gilgamesh of Uruk, it is believed, was already being written down around 2100 BC, and probably predates that time by several centuries as oral storytelling. A complete version of King Gilgamesh's life was kept in the royal library at Nineveh by the last Assyrian king, Assurbanipal, who had sent collectors across the then-known world to copy and translate such literary texts. The poem was lost after the fall of the Assyrian empire in 612 BC, and was only discovered by the Mesopotamian archaeologist Hormuzd Rasson in 1853 AD, working with A.H. Layard in his celebrated Nineveh excavations. However, it was only when George Smith, an English working-class banknote engraver, took to studying Layard's cuneiform tablets in his lunch hours at the British Museum, and then joined Layard and Rawlinson's excavations in the Middle East, that the full poem was successfully pieced together: a depiction of the life of the famous ruler of Uruk, mentioned in many other clay documents. In an age of Victorian religious missionary zeal and biblical scholarship, the very mention of a 'great flood,' in particular, described in the eleventh tablet of the Gilgamesh epic, aroused huge public interest – the prime minister of England, William Gladstone, having attended Smith's lecture to the Society of Biblical Archaeology in person in December 1872. Told to Gilgamesh by Utnapishtim, the Noah-like character in the epic, it begins warily: 'You know the city of Shurrupak, it stands on the banks of the Euphrates?' and proceeds to relate how the great god Anu, lord of the firmament, warned Utnapishtim to build a boat – described in great detail – and save himself and 'the seed of all living creatures' from the tempest about to befall the city.

Smith died of dysentery on his second trip out to the Nineveh site in 1876, aged 36. *The Epic of Gilgamesh*, however, may be considered the First Biography: recounting the life, fortunes and death of a real individual. It recounts this story, in verse, with haunting attention to detail, emotion and moral judgement – its account of Gilgamesh's relationship with his friend Enkidu, and Enkidu's eventual death, being especially moving. 'When Gilgamesh touched his heart,' the biographer relates, 'it did not beat. So Gilgamesh laid a veil, as one veils the bride, over his friend. He began to rage like a lion, like a lioness robbed of her whelps. This way and that he paced round the bed, he tore his hair and strewed it around. He dragged off his splendid robes and flung them down as abominations…'

Over the 4,000 years that have elapsed since the writing of the Epic of Gilgamesh, biographers have sought on the one hand to commemorate the lives of real individuals such as Gilgamesh, and on the other to satisfy the public's appetite for strong storytelling. Rarely, however, has the literary art of such biographical storytelling reached the level of the Gilgamesh-authors' magic realism. The need for verification came to pose an insuperable problem for biographers working in a genre that was developing increasingly as history – the history of an individual – not as art. Invention, imagination and high-storytelling were left to fiction authors, from poets to dramatists; and, from the late eighteenth century, to novelists.

Working with only non-fictional literary means (the term non-fiction was first used in 1867), the historical biographer had had to do his best to stay within the parameters of evidence and verifiable fact or information. Victorian fiction writers, especially, were not so encumbered. Increasingly, they simply borrowed the narrative chronology, structure and narrative approach of biographers, applying them to the telling of invented biographies or autobiographies – leaving fact-constrained biographers to toil with real lives. Since the narrative quality of many of the biographical-style novels written in the nineteenth century in Russia, France, Germany, Britain and America was so high, and the 'theft' of the life-story paradigm so frustrating for biographers with a literary sensibility, it was perhaps inevitable that, by the end of the Victorian era, one of them would revolt: Lytton Strachey.

In fact, there had been much soul-searching during the previous century over the tyranny of fact in biographical storytelling, as Bruce Nadel would point out in *Biography: Fiction, Fact and Form* in 1984; there was also much fine, clear nineteenth-century narrative prose, too. Nevertheless, the fact remained: biographies had simply failed to match the competition. Virginia Woolf, especially, found herself tormented. In 1929 she wrote an essay, 'The New Biography,' which memorably lauded the value of factual truth in real-life narration – truth which 'has an almost mystic power. Like radium, it seems to give off forever and ever grains of energy, atoms of light. It stimulates the mind as no fiction, however artful or highly coloured, can stimulate it.' Yet even with her virtuoso storytelling skills, Woolf could only write one actual biography, of her friend Roger Fry, which proved a literary and biographical dud.

Woolf's conundrum – how to deal with facts and truth, rather than writing truth-sounding fiction (a conundrum that led her to write a brilliant spoof-biography, *Orlando*) – remains unsolved today. Many literary devices were tried in the twentieth century, the most prominent of which was the 'non-fiction novel,' a designation used by Truman Capote for his biographical narrative of a real murder, *In Cold Blood*, in 1966. In turn, this led to the designation 'Creative Non-Fiction': a new classification used for prose writing that is based on facts and real lives, but not rigidly followed. These designations permitted authors to pivot their work on the 'mystic power' of true facts, but also to ignore them, elide them and manipulate them as suited the author, in pursuit of his primary goal: to better shock, awe and entertain the reader.

Fact became, in effect, a new spice in the cuisine of fiction authors seeking to profit from the growing public fascination with real people and the radium-like quality of true facts. In a celebrity culture in which, as Andy Warhol claimed, everyone was entitled to his own fifteen minutes of fame, the new genre of 'non-fiction narrative' offered a free launchpad: employing the name-power and energy-grains of real lives to provide an instant connection with the reader, without the author first having to create, by literary artistry, initial curiosity. Curiosity about real people and their real lives, in a burgeoning celebrity culture fanned by myriad gossip magazines and press stories, was too enticing, in other words, for the otherwise fictive author to pass up. Licensed by college professors as the new field of 'creative non-fiction narrative,' practitioners could now re-order, merge, re-fashion and invent facts where considered necessary, at will. As for the ethical question of whether this was right, or its potential consequences for the public perception of what Woolf had called the 'granite-like' substance of facts and truth: who could complain when biographers were failing sufficiently to *entertain* their readers? Whose fault was that?

Non-fiction narrative thus became, by the end of the twentieth century, a growing commercial success, as well as offering valuable teaching posts to practitioners – inspiring yet more potential authors in college classrooms and spawning a cascade of virtuoso works that were, from a literary point of view the equal of any modern fiction. Or its superior. As Tom Wolfe pithily put the matter: recent non-fiction had, he wrote, 'wiped out the novel as American literature's main event.'

It was, of course, a ruse. So-called 'creative non-fiction' was, in truth, fiction in all but name. As entertainment and literary self-expression it was no worse for that, in fact it was often better. But it certainly moved the goalposts of what had once been considered simply the inviolable rules of non-fiction. Rules that were to be disregarded in the drive to provide great entertainment.

Biographers could hardly complain, since in open commercial competition they had been outwitted and outclassed by their competitors in terms of entertainment – authors of non-fiction stretching from Truman Capote to Thomas Keneally (*Schindler's List*), Erik Larson (*In the Garden of Beasts*), Laura Hillenbrand (*Unbroken*) and Daniel Brown (*The Boys in the Boat*). Lytton Strachey had referenced size as the major problem in biography – but not even Strachey was able to reduce his biography of Elizabeth I to less than 296 pages. And besides, size did not matter. The pages of his *Elizabeth and Essex* simply failed to match the excitement and dramatic, entertaining qualities evinced by fiction writers – and so-called 'creative non-fiction' authors.

Did this mean that biography, as a non-fiction genre, was doomed to be the journeyman of Strachey's lament – unrespected and untaught in academia, and unable to match the commercial success of 'creative non-fiction' works – even in literary prizes, where biographies and non-fiction narrative works were conjoined or lumped together under the same jury?

Curiously it did not, or not entirely.

True, there was a university conference held in Britain in 1985 to address the situation – the panellists' papers printed under the mournful title *The Troubled Face of Biography*. Yet the sense of crisis was premature. In succeeding decades biographers finally recognized that Strachey was, in fact, wrong – or partially so. Far from avoiding length in a vain attempt to compete with fiction writers and 'creative non-fiction writers,' biographers only needed to recognize that what they were doing was actually *more important* in modern society, in the long run: more deeply and intellectually rewarding as a challenge to the author, and of inestimable value to society as corrective as well as commemorative history. And that by setting higher storytelling and truthtelling goals, biographers did not need to reduce their size. Rather, they needed to *write* better – and take advantage of the new culture in which legal, moral and other protections of privacy were flying out the window.

It meant learning from storytellers in other media, such as film and television; meant harder work; better interviews; better quotations; more selectivity; deeper focus; and paying more attention to the reader's attention span, patience and curiosity. In short, composition, composition, composition,* not simply recitation, or the attempt to be 'definitive' – an aim which was inherently impossible to achieve, since every biography is a provisional account and will be superseded over time by others.

By the late 1980s, the word 'definitive' had in fact been expelled from the biographical lexicon. Though Janet Malcolm's own attempt at biography – *Two Lives*, a life of Gertrude Stein and her partner Alice Toklas, published in 2007 – was as brief and neatly designed as Strachey had wanted, it was ridiculed as tedious, self-regarding, prurient and utterly without merit as modern biography. Instead, big biographies came out that were brash, critical, penetrating, fascinating, controversial, revelatory, insightful – and brilliantly written, with remarkable pacing and attention paid to suspense, point of view, scaffolding, poignant detail, and what Virginia Woolf, in an essay in 1938, had called 'the creative fact; the fertile fact, the fact that suggests and engenders.'

Biography, in short, finally came of age, welding truth and personality – a challenge Woolf had considered such a 'stiff' problem that it might never be solved – in a new golden age, as major scholarly yet compellingly readable biographies by Richard Holmes, Victoria Glendenning, Deidre Bair, Claire Tomalin, Robert Caro, Hermione Lee, Edmund Morris, Ron Chernow and others across the biography-world demonstrated the power of truly New Biography, as distinct from fiction and 'creative non-fiction.'

What had happened? Doubtless future historians of biography will draw their own conclusions, but two or three preliminary explanations might be adduced.

First, by the latter part of the twentieth century many writers of biography saw themselves proudly as an endangered species – ignored within an academia beset by deconstructionism and postmodernism, but also threatened by rising competition from writers of 'creative non-fiction' and 'non-fiction narrative.' Only then did biographers rise to the narrative challenge by writing prizewinning works of modern non-fiction themselves. And not for entertainment or sales value, but for the cause and fulfilment of the biographical genre – however long, or in however many volumes it took to tell the story.

Second, they appreciated that the ever-increasing popularity of fiction, film, drama and television in modern entertainment culture made their own work and role as biographers important in a way that it had not been before. Biographers were increasingly seen as the guardians of truth about real lives in an age of superficiality. Not definitive guardians, or perfect guardians, but guardians nevertheless. Their attention to solid research, factual detail, verification of sources, and serious attempts to grapple with the complexity and contradictions of real lives in history and in contemporary society gave them a standing that university historians had once held – in fact, biographers of US presidents such as Michael Beschloss, Doris Kearns Goodwin and Robert Caro became lauded as the 'premier historians' of their time, rightly or wrongly – a stature unthinkable a generation previously.

Third, biographers did not fall into the trap that 'creative non-fiction' writers had succumbed to in chasing modern society's fickle audience for entertainment. Where the works of 'creative non-fiction' writers such as Frank McCourt (*Angela's Ashes*, 1996) came and went, remunerated but soon forgotten, the work of serious biographers remained lauded and appreciated as a lasting contribution to modern culture and history. When the new era of Breitbart News, 'fake news,' 'alternative facts' and the trashing of science threatened to overturn civilized discourse in America in the wake of the election of its 45th president, 'creative non-fiction' was seen as in part responsible, or at the very least, a contributor.

And last, but not least: mid-level biographers – i.e. those of a lower commercial and literary profile than the David McCulloughs, Robert Caros, Antonia Frasers and Edmond Morrises of the genre – recognized that they might not have reached the giddy literary heights they had aspired to in their youth, but that this didn't matter. For what they were doing as biographers required a degree of maturity that young people simply did not recognize, yet which, when applied to the task of researching and narrating the course of a real life, was fulfilling in a way that very few works of fiction or 'creative non-fiction' could be, in the long run.

Biography as Fulfillment. The professor of English and jazz-biographer Philip Furia put this point best, perhaps, in an essay he wrote in 2001: 'As Time Goes By: Creating Biography.' Rejecting a colleague's suggestion that he should write the biography of Hedy Lamar, 'the sex goddess' of 1940s Hollywood who intrigued him but did not resonate with his deeper interests, Furia realized he was 'still passionately committed to the lives of the people I first discovered' as musical demigods when growing up in the shadow of the 'blast furnaces of the Pittsburgh steel mills.' As a teenager and student, he had dreamed of becoming a writer, tapping out 'poems, plays, and stories on my father's huge Underwood' typewriter, and 'writing a biography had never occurred to me.' In due course, he had become a literature professor and instructor, unaware that it was the lives of the composers and lyricists behind the music he had listened to as a teenager that he *really* wanted to write about. After winning a Fulbright scholarship to Austria, he had realized 'how little had been written about these brilliant lyricists,' and 'I burned to celebrate their lives' by writing about them. When a colleague said 'We need a book about Ira Gershwin and Cole Porter – we don't need any more books about Milton and Pound,' Furia was inspired to start. Researching and writing a series of excellent biographies of Gershwin, Porter and Johnny Mercer in the years thereafter made his own life worthwhile, as well as contributing importantly to the history of jazz in America, being read with lasting appreciation by those who cherished their music. 'So the passion to write biography can feed both your altruism and your ego,' Furia commented wryly, in retrospect.

Biographers, *en bref*, are not 'creative non-fiction writers.' They are biographers: seeking as their goal not to entertain, per se, but to learn and impart their biographical learning entertainingly, in prose that unashamedly abides by the facts and the truth, as best it can be researched and written, via non-fiction storytelling.

Sources: Philip Furia, 'As Time Goes By,' in: Carolyn Forché and Philip Gerard (eds), *Writing Creative Nonfiction*, (Cincinatti: Story Press, 2001); Theodore Cheney, *Writing Creative Nonfiction: Fiction Techniques for Crafting Great Nonfiction* (Berkeley, CA: Ten Speed Press, 2001); Ira Bruce Nadel, *Fiction, Fact and Form* (New York: St Martin's, 1984); Paula Backscheider, *Reflections on Biography* (Oxford: Oxford University Press, 1999); Janet Malcolm, *Two Lives: Gertrude and Alice* (New Haven: Yale UP, 2007); *The Epic of Gilgamesh*, tr. N.K. Sandars (London: Penguin, 1972); Lytton Strachey, *Eminent Victorians* (New York: Modern World Library, 1918); Eric Homberger and John Charmley, *The Troubled Face of Biography* (New York: St Martin's Press, 1998).

is for Obituary

The obituarist resembles an undertaker. It is his job to bury the dead – in words. In this task, the obituarist is a mini-biographer, working against the clock to present an embalmed likeness of the deceased to the general public: showing the corpse if not at his best, then at least recognizable as a once-real human being, and an individual, before the earth or flames engulf his memory.

Some form of such historical record has accompanied death, or followed immediately after it, probably since the beginning of written language. Graveside encomia or funeral orations were reduced and chiselled onto monuments or stelae, or clay tablets, or sarcophagi – their earliest preserved necrological form. With the advent of journalism, however, in the eighteenth century AD, the obituary – from the the Latin *obitus*, going down, and mediaeval Latin, *obituarius* – became a popular sub-genre: a death notice accessible not just to immediate relatives, but also to the wider world. As such it grew into a traditional, recognized format or text, balancing society's need to honour the dead against the curiosity of the wider public. Known as necrologies in much of Europe, and varying in the attention given to the life of the deceased as opposed to the manner of his death, for centuries the obituary continued largely unremarked as a literary craft.

Until, that is, the example of 'major biographers' caused such 'mini-biographers' to also turn against the traditional *modus scripturae*. Thus, in the 1980s, the obituary advanced from the basement of journalism to the upper level. The obituary became a new media star in journalism – the London *Independent* even daring to give a by-line to the hitherto anonymous author. And with this, the obituary, or Obit, finally came of age.

In the world of journalism, the Obit is now considered the acme of good, swift research as well as compact, fine prose: encapsulating the life of a real individual in a text that will satisfy as a memorable likeness those who knew the deceased, but also those who did not, and are curious. For the life of another human being may have many lessons, good or bad, to convey – as every biographer is aware.

If journalism may be said to be 'the first rough draft of history' (according to Jeremy Bentham, quoted in 1859), then the obituary, as mini-biography, may be said to be the first rough draft of major biography – and is often today as transgressive as its larger, later version of 'a life.' Not only are such mini-biographies widely read and enjoyed, but they are collected – *The Times* of London, for example, publishing an annual volume of necrologies. The obituarist had even entered fiction, though only in his guise as the occupant of a backwater desk at a newspaper. By the 1980s, however, this, too, changed, as novelists played catch-up in works such as Robert Chalmers' *Who's Who in Hell*, or Peter Shreve's *The Obituary Writer*, where the detective skills of a good obituarist were used to uncover crime – much as A.S. Byatt paid a backhanded compliment to the forensic work of biographers in her 1990 novel, *Possession: A Romance*.

It was not simply the biographer's remarkable forensic research skills that led to a renaissance of mini- and major-biography, though; it was a major shift in public expectation. Readers wanted not only greater truth-telling, but greater telling. And where better to demonstrate those skills than on the corpse of the recently deceased, who could no longer sue the newspaper, or author? In the traditional intersection between the obituarist and the audience, a huge change became apparent in the 1980s. The public had always had an almost fetishistic fascination with the *details* of death, and in the memorializing of the dead. These details were now honed by obituarists to become, literally, telling details. Insightful, amusing or surprising, they became part and parcel of the 'Biographical Turn,' as it has been called – the challenging cultural changes that commenced in the 1980s and which swept away the notion of biography as literary backwater.

In their new role as mini-biographers, professional obituarists now saw their trade as one that directly confronted readers' prejudices, curiosity, ignorance and willingness to be teased. And entertained. 'Canon Smith expired after suffering an unfortunate disagreement with his bishop,' had been a late nineteenth-century Australian obituarist's tease, tucked away in the usual reverential column. A century later, though, the biographical gauze, like the wrapping of an exposed mummy, was wearing thin, and was bound to fall away once major-biographers led the way. As biographers challenged the guardians of the dead (and even the living, after *The New York Times* succeeded in overcoming the American law of libel, citing the First Amendment, in 1964), so too did obituarists, citing legitimate public interest in the truth, not simply decorum. The life of the deceased, especially if a celebrity, thus became a test of the modern obituarist's research and detective skills as well as his writing ability. As one distinguished American obituarist (of Katharine Hepburn, Marlon Brando, Jackie Onassis and Princess Diana, among others) wrote in her survey, *The Dead Beat: Lost Souls, Lucky Stiffs and the Perverse Pleasure of Obituaries, as witnessed and faithfully recorded by Marilyn Johnson*, necrologies came to form 'a tight little coil of biography,' reminiscent to her of 'a poem. Certainly it contains the most creative writing in journalism.'

As Ms. Johnson noted, the 'florid nineteenth century' had traditionally entertained readers with 'lots of gruesome descriptions of death scenes' – such as: 'Within the short period of a year she was a bride, a beloved wife and companion, a mother, a corpse!' And things had not got much better in the twentieth century – in fact, they could be said to have got worse, as Ms. Johnson mocked. Perhaps, she speculated, 'it was all those wars. A few stray writers and the occasional publication tried to jazz up the obit, working up something more than the lists of white men, their jobs and descendants, but it was a grey and dusty and depressing beat for years. It wasn't just the subjects who were dead, but the prose, too.'

Impelled by readers of biography, newspaper editors began to follow publishing house editors in departing from the trope of slavish memorial – which could, in any case, be left to the families of the deceased in 'death notices,' or paid advertisements. 'The equivalents of Elvis and The Beatles rose up in the United States and the United Kingdom,' Ms. Johnson chronicled, proudly, as a veteran (in *Life* magazine and *Esquire*) 'to give the Dead Beat a beat. Our own glorious era has been a time of expansion, innovation, entertainment, and world-class one-upmanship. In one generation, a boring, moldy old form has sprung to life' – ironically, while burying the dead. Undeterred by postmodernist deconstruction or the pratfalls of faux memoir, and avoiding the controversy and legal blowback often facing modern major-biographers, obituarists found themselves miraculously safe in the new world. Potentially aggrieved and grieving families were reluctant to sue a newspaper, or organize a literary counteroffensive using paid puppets (as the Kennedy family tended to do whenever a critical major-biography appeared, contesting the family's myths), to combat a 'mere' column in an obituary section of a newspaper.

The 'tight little coil' of modern mini-biography, the Obit, thus became established – too small to be lethal in the eyes of the 'Keepers of the Flame' (as the censored would-be biographer of J.D. Salinger, Ian Hamilton, called his protest history in 1992), but important enough as unique, well-researched information, to impel many readers to go out and buy a newspaper: an *amuse-bouche* with a coffee and a croissant or bagel every morning. More and more readers, indeed, found such mini-biographies addictive, like crosswords, so that newspapers began to increase the staffing of their obituary desks – their top authors becoming newspaper wizards, able to make readers laugh at a remembered, or forgotten, or never-known tale or irony, or quoted remark, or to feel sad at the premature departure from this life, owing to disease or accidental death.

So important did the modern Obit become, in fact, and so good the research done to ensure its accuracy and depth for competitive, instantaneous publication on the passing of a national or international figure, that newspapers began to commission them well in advance of the day of judgement. Thus, when the Dutch newspaper *Het Parool* published Paul van 't Veer's necrology of Simon Carmiggelt in 1987, it added a note, namely that the author had already predeceased his subject by eight years – as also happened with *The New York Times*'s theatre critic, Mel Gussow, whose obituary of Elizabeth Taylor appeared six years after his own demise.

It was not only well-researched information and the tone of respect – or disrespect – that changed obituary or mini-biography, however. It was also, as in major-biography, the structure.

Obituarists could pride themselves on their swift research skills and their determination to find out the truth, to check all sources before committing to print, and their ability to encase a whole life in a literary casket comprising a few hundred, or at most a few thousand, words. What made mini-biography so modern, though, was the compositional *structure*: the shaping and ordering of the material, as in major-biography. Just as modern biographers had begun to cast off the traditional biographical form in the 1980s, no longer beginning with the birth of the subject, so obituarists sought to start their work by surprising the reader while pivoting on an aspect of the life that might nevertheless be well-known (if for the wrong reasons!). The London *Daily Telegraph*, for example, began its obituary of William Donaldson by mention of the theatre critic Kenneth Tynan, who had memorably dismissed Donaldson as the product of a top English private school who went on to become only a 'moderately successful Chelsea pimp.' Quoting this, however, the *Telegraph*'s obituarist was willing to go far further, right off the bat. Tynan's sniffy put-down might have been perfectly 'true,' the obituaritst allowed, but Tynan had not gone far enough. He had omitted the fact that Donaldson 'was also a failed theatrical impresario, a crack-smoking serial adulterer' – and the 'writer of autobiographical novels,' under the pseudonym 'Henry Root.'

Name-dropping could also be relied upon to draw the reader's attention, even if the subject of the obituary himself was a forgotten figure, or not considered front-rank. The introductory paragraph to the obit of an unusual musician thus began, in the *Telegraph*: 'Jeanette Schmid, the professional whistler who has died in Vienna aged 80, performed with Frank Sinatra, Edith Piaf and Marlene Dietrich; she had been born a man and fought in Hitler's Wehrmacht before undergoing a sex change in a Cairo clinic.'

Few major-biographers could have improved on such a start. Moreover the style became global. For example an Australian obituary of American playwright Arthur Miller, who died in 2005, began: 'There was a lot to dislike about Arthur Miller, the giant of twentieth-century American literature and one-time husband of Marilyn Monroe...'

For the biographer, of course, obituaries had always provided invaluable data – and not only because of the information they contained. The very approach of the obituarist, through the centuries and across different cultures – even sub-cultures and religions – gave a flavour and clue as to how the deceased had been seen, valued and judged in his time. American Civil War necrologies, for example, showed how war affected the style and the ideological bias of the obituarist. How an individual was judged or weighed by his contemporaries could reveal a great deal. Exclusions, too, could be revealing about a society. Murderers and criminals were seldom granted a necrology, for moral reasons – but then, most women, too, were denied an obituary. Black people – 'negroes' – also lacked necrological notice. Or, when they were given space, it was most often because they had served, met or been associated with a white figure, such as having shaken hands with Thomas Jefferson, as Janice Hume noted in her *Obituaries in American Culture*. Moreover, if necrologies reflected differing religious, parochial, even sporting cultures, as Marije Zomerdijk showed in her study of Dutch newspaper necrologies, so too did necrologies collectively influence whole national cultures, as James J. Farrell wrote in his *Inventing the American Way of Death*.

To the biographer, then, necrologies could thus be revealing in many ways – and decidedly helpful. Name-dropping in obituaries could alert the keen biographer to other figures who might possess papers and materials of interest in reconstructing the individual's life. The factual content of necrologies, moreover, could often provide important detail for later biographers to recycle. The manner of death, as recorded in an obituary, can, for example, provide an excellent end to a major-biography – especially French necrologies. 'Mr. Lanjuinais did not say a word and gave no cry. A slight convulsion occurred, and that was how it ended. His face remained calm and he smiled,' *La Presse* reported on 4 January 1869. 'He died almost suddenly at ten o'clock in the evening, in full possession of his great intellectual faculties,' the *Figaro* reported another death, on 4 January 1899. Humorous anecdotes, coincidences, and above all detail, detail, detail: these could furnish major-biographers with valuable death-blood, so to speak.

Mini-biography, or obituary, in short, has moved in recent decades very much in line with major-biography, covering more and more people who were not previously considered important enough to be recorded or remembered.

Even the profession of obituary-writing has grown in stature – as has biography. Just as biographers finally created – after 2,000 years – an organization to provide themselves with a platform and annual conference (the Biographers International Organization, or BIO, founded in 2010), and the *Société de Biographie,* founded in 2016, so too have mini-biographers. Beginning with a First Great Obituary Conference in 1999, and the founding of the Society of Professional Obituary Writers in 2007, they are going from strength to strength as a professional trade body. Awards are given for Best Obituary Writer of the Year, Best Short Form

Obit, Best Long Form Obit, Best Obit of an Ordinary Joe/Jane, and Lifetime Achievement in Obituary Writing at their annual conferences.

Perhaps the most public accolade of our time, though, is in film. Vanessa Gould's 2017 documentary *Obit* thus followed *The New York Times*'s modern necrology team at work, in order to reveal its highly professional process behind the scenes (or black drapes). The camera follows Bruce Weber, its star obituarist, as he assembles an obituary in 2014 of the forgotten TV coach, William P. Wilson, who helped Senator John F. Kennedy prepare for his historic, first-ever televised debate with Vice-President Richard Nixon in the 1960 presidential campaign – using material from the newspaper's own aptly-named 'morgue,' or archive, as well as phone calls made to grieving relatives and others. The documentarist also peeped into editorial conferences in which decisions were made about the length of the text, its content, the positioning of the Obit in the newspaper, and its illustration.

To the chagrin of obituarists, however, the *Obit* documentary was replicated in drama or feature film – but, typically, mangled for its entertainment value, not its truth-telling. The same year, 2017, thus saw the screening of a Hollywood movie, *The Last Word*, starring Shirley MacLaine. The plot concerned a young journalist who is commissioned by her newspaper editor to write the necrology of a retired and domineering local celebrity, who is willing to pay for its composition in advance, as long as she can supervise it.

As *The New York Times*' Bruce Weber objected, the movie was irritatingly ignorant of the field it was describing – despite starring Shirley MacLaine. As Weber noted in a protest article, published in *The New York Times* on 11 March 2017 and addressed to Ms. MacLaine, he himself had, in truth, written Ms. MacLaine's advance obituary for the *Times*, and felt compelled to point out that modern obits are not composed in the way portrayed in the film – the obituarist failing to 'extract a single distinctive fact' about the character's past, or even to look her up 'in the files of her own newspaper.' What the real writer of a professional obituary is interested in when interviewing people who have known the deceased,

> is factual information – the specifics of the subject's education, for example, or where she was born and grew up – so that some connection might be made between the person's background and the reason the obituary is being written in the first place. Which is why most of the time you do your research before, not after you call the friends and family. The last thing you want is for them to think you don't know anything about the person you're asking about.

Anecdotes were important, too – though also absent from the film.

Thus, like biographers among their literary (and academic) colleagues, the obituarist is still not really understood, or not as highly regarded as other journalists are in his profession. This is perhaps as it should be. At most, biography can influence society's knowledge and judgement of a single individual, whereas other disciplines offer and shape much larger, broader judgements.

Weber, however, was not willing to let such an ignorant movie pass without comment – from a professional obituarist. As he pointed out to Ms. MacLaine, 'when you're writing an actual advance obituary, you tend not to approach friends and family at all, lest you freak them out.' He went on to laud Ms. MacLaine for her lifetime's work in film (*The Trouble With Harry, The Apartment, Terms of Endearment*, etc.), as well as the books she had written, her political activism, even her 'loopy philosophical exploration.' Why she had agreed to act in a film fiction about an obituarist whose work belonged on Legacy.com, rather than a real newspaper, defied Weber's understanding. The movie was 'fake news,' as opposed to obits that 'are real news.' 'Which makes me want to ask: Why did you want to add this misleading trifle of a movie to your genuine achievements,' he wrote sadly, if rhetorically. 'Now I have to add it to your obit.'

Sources: Marilyn Johnson, *The Dead Beat* (New York: HarperCollins, 2006); Nigel Starck, *Life after the Death: The Art of the Obituary* (Melbourne: Melbourne University Press, 2006); Janice Hume, *Obituaries in American Culture* (Jackson: University Press of Mississippi, 2000); Arina Makarova, 'Necrologieën in de Franse pers 1800-2000', in: Hans Renders (ed.), *Het leven van een doodsbericht. Necrologie en Biografie* (Amsterdam: De Bezige Bij, 2005), 43-59; Marije Zomerdijk, 'Een ideaal lijk. Necrologieën in de Nederlandse krant', in: *Het leven van een doodsbericht. Necrologie en Biografie*, 140-155; Gabriel Riblet, *Ces chers disparus. Essai sur les annonces nécrologiques dans la presse francophone* (Paris: Éditions Albin Michel, 1992).

is for Psychology

Psychology is as old as the Egyptians and the Greeks; in fact, the Greek word for mind or soul, 'psykhe,' gave the discipline its birth-name. During subsequent millennia, the study of the mind influenced almost every science and branch of knowledge, from medicine and philosophy to law and economics, as doctors, thinkers, criminologists and chroniclers sought to interpret their own specialties in relation to what was known as 'grey matter.'

And then came Freud. Today, Freud is often considered a fraud by medically trained doctors of the mind. Psychoanalysis, his revolutionary contribution to the medical field as a treatment for the mentally ill, is regarded by many as passé, just like Marxism, which had predicted a 'withering away of the state' under communism. In other words, born of idealism, 'psychoanalysis' was disproven by human reality, having helped too few to sanity while wrecking quite a number of lives.

In 1909, however, when Professor Sigmund Freud launched his bid for the world's attention ('It was no small thing to have the whole human race as one's patient,' he wrote in 'The Resistances to Psycho-Analysis'), there was no stopping him. In October of that year he wrote to Dr. Carl Jung, his intended heir in establishing an international psychoanalytic organization, that the 'domain of biography, too, must become ours.' His secret weapon? A counter-biography: namely, a new psychoanalytic interpretation of Leonardo da Vinci's life that would blow conventional biography apart. Lauded by Victorian biographers and art critics as the greatest artist of the early Renaissance, Leonardo da Vinci would, in Freud's exposé, be revealed as a common, deeply repressed homosexual. The basis for this insight, moreover, came straight from Freud's own personal consulting room: 'a neurotic' Freud had 'recently encountered' in his work as a private neurologist.

It is impossible to overstate the intention and impact of Freud's Leonardo-missile on the palace of biography. In 1882, Gabriel Seailles had published *Leonardo da Vinci: The Artist and the Scholar: Essay in Psychological Biography*. This – like the poet Paul Valéry's 1894 essay on Leonardo – had treated da Vinci's psychology entirely as a matter of his mind: a mind which seemed to late Victorians to combine the best of art and scientific genius, arriving together at a unifying, almost mathematical beauty in his work. As the art critic Walter Pater had described da Vinci's Mona Lisa painting, the model was

> older than the rocks among which she sits; like the vampire, she has been dead many times, and learned the secrets of the grave; and has been a diver in deep seas, and keeps their fallen day about her; and trafficked for strange webs with Eastern merchants: and as Leda, was the mother of Helen of Troy, and, as Saint Anne, the mother of Mary; and all this has been to her but as the sound of lyres and flutes, and lives only in the delicacy with which it has moulded the changing lineaments, and tinged the eyelids and the hands...

In Freud's view (and that of others) this was hogwash. Mindless Victorian hero-worship had overtaken the public mind, and Freud considered it his duty to apply an emetic or purgative.

On 30 March 1910, Freud – who had been writing his da Vinci psychobiography all winter – therefore addressed a gathering of would-be psychoanalysts in Nuremberg to launch his International Psychoanalytic Association. He was convinced that the root cause of neuroses, especially hysteria, was to be found in infantile and early childhood sexual experience – and that in order to cure such patients, an analyst must get the analysand to overcome his or her inhibitions – as, in due course, future society must also do, if it was to become less neurotic. At a picnic, for example, if ladies wishing to urinate were to say they were merely going to 'pick flowers,' they would be mocked by their companions who knew the truth, he said – namely, they were off to take a piss. He therefore wanted society, he told his would-be disciples in Nuremberg, to face up to the sexual taboos repressing them – locating the origins of such repression in early childhood. His new version of Leonardo, the greatest artist of the early Renaissance, would take on the most prominent, famous and iconic figure in the history of art and achieve this: a kind of mock public execution.

Sigmund Freud's *Leonardo da Vinci and a Memory of His Childhood* was published two months later – and it duly shocked polite society, as he had hoped. 'If a biographical study is really intended to arrive at an understanding of its hero's mental life it must not – as happens in the majority of biographies as a result of discretion or prudishness – silently pass over its subject's sexual activity or sexual individuality,' Freud claimed in the new book. The 'psychological approach' to telling lives was 'often very alien' to biographers. 'So resolutely do they shun everything sexual that it would seem as if Eros alone, the preserver of all living things, was not worthy material for the investigator in his pursuit of knowledge,' he claimed – and the squeamishness of readers was pathetic. Were not the 'erotic' and 'even crudely obscene' part and parcel of the work of great artists? Yet the absence of such material in da Vinci's work, and his well-known lack of sexual or erotic interest in women, could mean only one thing; he was a repressed homosexual – and to 'demonstrate' this the Professor produced a magic proof: namely, a memory of a dream da Vinci had had as an infant, of a vulture wagging its tail in his mouth. This was, Freud inferred, a clear indication of fellatio, and thus his homosexuality. Carl Jung, Freud's intended disciple to run the IPA, felt likewise; the vulture in the 'pubic region' was, Jung wrote to him, overwhelmingly indicative.

The book, published in an edition of 1,500 copies, did not immediately lead to psychoanalysis overtaking the 'domain of biography.' Freud thought it a *'halb' Dichtung,'* one of the dearest things he ever wrote, but friends informed him that it was arousing 'horror,' even 'in persons "favourably disposed to psychoanalysis."' As the editor of a book of published responses to Freud's work, *Freud Without Hindsight*, later wrote, by August 1910 the knives were already out. 'Carried away by pained outrage, civility disappeared,' as the daring analyst was himself outed, but as a fraud. Freud was an ignoramus, one contemporary critic sneered, who knew nothing of art or painting. 'But if he doesn't dare to touch his [Leonardo's] paintings, he consoles himself by touching Leonardo's genitals.' Such a counter-biography reminded the critic of the Inquisition. 'No matter who you are, an analyst will find you guilty of incest with your mother or sister or of homosexual love for your father or brother' – with men like Freud turning 'into necrophiles and necrophagi. The psychoanalytical hyenas have invaded the literary churchyards...'

Jung commiserated. 'It was only to be expected that *Leonardo* would meet with opposition,' he reassured Freud from Zurich, 'since the intellectual freedom of this work far exceeds that of its predecessors. What the rabble say about it is neither here nor there,' he added, for the professor was 'God knows how many decades ahead of these duffers.'

Such assurances, unfortunately, only fanned Freud's increasing megalomania, and within a couple of years Jung and Freud themselves had parted company. But Freud's challenge to the field of biography could not be undone. The vulture-theory turned out to be phony, since the bird in question (which Freud had found in a Russian novel about da Vinci) had not been a vulture at all, but a kite: a pointed-winged raptor. Jung had remarked that it did not matter: 'Only simpletons will stumble over the difficulties of detail.' But in a still-deeply repressed bourgeois society, the ramifications of Freud's essay were devastating to da Vinci's reputation, which was ruined. The Mona Lisa was stolen that year – and by 1916 the famous art critic Bernard Berenson was declaring that, if it were never recovered, it would be no great loss. Berenson now declared da Vinci had had no influence on the Renaissance, or upon subsequent art – that 'no Tuscan painter born after Leonardo's death produced a single work with the faintest claim to any general interest.' Moreover, to add insult to injury, the only artist who did acknowledge a debt to Da Vinci, namely Marcel Duchamp, produced in 1919 his famous postcard of the Mona Lisa with a moustache and goatee, entitled 'L.H.O.O.Q.' – phonetically signifying 'Elle a chaud au cul,' or in English, 'she has a hot ass,' beneath her enigmatic smile.

Despite his urge to make a *grand éclat*, this was not quite what Freud had intended. His hope that 'the domain of biography will become ours' certainly inspired many attempts at psychobiography, however. Over subsequent decades, one psychologist after another attempted to use quasi-scientific research and reasoning to 'explain' individual lives by penetrating the subject's unconscious. 'Psychobiography' (a term invented by the psychiatrist and psychoanalyst L. Pierce Clark in the 1920s) was pushed in American universities along with 'psychohistory.' They formed the subject of whole college courses at one point in the 1970s, and an academic journal, *The Psychohistory Review*, was launched. This fared as badly as Freud's Leonardo essay, however – despite a number of interesting attempts by psychologists. Walter Langer's *The Mind of Adolf Hitler: The Secret Wartime Report*, was one, followed by Erik Erikson's *Young Man Luther: A Study in Psychoanalysis and History*, and *Gandhi's Truth: On the Origins of Militant Nonviolence* (1969). The historian Bruce Mazlish also tried his hand with *In Search of Nixon: A Psychohistorical Inquiry* (1974) and *James and John Stuart Mill: Father and Son in the Nineteenth Century* (1975). Journalists, too, weighed in – *The Kennedy Neurosis* (1973) by the journalist Nancy Gager Clinch being a less than notable and soon forgotten example. Perhaps inevitably, *The Psychohistory Review* itself died in 1999.

The problem was not simply prudery; it was Freud's fundamental misunderstanding of biography as a 2,000-year-old genre. As Mazlish himself wrote, psychohistories and biographies fell 'outside the common the circle of common scholarship and between the proverbial two stools.' Trying to apply a new psycho-forensic template to the study of real individuals – especially when based on a neurotic patient's confession of fellatio and an infantile dream – could only demean the individual as a complex, distinctive human being, and diminish the stature of the noble scientist, masquerading as serious biographer.

Freud's ultimate influence on society and on biography, nevertheless, extended way beyond psychoanalysis – a pseudo-medical approach that was not accepted by the medical profession as effective in helping the sick. Freud's *cultural* impact, by contrast, when set alongside modernism of every stripe in the twentieth century, was undeniable. His cigar and couch became symbolic of a new post-war Western world in which every tenet of previous civilization was contested, from democracy to morality.

Ironically – and tragically – Freud himself did not benefit from this. Democracy in Europe wilted before fascism, and Freud, having procrastinated in a way similar to his description of Leonardo's inability to complete a task, left it too late to leave Austria after Hitler's Anschluss. Only with great difficulty was he able to emigrate to England, where he died in 1939 – a victim not only in his own life, but also in his post-life, as the monumental, sycophantic multi-volume portrait painted by his acolyte and biographer Ernest Jones (a work that contradicted Freud's own excoriating criticism of conventional biography) was found to be seriously wanting.

In 2017, Frederick Crews' *Freud: The Making of An Illusion* was published. In a 746-page assault on what he termed 'Freudolatry,' Crews finally cut Freud down to minuscule size, as Freud had once cut down da Vinci: exposing Sigmund Schlomo Freud's childhood travails, his obsessive opposition to masturbation, his belief in nasal reflex neurosis (and his friend Wilhelm Fliess's disastrous nose surgery to 'cure' it), his messianic determination to succeed as Superman despite his grave failings as a practising doctor, his supposed adulterous sex with his sister-in-law Minna, and his utter contempt for his actual patients... So extensive was Crews' list of Freud's failings, the author did not even find space to mention Freud's failure to colonize biography, or the spluttering invention and demise of 'psychobiography.'

Leonardo da Vinci's posthumous reputation, once trashed by Freud, meanwhile soared. Its ascent was marked by publication of an ecstatic biography by Walter Isaacson; a Hollywood feature-film, based on the Isaacson biography, starring the appropriately-named Leonardo DiCaprio; and a newly discovered da Vinci painting of Christ, his *Salvador Mundi*, or Saviour of the World, auctioned for a record 450 million dollars ...

And yet...

Freud could not easily be written out of modernity's canon – or the history of biography. There had certainly been other courageous investigators of sexual life and identity before Freud – sexologists such as Richard von Krafft-Ebing – but no other writer, philosopher or intellectual challenged the pursuit of biography in terms of biographers' failure to delve into the hidden mind as Professor Sigmund Freud had done in 1910.

It helped, of course, that Freud was a clinician, a doctor, with a long track-record of 'cases' that he had written up – the 'Dora Case,' 'Little Hans' and 'Rat-Man.' As Jung had pointed out, his details might be wrong, but who cared? His determination to lift at last the veil of hero-worship – a veil that had famously infuriated biographers like Samuel Johnson – was what counted. It was small wonder Freud corresponded amicably with Lytton Strachey; together they were knocking down the bulwarks of 'pure' or hagiographical lives, and exposing what was underneath. Laws of obscenity, libel, copyright and rules of social convention would continue to dam (and damn) the biographical quest, but psychology and sex went together hand in hand, as Freud pointed out – suppression and repression being the inevitable manifestation of what he called (and published as) *Civilization and Its Discontents* (1930).

It was Freud's insistent efforts to dig below the surface of supposedly 'civilized' lives, motives and consciousness that both shamed and inspired biographers after World War II. Psychobiography failed to catch on, since it was, essentially, reductive and formulaic, but Freud's appeal to biographers to peer under the proverbial stone began belatedly to change the entire genre. As Peter Gay – a former avowed psychohistorian – noted in 1988, 'Freud pervades our culture to such an extent that we often use Freudian language – narcissism, sibling rivalry, ambivalence, neurosis – without even noticing it.'

Novelists such as Arthur Schnitzler, Henry Miller and Robert Bloch certainly took on the tropes and influences of Freudian X-rays, so to speak, of the mind, but none had pretended to be 'proving' the truth of Freud's theories. And the same was the case with biography, where – however ridiculous they found psychobiography – biographers did slowly begin to use Freud's approach to the unravelling of an individual's real mind. In other words, biography became a psychological as well as an historical *quest*. That new curiosity, on behalf of the reader, enabled them to unravel, with candour, at least some of the mummy-like layers that wrapped the lives of others. At the most populist level were books like *The Intimate Sex Lives of Famous People* (1981), but at the most serious was Michael Holroyd's *Lytton Strachey: A Critical Biography* (1967 and 1968). With access to the Strachey family's voluminous papers, and by interviewing candidly everyone living who had known Strachey, Holroyd was able to describe both the inner and outer life of a homosexual author with complete candour – and sympathy. Richard Ellmann's *Oscar Wilde* followed in 1987. Biography had turned a new leaf: a fig leaf.

On leaving the Vienna General Hospital in 1886, Freud had become obsessed by Charcot's *secrets d'alcôve* and the growing attempts to uncover the unconscious mind, whether by Mesmerism or hypnosis or plain interrogation. In truth, however, Freud did not lose all interest in the physiology of the brain. For his work on childhood palsies he was made Professor Extraordinarius in 1902 – and ultimately it was the realm of physiology and pharmacology which offered breakthroughs not only in treating diseases of the mind, but understanding its mechanics. By the end of the twentieth century, research into the neural structure of the brain had completely overtaken the field of psychology

– and this, more than Freud's psychoanalytic spotlight on the unconscious, began to have an interesting effect on biography.

Where Freud's dogmatic focus had been on early childhood as the source of all later achievement (and problems) in life, the new emphasis on the brain as the point of impact relating to an individual's traumatic life experiences and disease now shifted attention to the later years of an individual's life, especially with respect to memory, dementia and Alzheimer's disease. Where Freud had ridiculed biographers for ignoring sex as a prime component of life studies, so psychologists now waded back into the field in order to show what biographers were *still* missing: namely the medical life, as it pertained to the mind. The effect of drugs on the mind was an especial area of investigation of hidden life, with a cascade of new biographies of Hitler, such as *The Secret Diaries of Hitler's Doctor* (1983), *Patient Hitler* (1989), and *Hitler: Diagnosis of a Destructive prophet* (1999).

A similar trend could be seen in biographies of Franklin Roosevelt around the turn of the millennium. Whereas in the 1960s it had been Franklin Roosevelt's sex life that had drawn great attention – biographers highlighting a secret mistress who had been with him at Warm Springs when he died in April 1945 – it was now his ultimate *medical* condition (undisclosed heart failure as early as the spring of 1944) that attracted interest and speculation, with books such as *The Dying President* (1998), *A Conspiracy of Silence: The Health and Death of Franklin D. Roosevelt* (2007) and *FDR's Deadly Secret* (2009). How that medical condition affected FDR's mind, affecting decisions he then made involving millions of human beings, made the matter – as with Hitler – one of grave import in modern biography and history, especially in terms of the American presidency and safety of the world.

Et sic vadit. The Dangerous Case of Donald Trump: 27 Psychiatrists and Mental Health Experts Assess a President* (2017) is merely the latest example of psychology's place – sometimes shocking, always challenging – in the modern study of real lives.

Sources: Nigel Hamilton, *Biography: A Brief History* (Cambridge, MA: Harvard University Press, 2007); A. Richard Turner, *Inventing Leonardo* (Berkeley: University of California, 1992); Peter Gay, *Freud: A life For Our Time* (New York: Norton, 1988); Frederick Crews, *Freud: The Making of an Illusion* (New York: Henry Holt, 2017); George Makari, *Revolution in Mind: The Creation of Psychoanalysis* (New York: Harper Collins, 2008); Arthur Eaton, *History Telling: The Rise and Fall of Psychohistory* (Boston/Leiden: Brill, forthcoming); W.M. Runyan, *Life Histories and Psychobiography: Explorations in Theory and Method* (Oxford: Oxford University Press, 1982); Alan Elms, *Uncovering Lives: The Uneasy Alliance of Biography and Psychology* (Oxford: Oxford University Press, 1994).

 **is for Quotation**

Some years before Samuel Johnson died, his friend James Boswell, Esq., the Laird of Auchinleck, a barony in Ayrshire, Scotland, began to reflect on how he could best tell the story of Dr. Johnson's life. Since Johnson had not been a soldier or a politician or a religious leader, but had led an outwardly undramatic life, Boswell hit upon the notion of chronological 'scenes' in which the reader could meet the master-conversationalist of his age, and get to know his character in all its quirks and dimensions.

As Boswell's own biographer, Adam Sisman, later explained,

> readers would be able to watch the progression of each scene, like fellow guests at the dinner-table. Johnson's remarks, and those of his companions, would be reported, as if in full; and rather than being given in indirect speech, the most dramatic exchanges could be cued to the speaker's name like an actor's lines, sometimes with stage directions to indicate manner or inflection.

For it was well established, Boswell claimed as a biographer, that the conversation of a celebrated man 'will best display his character.' And to prove this, Boswell included, as Sisman noted, 'extracts from a vast range of documents, including working notes and discarded drafts: letters, prayers and meditations, essays, biographies. Pamphlets, definitions, parodies, fables and allegories, decisions on literary disputes, legal opinions, an appeal for votes, poems, a novel, dedications, obituaries and epitaphs.' Thus began the greatest biography in the English language – based substantially on quotes or quotations.

If storytelling is the heart-pump of biography, then quotation is the lifeblood. The reader of a biography is curious about a person, an individual – a real individual. Moreover, as Boswell appreciated, the reader would probably like to meet him on the page. By quoting what the individual said or wrote, or how he was described or remembered by those who knew him, in their own quoted words, the reader is able to get as close as possible to the course and reality of a lived life. Without quotation, biography would be like entering a room devoid of people. Quotation of speech, of documents, of memoranda, of diaries, of correspondence, of interviews, even of gossip, is thus not only integral to the business of biography, it is a defining virtue; one that distinguishes it even from history. For a history of a time, an event, an idea or a society can be written without quoting a single person, but a biography is dead without such material – and has always been so, since the Greeks and Romans.

Suetonius provided perhaps the best early template for this. He had, it is believed, been an archivist and senior secretary at the imperial court in Rome at the time of Trajan and Hadrian; certainly, he seems to have had access to diverse libraries and witnesses when writing his account of the first Roman dictators, *De Vita Caesarum*, or *The Twelve Caesars*, the greatest group biography in literature, written 1,600 years before Boswell's masterpiece. Through Gaius Suetonius Tranquillus's mix of factual information, authorial judgement and quotation, we get to meet his chosen dictators with far more shocking candour, in fact, than Boswell's heroic portrait of his friend – whose intention to remarry, a year after the death of his wife, Tetty, Boswell found too unheroic to include in his *Life of Samuel Johnson, LL.D.* Much of Suetonius's rogues' gallery of the first Caesars is shockingly candid, and deliberately so – for Suetonius was determined to show he had both an open mind as a biographer, and a wickedly candid quill: one that was responsible, it is said, for his being exiled, eventually, from Imperial Rome. (Rumoured intimacy with Hadrian's wife was another.)

Regarding the sexual aspects of Augustus Caesar's early years, Suetonius wrote, for example, that Augustus was

> reproached with various sexual improprieties. Sextus Pompey taunted him with the charge of effeminacy, while Mark Antony accused him of unnatural relations with Julius Caesar as the price of his adoption; and Lucius Antonius claimed that not only was that accusation true, but that he had submitted to Aulus Hirtius in Spain, for three thousand gold pieces, and that he used to soften the hairs on his legs by singeing them with red-hot walnut shells.

Then came the *coup de grâce*: 'Furthermore, on one occasion in the theater, the following line, said of a eunuch priest of Cybele [goddess of earth] striking a tambourine, was loudly applauded, as referring insultingly to Augustus: "See, how this sodomite's finger rules the orb!"'

For many historians and readers in later centuries this was too much, and Suetonius was often disparaged as an incorrigible gossip. Among biographers, however, he became a kind of patron saint – for he did not use such quotations simply as confetti, but as part of a distinctive, open-minded frankness in describing and assessing character. His quotation of the eunuch priest was followed immediately, for instance, with an appreciation of Augustus's sexual behaviour as an adult – and its role in his political fortunes. 'Not even his friends denied he was given to adulterous behavior, though they justified it as a matter of policy not passion, claiming he discovered his enemy's intention through their wives and daughters,' Suetonius recounted. 'Mark Antony accused him not only of marrying Livia with indecent haste, but of maneuvering an ex-consul's wife from the dining room to the bedroom before the man's eyes, and returning her blushing and with her hair in disorder,' and even

> stripping wives and young women of their clothes in the manner of Torianus, the slave-dealer, and inspecting them as if they were up for sale. Mark Antony also wrote familiarly

to Augustus, before his quarrels with him: 'Why the change in you? Because I'm rutting with Cleopatra? She's my "wife." After nine years is it news? Do you rut only with Livia? Be hanged if, by the time you read this, you've not had Tertulla or Terentilla, or Rufilla, or Salvia Titisenia, or the whole lot of them together! What matter where or whom you pleasure?'

No biographer of President John F. Kennedy – an American Caesar – or the powerful men whose careers were brought to a halt in 2018, the year of #MeToo, would be doing his job properly, almost two millennia later, if he did not re-read *The Twelve Caesars* and see how deftly Suetonius had married the personal and the political, sex and power, ambition and social context. The search for personal material that can be quoted in order to help make an authorial point is an essential ingredient in biography. Quotation by no means makes an assertion true, necessarily, but it undeniably contributes to the biographer's evaluation of the truth about a chosen individual, helping to authenticate it.

Given its importance in biography, it is all the more surprising that quotation so seldom features in studies of biography as a genre. A twenty-first century textbook on Biographical Research, by Professor Brian Roberts, does not even mention quotation. To be sure, to some extent this reflects the central status of quotation in biographical storytelling and thus needs no further comment; but if so, it skirts a vitally significant feature today: one that is increasingly dividing Western democracies from autocracies and dictatorships. This concerns the matter of evidence, whether in environmental science, as in global warming, or the repeated gassing of innocents in the war in Syria.

What then is quotation, exactly?

Quotation is generally understood to mean the use, in quotation marks or by typological highlighting, of a passage from a text, book, or source that helps succinctly to support an argument: part of an evidentiary trail.

In biography, let us be clear, quotation was never used as proof. No biographer ever saw himself as a scientist, but rather as a quasi-lawyer, presenting evidence to be taken into account by the jury (i.e. the reader) when arriving at a verdict. The 'discovery' process itself, including authentication and verification, was thus part and parcel of establishing the validity of the evidence, and its role in forming a judgement. As Sisman noted, Boswell's life of Johnson was an extraordinary achievement in terms of the lengths to which the Laird went to find material, in competition with other writers and editors anxious to capitalize on Johnson's posthumous reputation, such as Sir John Hawkins and Mrs. Piozzi. But Boswell's diligence, across many years of research, produced material that was 'by its very nature miscellaneous, provided by many different individuals and supplied in many different forms. It included Boswell's own assorted anecdotes and Johnsoniana collected in notebooks; his notes on interviews with friends and colleagues of Johnson's; and material supplied by other hands.' Taken as a whole,

> this material presented a number of problems to the author. It was variable in quality: some appeared to be authentic, while other parts seemed unreliable, second-hand, or indeed little more than gossip. It was inconsistent, or contradictory; the same anecdotes were duplicated, often with different details or different emphasis. Many of the anecdotes were undated. Much of it was unusable, for one reason or another.

Boswell's 'problem,' in other words, was the problem that had faced every serious biographer since classical times – and it would be the same for every serious biographer who followed him. Boswell had seen himself as a 'compiler' of such material, using his own judgement to decide its merit, as well as its possible usefulness in showing the range of Johnson's intellect and character over the course of his life. Certainly, no biographer since Boswell has failed to read his *Life of Samuel Johnson, LL.D.*, as a model of the biographer's task: a job in which quotation is the crucial haemoglobin. Even as the writing and sending of letters decreased in the late twentieth century, the loss was largely made up by electronic correspondence such as emails and text messages, as well as by other electronic devices such as the tape recorder and dictation, or even telephone recordings. Successive US presidents, from Franklin Roosevelt onwards, had begun using hidden microphones – indeed the 34th President, Richard Nixon, would be brought down by his secret White House tape recorder, which he had wanted as a means of quotation when one day he left office and hoped to write his memoirs.

Openly-taped interviews provided another source of evidence and insight – so much so that, when the tape recorder malfunctioned, as in the case of Janet Malcolm's 1982 interviews with the then recently-dismissed director of the Freud archives, Jeffrey Masson, it led to a high-profile lawsuit and two trials that lasted twelve years, for alleged libel. 'The proceeding felt more like the end of a bad marriage than a libel trial,' wrote Robert Boynton, in *The Village Voice* in 1994, after the second trial.

> It had grown beyond a mere libel suit, becoming a signifier for some of our society's most bitterly fought cultural battles, about the press, psychoanalysis, the roles of men and women. By the second trial, popular attention had exhausted itself. The onlookers this time were a reserved bunch: First Amendment lawyers, media consultants, court buffs, journalism students, the occasional stray analyst. Outside the courtroom, nervous journalists milled around, comparing notes to make sure they got all the quotes right. Still, even in its widely overlooked denouement, the Malcolm case continually forces us to face uncomfortable truths and moral chaos we would just as soon ignore.

The problem was that Malcolm had portrayed Masson, whom she had interviewed for many hours in different locations, as 'a stupendously promiscuous braggart and narcissist,' as Boynton described, comparing the more-than-a-decade-long lawsuit to Jarndyce v. Jarndyce in Dickens's *Bleak House*. Malcolm, a journalist with a deeply problematic view of privacy, had become celebrated for skewering her own kind, as when she had written of journalist-biographer Joe McGinniss that 'every journalist who is not too stupid or too full of himself knows that what he does is morally indefensible' – a view she attached to biographers, too, in *The Silent Woman*. When directed at Masson, however, she had 'triggered a deluge of psycho-speculation about what made Malcolm tick. Masson's own lawyer tried (unsuccessfully) to introduce the inflammatory passage at trial in order to show that Malcolm, contrary to her testimony, knew full well that she had betrayed her client.'

Betrayal, respect, honour… Both journalism and biography involve a writer-subject relationship that can hinge on quotation, when challenged in libel cases. As Boynton rhetorically asked: 'Do quotation marks indicate what was actually said, or are they only an approximation? Are women who claim to have been sexually abused telling the truth, or simply fantasizing? Had Masson's reputation been destroyed by his verbal indiscretion,' when agreeing to be interviewed by Janet Malcolm, 'or by Malcolm's unscrupulousness?' All too cruelly, the issue came down to quotations.

The 'legal issue at the heart of Masson v. Malcolm was fairly simple,' Boynton summarized:

> Had Masson uttered the five disputed quotes [when publishing her interview in *The New Yorker*] – one of which appears on tape in a slightly different form, three in her typed notes, and one in her memory – or not? And, more important: Did the quotes hang from Malcolm's artfully devastating portrait, or does the portrait itself dangle precariously from one or more of the five damaging quotes? This last question carried very real consequences since, if the latter were true, Masson might receive the $7 million in damages he was requesting.

It was Malcolm's deliberate and incendiary inclusion in her published article of Masson's sexual admissions and self-revelations

– which he had thought were 'off the record' – that had so stirred him to judicial revenge, however: the very reason Boynton likened it to divorce. As Boynton afterwards mused, 'It seems strange that two such ardent students of Freud had no clue that their collaboration' – involving fifty hours of tape-recorded interviewing – 'would end up such a disaster.'

The bigger disaster, in terms of quotation, was elsewhere, however – as Professor Boynton's use of the word 'signifier' (he became a professor of Literary Reportage at New York University's Journalism Institute) intimated. By the time the Malcolm trial (which Malcolm mercifully won, the second time) took place in 1994, the twin movements of poststructuralism and deconstruction had swept academia, and Boynton's fellow professors were fighting a rear-guard action to maintain the distinction between truth and falsehood.

One such professor was Daniel Lehman of Ashland University, Ohio, who had trained and worked for many years as a reporter, but then entered academia. Once in the college classroom, Lehman found theoretical criticism had blurred, if not demolished, the traditional meaning of 'truth,' which had once been the goldstone of his profession. In his *Matters of Fact* in 1997, Lehman tied himself in knots over the validity and implications of new deconstruction in public life. The focus on 'text' as a dubious receptacle and purveyor of even more dubious meaning, pace deconstructors, was in danger of demeaning human interaction and the ability to think straight. 'Nonfiction is a form of communication that purports to re-enact for the reader the play of actual characters and events across time,' Lehman wrote. 'What counts is not so much whether these phenomena can be empirically known but that they are also available and experienced by the reader outside the written artifact' – in other words, *in real life* – with life and death consequences. Deconstructive theorists had subverted the 'putative equation of historical text with truth and fictional truth with falsity,' he lamented; it was a war on 'truth' that could only end badly...

It did. In fact it ended seventeen years later with 'fake news': not only as a term of cursory dismissal by an elected US president, but one that would be replicated across the world in 2018 whenever autocrats and dictators faced reportage and quotation they disliked – the tweets of the 45th US President against CNN and *The Washington Post* as arch-purveyors of 'fake news' being mirrored in Moscow, as the Russian government brushed off horrifying photographic evidence of mass murder by Russian-supplied chemical weapons close to Damascus on the front page of *The New York Times* as merely more 'fake news.'

Having managed to ignore the poststructuralist semioticians for decades, biographers could at least claim innocence for this demise. Nevertheless it was a tragic example of man's gullibility and short-sightedness: one that could only re-affirm the biographer's honourable quest for practical, verifiable truth – truth with real consequences – as James Boswell had recorded in his life of the Great Doctor.

'After we came out of the church, we stood talking for some time together of Bishop Berkeley's ingenious sophistry to prove the non-existence of matter, and that every thing in the universe is merely ideal,' Boswell recalled. 'I observed, that though we are satisfied his doctrine is not true, it is impossible to refute it. I never shall forget the alacrity with which Johnson answered, striking his foot with mighty force against a large stone, till he rebounded from it, "I refute it *thus*."'

Ouch.

Sources: Tristan Power and Roy Gibson, *Suetonius the Biographer: Studies in Roman Lives* (Oxford: Oxford University Press, 2014); Daniel Lehman, *Matters of Fact: Reading Nonfiction over the Edge* (Columbus: Ohio State University, 1997); Adam Sisman, *Boswell's Presumptuous Task: The Making of the Life of Dr. Johnson* (New York: Farrar Strauss, 2001); Brian Roberts, *Biographical Research* (Buckingham: Open University Press, 2002); Robert Boynton, 'Till Press Do Us Part: The trial of Janet Malcolm and Jeffrey Masson,' *The Village Voice*, November 28, 1994; Suetonius, *The Twelve Caesars*, numerous editions; James Boswell, *The Life of Samuel Johnson LL.D.*, 1791.

 is for Religion

Religion features very little in the theory of biography, for it is considered antithetical to the pursuit of verifiable truth – the cornerstone of modern biography. Yet, as with the history of art, the history of biography would be immeasurably thinner without the contribution of religion – a contribution made in myriad ways, from the drama of conversion and martyrdom to religious wars, jihad, repentance, the Last Rites and memorial services.

In his book *God is Not Great: How Religion Poisons Everything* (2007), Christopher Hitchens, the essayist and critic, memorably inveighed against religion before his own death from cancer. Not only were religious teachings about creation and the cosmos unscientific, he stated, but the practice of religion had led to wars and bloodshed on a scale which vastly outweighed any individual solace it had given – wars that were still being waged by Al Qaeda and Islamic fundamentalists in the twenty-first century. For Hitchens, the existence of God was pure sophistry, leading him to rail against the very concept, and against death – raging 'against the dying of the light,' *pace* Dylan Thomas.

The biographer, however, works on a different plane than the essayist. He is not concerned with making a point about history or existence, but simply the recording of an individual's life – and religion has always played a part in those narratives, whether as background or spiritual battlefield. Especially the battlefield. For although the facts of a life can be interesting, even sensational, they are meaningless without meaning, as in the individual subject's struggle to find meaning, sense, comfort, happiness, fulfilment, joy, sorrow, or merely stability. In this respect, religion is at the very core of biography, however unacknowledged – furnishing not only outward events to chronicle, but inner ones, too. Inherently or overtly, it is the spiritual dimension and development of an individual – his conscience and his moral conduct – that a serious biographer attempts to delineate. And judge.

In this sense, religion – embodied in the quest to find meaning in a real individual's life's journey – is a defining aspect of biography, distinguishing it from history or sociology. Even from psychology – for where the psychologist may seek to explain the evils committed by Joseph Stalin by reference to his childhood and psychologically-defined traits of character and behaviour, the biographer is not driven simplistically to 'explain' such a life. Psychological precepts may offer insights into Stalin's career, but they can neither be definitive as explanations, however supposedly scientific, nor can they explicate why he chose any one direction rather than another. The biographer, by contrast, attempts to research the life carefully, and ultimately to judge it: what it meant for the subject, as far as possible, what it means to the biographer, and what it conveys to readers of the biographer's era. The biographer's task, in other words, is a moral one – deriving, inevitably, from religious concepts of good and evil, forgiveness, judgement and reckoning. How Stalin saw his own life, how others saw it, how we see it today, how we judge it: these are the dimensions in which the biographer works, uniquely – which in its spiritual aspect is a religious endeavour, and true of every biography, whether of a saint or a tyrant, an artist or an ordinary individual, in attempting to explore and assess the meaning, the moral meaning of a real life.

Though the first golden age of Western biography took place in antiquity, in Greece and Rome, when a plurality of gods helped people to understand the universe and the fates of men, it was only in the decades after the death of Jesus of Nazareth in 33 AD that the quest for meaning in biography took a more direct role. The four canonical Gospels of Matthew, Mark, Luke and John remain remarkable in biography's long history for the intensity with which they focused on what had become the cardinal elements of biographical narrative: birth, background, relationships, ministry or service, quotation, confrontation, trial, death and afterlife. It was in the search for moral meaning in Jesus's life, however, that the Gospel writers breathed new life into the business of biography – Jesus's lament, 'My God, My God, why hast thou forsaken me?', being perhaps the most heartbreaking example of its quest.

Why indeed? The Gospels, as we have noted elsewhere, are ultimately too ideological in purpose, and too unverifiable, to qualify as standard biographies, but they had a huge impact on biographical narrative, for they were replicated in subsequent centuries in myriad lives of saints that we know as hagiographies – interesting accounts, especially of ministry and martyrdom, but lacking quite the same divine inspiration. They were designed, however, as educational texts to reaffirm Christian religious faith – and doubtless for many they did.

With the advent of the Renaissance and the Reformation, however, biography became once again a predominantly secular undertaking, even if they followed for the most part the Gospel prescription in terms of narrative structure, focus and drama – weighing, ultimately, the good and the bad in the record of an individual's life.

Once the authority of religion faded in the twentieth century, and the very existence of God became widely questioned in the Western world, writers felt compelled to seek meaning outside of religious faith – the starting point, as it were, of existentialism. This was followed by an even greater investigation of meaning – some would call it an assault – by poststructuralists and deconstructionists in the 1970s. Paradoxically, this led to a new golden age of biography, since practising biographers expressed no interest in academic or nihilistic theorizing. Instead, watching the fields of history, sociology, anthropology, linguistics and psychology being ravaged by self-important, self-regarding critics – none of whom was capable of writing more than a few intelligible sentences – biographers took on with gusto the discarded mantle of *le grand récit*. Not only of *grand récit*, moreover, but the role, too, of Grand Inquisitor, in terms of the meaning of a life. For if all other examiners of the human condition, from a moral perspective, were now tongue-tied, so to speak, who else in non-fiction would record, interpret and judge a real human being's life? Sartre tried, in his indigestible four-volume biography of Gustave Flaubert, *The Family Idiot*. Even the novelist Julian Barnes, famous for his spoof biography, *Flaubert's Parrot*, called Sartre's attempt at biographical narrative a 'mad' book, 'couched in a lazily dense style' – an attempt at 'reinvention of the genre' which exceeded 'in wordage all the major works of its subject put together,' that took Sartre ten years to write, and was read by only a handful. Derrida? Saussure? Lacan?

Emboldened and unfettered by paralyzing theories of meaning, biographers thus stepped forward in the 1980s to address the more practical question of meaning in an individual's life – and more than willing, moreover, to research it, chronicle it, and judge it morally, without existentialist, Marxist, psychological or poststructuralist inhibition. They accepted, as they always had done, that their own authorial views had been formed by their own background, upbringing, education and life experience, even religion – but this had always been so, and it had not inhibited the practice of biography more than any other prohibition, from libel to censorship. It was something *understood by the reader*, as part of the social contract between author and lector – just as readers accepted fiction as fiction. What had changed was the biographer's vestment as Grand Inquisitor – for the biographers of the 1980s certainly felt a new freedom to investigate, question and direct the camera, so to speak, on what they saw as the significant features of their chosen subject's lives with the same moral candour as the great quasi-biographical novelists of the nineteenth century, from Balzac to Dickens, Tolstoy to Dostoevsky. Where late twentieth-century fiction writers still found themselves hamstrung by the dictates of postmodernism, then, *le grand récit* seemed to biographers a perfectly admirable way to research, recount, review and judge a real life. The barbed wire surrounding the castle of Xanadu, in Welles's epic *Citizen Kane*, had largely been removed in terms of libel, sexuality, censorship and judicially-policed privacy. Biographers were now free at last to write openly about real lives – encouraged by readers to pry, expose, reveal, investigate, ridicule, mourn and judge no differently than Thackeray, George Eliot or Thomas Hardy had done, overtly or inherently. There would be those who would protest, or claim – like Janet Malcolm – that there was too much looking through the keyhole rather than the looking glass in biography, and to be sure biographers provided plenty of sensational revelations that the media could seize upon and highlight. But the very controversy fuelled by such biographies indicated that biography had reached a new era, for biography had hitherto only really been controversial around the edges, given punitive law and negative social attitudes on what it was proper for a biographer to reveal. Relations of adultery, murder, suicide, prostitution and darker secrets were now front and centre in biography, as in great Victorian novels such as *Anna Karenina, The Brothers Karamazov, The Mill on the Floss, Tess of the D'Urbevilles*, or *Heart of Darkness*: investigations of an individual's development and life-course from a larger, more life-encompassing moral perspective than before. Decades ahead of the hashtag #MeToo or #BalanceTonPorc, biographers dared investigate and record the moral contradictions, evasions, short-cuts, obsessions and depravities that accompanied great artistic or scientific, political or economic achievement in the lives of supposedly well-known real individuals.

The modern, late-twentieth century biography, in short, did not recoil from telling the truth about an individual's whole life story as a moral endeavour, moreover in authentic, realist detail – just as the great Victorian novelists had done. Robert Caro's life of Lyndon Johnson, for example, never flinched from revealing the sexual appetite of what he called his 'Jumbo.' Or the financial antics of the man who would almost single-handedly push Civil Rights legislation through Congress after a century of white-supremacist lynching and backpeddling, but who also, as an impetuous US Commander in Chief, began the Vietnam War, resulting in the deaths of hundreds of thousands of Vietnamese and Americans on the flimsiest of premises.

Similarly, in the field of literature, the biographer of Tennessee Williams, John Lahr, would subtitle his 765-page reconstruction of the playwright's life *Mad Pilgrimage of the Flesh* in 2014: detailing in a series of spellbinding reconstructions not only the genesis of Williams's greatest plays – *A Streetcar Named Desire, Glass Menagerie, Cat on a Hot Tin Roof* – but also the price which the homosexual author paid for his freedom to create, and to garner fortune and fame. Drawing on Tennessee Williams's diaries, letters, tapes, conversations, and the witness of many hundreds of relatives, colleagues, enemies, lovers and observers, Lahr delineated the tormented soul of Tennessee Williams and, *pace* Gosse, recounted his 'adventures through life': a story as morally bracing as any Dostoevskian tract, and as impossible to put down. 'Grabbing both the brass ring of success and the trapeze of the flesh,' Lahr ended his version of Williams's trajectory, 'Williams swung high and low. His passage through time was sensational. He contended doggedly with his own roiling divided self. In him, until his last breath, the forces of life and death were pitched in clamorous battle. Art was his habit, his "fatal need," and his salvation.' In his plays, too. 'Foraying into those ineffable realms of sensation where language has little purchase, he uncovered our sorrow, our desire, our hauntedness,' to remake American theatre.

As Grand Inquisitor in the new century, the biographer as moral jurist had once again come of age, with similar moral inquisitions of Pablo Picasso, Eleanor Roosevelt, Zelda Fitzgerald, Ernest Hemingway, Albert Einstein, Alexander Hamilton and other notable figures – bringing the unique *moral* biographical lens of biography to the history of an individual. An individual, moreover, examined in retrospect by another individual: an author situated somewhere between confessor and judge, acting not on behalf of a church or sect, but simply applying the morally-inquisitive perspective of a biographer, tasked by the modern reader with telling the truth, and with forming a personal judgement based upon all the evidence, carefully researched and subjected to rigorous, disciplined examination.

Which leaves the biographies of religious leaders, from Martin Luther to Martin Luther King, Jr., and also the specific element of religion in the life of the biographee. Here the status of modern biography is not so high.

There have been memorable accounts of religious conversion as turning points in the lives of Cat Stevens, Mohammed Ali, or Malcolm X, for example, and rich examples of individuals turning to formal religion at the end of their lives – such as Napoleon – for absolution of their sins. But how religious faith has moulded, changed, affected or developed in the lives of most biographees is often a blank page in biographies. Conversion to Catholicism clearly had a major impact on the life of Evelyn Waugh, but how it developed – i.e., the spiritual and doctrinal trials it went through – is seldom pursued by his biographers, or by those of Graham Greene, another novelist-convert.

Doubtless such daintiness reflects the modern biographer's wariness in addressing formal religion, lest the biography be deemed ideological – and thus best left to a real confessor, or to God. In some ways, though, it reflects our continuing uncertainty as to what exactly we understand by religion, whether as doctrine, rules, worship, church or church-affiliation. For many years, there were objections, especially in the Netherlands, to biographies of political or other figures if they were not written by writers of the same religious background. The field was thus divided up, so to speak: Catholics covered by Catholics, Protestants by Protestants, Socialists by Socialists, atheists by atheists. Evelyn Waugh's biography of Ronald Knox in 1959 was a prime example of the problem – Waugh hoping for a knighthood for his devout work. Instead of abating, however, the problem became worse. 'Cultural appropriation' – the attempt by someone of a majority culture to address someone of a minority culture as exotic – was not only declared a sin in academic sociology and anthropology departments, but the campaign against it swept through public discourse, too.

For the biographies of men and women in terms of their faith this proved discouraging, even disabling. The American sociologist Gaye Tuchman once explained how 'fraught by meaning' can be a social environment characterized by uniformity. In such an environment, there is a tendency to consider moral values within that environment as objective, and therefore not interesting as themes for discussion or examination. Yet the actual expression of religious belief by politicians, across their careers, marks the intersection of faith and practice, the inner life and the outer life, which are of abiding interest – or should be – to biographers. John F. Kennedy's candidacy for the US presidency was put in doubt owing to his Catholicism – a matter he confronted head-on by famously addressing the Greater Houston Ministerial Association in his 1960 election campaign. But other confessions of faith or doubt can catch up with a politician, as happened with the liberal Dutch prime minister Mark Rutte. Rutte had told a journalist from the *Reformatorisch Dagblad* newspaper in 2005, when he was a Member of Parliament, that he was a member of the Dutch Reformed Church. It was part of my upbringing, he explained. 'I am grateful for that, although I sometimes doubt whether God exists. Faith remains a struggle for me.' Five years later, media journalist Peter Dekker returned to the statement. Rutte – in the meantime Prime Minister of the Netherlands – was accused of having pleaded for the abolition of the blasphemy prohibition, and 'so we may also curse the Lord God as much as we like,' Dekker commented – a live wire in the context of Islamic fundamentalism sweeping Europe.

Religious faith – the faith in which a biographee grew up, the faith he or she developed during his or her lifetime, and the faith, or lack of faith, in which the biographee died – is such a profound ingredient in the life of an individual that it surely cannot be excluded from modern biography. How it should best be included is, of course, another matter. Directly or indirectly? Head-on or peripherally? In terms of background culture, or as a direct influence on the biographee's life? There are no clear rules that the biographer can follow. Which compels him to adapt the memorable adage that William Somerset Maugham once coined for writing a novel: there are only three rules of thumb for writing it – only nobody knows what they are.

Sources: Christopher Hitchens, *God is Not Great: How Religion Poisons Everything* (New York: Grand Central Publishing, 2007); Richard A. Burridge, *What are the Gospels? A Comparison with Graeco-Roman Biography* (Michigan/Cambridge: Wm. B. Eerdmans Publishing Co, 2004); John Lahr, *Tennessee Williams: Mad Pilgrimage of the Flesh* (New York: Norton, 2104); Peter Dekker, blog, 16 October 2010; Gaye Tuchman, 'Objectivity as Strategic Ritual: An Examination of Newsmen's Notions of Objectivity', in: *American Journal of Sociology* 77 (1972) 4, 660-679; Mirjam de Baar, Yme Kuiper and Hans Renders (eds), *Biografie en religie. De religieuze factor in de biografie* (Amsterdam/Groningen: Boom, 2011).

is for Sex

For most of biography's long history, the matter of sex was a subsidiary theme: too private to be explored within marriage, scandalous enough to be of interest outside.

In Suetonius's group biography* *The Twelve Caesars* (c119 AD), for example, Tiberius's marriage to his first wife, Vipsania Agrippina, is described as 'happy' but short – poor Tiberius being compelled to divorce her. Instead he had to marry Caesar Augustus's daughter Julia, whom he came to hate. 'Tiberius came to regret the divorce so heartily that when, one day, he accidentally caught sight of Vipsania and followed her with tears in his eyes and intense unhappiness written on his face,' Suetonius described, 'precautions were taken against his ever seeing her again.'

Suetonius was a senior archivist, librarian and private secretary to the Roman emperor. His romanticized account then gave him leave, as biographer, to detail Tiberius' sexual activities outside his marriage to Julia – especially at his 'private sporting house' in Capri, 'where sexual extravagances were practised for his secret pleasure. Bevies of girls and young men, whom he had collected from all over the Empire as adepts in unnatural practices, and known as *spintriae*, would copulate before him in groups of three, to excite his waning passions.' 'Some aspects of his criminal obscenity are almost too vile to discuss, much less believe,' Suetonius wrote – while going on to record them.

Within the traditions and censorship laws of different countries, this intra- and extra-marital distinction held sway for almost 2,000 years: moralistic critics denouncing biographers who dared invade the sexual privacy of a marriage, and deprecating – but happily quoting – accounts of extramarital sex. For the most part the subject was considered off-limits, to be handled only in fiction – and then only if it avoided pornography laws. Those laws, however, began to wobble in the twentieth century, giving rise to some epic – and in retrospect amusing – legal sagas, especially in England and America. A very English, class-conscious version of Flaubert's *Madame Bovary* (perhaps even of Tolstoy's *Anna Karenina*), D.H. Lawrence's *Lady Chatterley's Lover* was published privately in Italy in 1928, then openly in France and Australia the year after. News of attempts to get it past English Customs officials, however, aroused the British popular press to paroxysms of disgust, inciting headlines such as: 'A Landmark in Evil' – the 'most evil outpouring that has ever besmirched the literature of our country. The sewers of French pornography would be dragged in vain,' *John Bull* had raged, 'to find a parallel in beastliness.'

Evelyn Waugh, for his part, found the image perfect for his comic genius. In 1930 he had published *Vile Bodies*, the story of a would-be autobiographer, Adam Fenwick-Symes, whose experience at the port of Dover, after a rough crossing of the English Channel, could be used to ridicule British problems with sex, memoirs and literature. 'Hullo, hullo, what's this?' the customs officer asks Adam, as he inspects the books in Adam's suitcase. 'That's a book, too,' Adam explains. 'One I've just written. It is my memoirs.'

Naturally, it is confiscated.

Pornographic novels like *Lady Chatterley's Lover* were bad enough – banned in the 1920s and 1930s in the United States as well – but they were at least fiction. Autobiography, Waugh recognized, was considered far more dangerous, for such writing purportedly recorded *real* life. Until the law on pornography was changed, biography – which relied heavily on autobiographical writings – was thus far more constrained than fiction.

The removal of the 'Chatterley ban' in 1960 marked a cultural turning point – one that the poet Philip Larkin immortalized in his poem *Annus Mirabilis.*

>Sexual intercourse began
>In nineteen sixty-three
>(which was rather late for me) –

> Between the end of the 'Chatterley' ban
> And the Beatles' first LP.

With the advent of the Beatles, and the introduction of the Pill as cheap and effective birth-control, the switch of social and legal Western culture finally flipped. The male 'shame' that had started for Larkin at age sixteen – one that had required a 'wrangle for the ring' of matrimony if he ever wanted to experience sex – had opened a new vista of intimate behaviour in which 'every life became / A brilliant breaking of the bank, a quite unlosable game' in 'nineteen sixty-three.'

Many historians and sociologists have taken issue with the date, since the 'Pill' was not universally available, nor always culturally acceptable. Moreover, the freedom it gave women proved a double-edged sword – one that thereafter favoured men, especially men with power, significantly more than women. However, it was the date of *publication* of Larkin's poem, in *High Windows* in 1974, that is more significant for students of English biography.

Several months before appearance of Larkin's poem, the writer Nigel Nicolson published his *Portrait of a Marriage*: a dual biography of his parents, Sir Harold and Lady Nicolson. The biography recounted in dramatic detail their homosexual and lesbian love and sex lives within their celebrated marriage: he a distinguished diplomat, diarist, historian and member of parliament, she a celebrated poet and gardener – as well as lover of Violet Trefusis and Virginia Woolf, among others.

Nigel's book certainly set the cat among the proverbial pigeons, since it was the final nail in the coffin preserving the literary sanctity of marriage in biography, with respect to sex. Memoirs by aggrieved and abused sons and daughters were one thing (and still are) – but a biography describing and eulogizing the "open" marriage of one's parents? (Several of the chapters were even written by Lady Nicolson, detailing her passionate affair with Violet Trefusis.) This was quite another.

Conservative critics still tut-tutted, but from that moment late in 1973, the biographer could only with difficulty be stopped from revealing and exploring the whole gamut of his subjects' marital as well as extramarital lives. Celebrity lives were increasingly on display, across all media; curiosity about their personal, intimate and sexual mores became unstoppable – adding a further erotic charge to their behaviour, as if to taunt the press. To give one example: Elizabeth and Richard Burton had famously starred in *Cleopatra* in 1963; their tempestuous and intemperate affair destroyed their marriages thereafter, and led them to marry each other, with mixed but very public results. In any event, every manner of sexual activity, desire and identity gradually became part of the discourse of society in the West, depicted at every level of society and in every ethnic, gender and economic context. To try and stem that tide in the West seemed a losing battle. Until the twenty-first century.

With the attack on the Twin Towers in New York in 2001, the world's cultural axis crashed. The backlash against liberalism and sexual licence became fierce and punitive, from the American West to the Middle East, as nostalgia, whitewashed memory and fear fanned the flames of neo-Nazism and ISIS radicalism; a countercultural political shift in which the sexual mores (or lack of morals) of the Western world were – and are – likened to those of Sodom and Gomorrah.

How that dialectic will play out in the future is unpredictable. But in terms of the history of sex in biography, it has once again altered the landscape. For almost 2,000 years, the place of sex in biography had been marginal, yet vital: biographers delicately skirting a taboo marked out by propriety, obscenity laws and the like. Then came Noah's Flood. And now biography, like journalism, is once again on trial in the US and elsewhere, as the very attainments of the past half-century – especially the expansion of biography's purview to encompass minority individuals, and those whose sexuality had always had to be concealed – may be rolled back by those who feel the trend has gone too far; that the issue of gender-access to school bathrooms in America, for example, should be dismissed, and Transgender recruits be rejected for service in the US military. The #MeToo movement, which began in 2017, has further pitted expectation against derogation.

The impact of this cultural backlash will inevitably affect biography, just as the matter of truth-telling has already done in the rise of 'alternative' facts* and so-called 'fake' news. This leaves us with the perhaps deeper question, though, which the biographer is still free to examine: namely, how important a role does sex really play in an individual's life, irrespective of whether that individual is a neo-liberal or a neo-Nazi?

It used to be said that men think about sex every seven seconds. A survey by the University of Ohio for *The Journal of Sex Research* in 2012 showed this to be false. It found that on average, men between the ages of 18 and 25 thought about sex only nineteen times a day, and women only half that, at barely ten; certainly, way less than they thought about food or even sleep. Should biographers rank the relative importance of sex in a life in accordance with such a scale, though – including food and sleep?

Clearly, biographers of individuals who are not chefs or restaurateurs, or brain or sleep scientists, tend to weigh and examine more 'important' matters when relating a real life. For it is not frequency of thought that tells us what is unique about a human life; it is what those thoughts may have caused the individual to *do* in – or with – his life. Biographers, in other words, are interested in agency – and though sex is not necessarily the predominant agent in the lives of most human beings, it can be a very powerful motive at moments of their lives, as biographers since Plutarch have attested.

Causality, as such, has long since disappeared from the lexicon of historiography – a victim of deconstructionism. It did not disappear from biography, however, for the simple reason that biographers rarely sought to 'explain' human choices and actions as direct consequences of anything specific, but rather to give a background or context for understanding possibly why an individual developed in a certain way, and behaved as he or she did. In that respect, sex helped to delineate character – and character helped the reader understand behaviour. Plutarch's depiction of Pompey is a prime example. According to Plutarch, 'no Roman was ever held in such affection by the people as Pompey was, and no Roman enjoyed an affection which started so early in his career.' Part of the reason, Plutarch believed, was his handsome face, which people likened to that of Alexander the Great. It was a 'youthful beauty': one that went hand in hand with 'a kind of dignity and sweetness of disposition.' Which led Plutarch to recount stories of how 'Flora the courtesan, when she was getting on in years, was always delighted to tell people about her early intimacy with Pompey: she always had the marks of his bites on her, she said, when she went away from having made love with him.' She was devastated when, after complaining to Pompey that his friend Geminius had sexually harassed her, Pompey shocked her by 'giving' her as a gift to Geminius. To her disappointment, Pompey never had sex with her again – but he must have mourned her caresses, for he had her portrait painted in a temple 'because of her remarkable beauty.'

Such stories help to humanize the portraits that we, for our part, maintain of figures in the past, and even the present, 2,000 years later. Consider, in this context, the figure of John F. Kennedy, who became the youngest American president ever elected: his good looks and dignity adding powerful ingredients to his ascent to the presidency, while his sexual magnetism and addiction would provide the fodder for many a subsequent tell-all biography.

The point is, in terms of the fuel of life, sex is one of the most powerful propellants, and arguably crucial in helping us understand a person's life story – even our own! St Augustine, for example, became determined, in his famous *Confessions*, to tell God – to whom he was addressing his life story – the truth about his early history of chronic masturbation and love of premarital sex, since this helped him to understand his growing sense of guilt, shame and need for redemption. 'From the nineteenth to the twenty-eighth year of my life, I was led astray myself and led others astray in my turn... In those days I lived with a woman, not my lawful wedded wife but a mistress whom I had chosen for no special reason but that my restless passions had alighted on her' (Book IV). Moving from Carthage to Rome, he led an existence he later regretted, for 'I was sinning more and more' – living with a mistress whom he adored, but whom he had to abandon in order to make a good marriage arranged by his mother. His mistress 'went back to Africa, vowing never to give herself to another man, and left with me the son whom she had borne me.' His bride-to-be was 'two years too young for marriage,' however, so the wedding was delayed – and Augustine found he could not wait in celibacy. Thus 'because I was more a slave of lust than a true lover of marriage, I took another mistress, without the sanction of wedlock' – only to be rescued, mercifully, by 'the fear of death and your judgment to come' (Book VI).

Augustine's honesty helps us not only to understand his character, but also reminds us of the extent to which biography depends on evidence. Although memoir* can unwittingly or wittingly be deceitful – and therefore requires critical handling – it is a true sibling to biography, as is correspondence (and email, *de plus en plus*, today). The task of the biographer is to lace together these and other sources in order to present a truthful portrait and understanding of the chosen individual, as far as possible. Given human shame, embarrassment and defensive privacy, not all lives will be as open to sexual examination as was St Augustine's, even today – but to imagine a world of biography in which sex plays no role is unimaginable; for to exclude sex is, as Augustine confessed, to gut a life of life. How, for example, can we imagine let alone discuss the personalities of W.H. Auden, Caesar Augustus, Balzac, Baudelaire, Beardsley, Sarah Bernhardt, Bernstein, Blake, Boccaccio, Anne Boleyn, Lucrezia Borgia, Boswell, Brecht, Robert Burns, Byron, Callas, Camus, Caravaggio – you get the idea – without being honest about sex?

Of course, the sexual character of a person is only the beginning of the biographer's interest. Biography is the chronicle of a character *in action*: character that is tested by the unfolding experience of life. Requited and unrequited romantic love; lust and sexual jealousy; erotic and punitive dreams; these themes inevitably feature in many a biographized life – as do also adultery, fornication, depravity, indecency and sexual abuse. Churchill's father, Lord Randolph Churchill, may or may not have suffered from syphilis – but if not, the biographer will have to explain the manner of Lord Randolph's sudden decline in health, and his treatment of his son Winston. By 1886, the man who had so recently been Britain's Chancellor of the Exchequer, a politician spoken of as a future prime minister, became ill; in fact so distressingly ill that he was eventually persuaded to leave the country. 'He is quite unfit for society,' his wife wrote to her sister, 'you cannot imagine anything more distracting & desperate than to watch it & see him as he is.' He died in 1895.

Sex, in other words, has consequences, both good and bad – the biographer's job being to record and interpret both the 'beautiful and the base,' as Dr. Johnson exhorted. But if the biographer is not to snuff out, but rather to examine the burning candle of real life, namely sex, he must undergo his own test: a sort of second-degree.

Biography is, after all, a compact between author and chosen individual, alive or dead. The biographer has always been required to decide the balance of ingredients in producing a biography – a balance largely defined by the audience, the law and the market; but also by himself and by his Augustinian conscience. A biography, for example, of Simone de Beauvoir, author of *The Second Sex*, or Giacomo Casanova, author of *Story of My Life* – or even Georges Simenon, the man who was not Maigret – is not going to find many readers if the author eschews sex as a primary theme. But what of the author himself – or herself? To what extent is the biography of such a subject, indeed of any biographee with a sex life, a test of the author's *own* intellectual, moral and psychological character: his sensitivity or arrogance, defensiveness or openness, curiosity or closed-mindedness, courage or cowardice?

We rarely ask. And yet in addressing sex, *authorial* agency will determine the result more than any other single biographical theme. For subjective as well as objective reasons, to seek is to find. As the reviewer of a new edition of Sylvia Plath's letters wrote in *The New York Times*, 'these early letters reveal something the journals don't' – something from which no self-respecting biographer should shy away. The 'governing hunger in her life was for a leading man, a colossus,' the reviewer described – a giant 'which she found in [Ted] Hughes. She met him in England, where she was on a Fulbright scholarship. She bit his cheek, he ripped off her earrings, they married four months later.' Her letters home, however, revealed her inner doubts. Ted 'has done a kind of uncaring rip through every woman he's ever met,' Sylvia confided to her brother in America. And to her mother, 'He is a breaker of things and people.'

Hughes broke her, as he did Assia Wevill, his mistress at the time, who would also commit suicide. And Sylvia's sad death, we recall, was ... in 1963.

Sources: Arthur Marwick, *The Sixties* (Oxford: Oxford University Press, 1998); Philip Larkin, *High Windows* (New York: Farrar, Strauss and Giroux, 1974); Nigel Hamilton, *Biography: A Brief History* (Cambridge, MA: Harvard University Press, 2007); Walter Kendrick, *The Secret Museum: Pornography in Modern Culture* (Berkeley: University of California, 1987); Nigel Nicolson, *Portrait of a Marriage* (London: Weidenfeld and Nicolson, 1973); Parul Seghal, 'A Writer Aware of Her Contradictions,' *New York Times*, October 11, 2017; Suetonius, *The Twelve Caesars*, tr. Robert Graves (London: Allen Lane, 1979); Saint Augustine, *Confessions*, tr. R.S. Pine-Coffin (London: Penguin, 1961); Plutarch, *Fall of the Roman Republic*, tr. Rex Warner (London: Penguin, 1958); Patrick Marnham, *The Man Who Wasn't Maigret* (New York: Farrar, Straus & Giroux, 1993).

is for Theory

For thousands of years writers recorded the lives of real people – aka biography – without much theorizing. Plutarch's famous distinction between history and the telling of lives had been a start; his reflections, however, were more observational than analytical: a brief attempt, in introducing his famous *Lives*, to describe his craft rather than questioning the underlying principles and significance of biography.

Plutarch's almost off-hand remarks have characterized the higher study of biography ever since. Biographers simply preferred to write biographies – often excellent, sometimes great biographies – than to think too analytically about the writing of them as a genre. Each generation of biographers thus tended to model its work on the example of other biographers, and it was left largely to occasional philosophers such as Dr. Johnson to question and to investigate not only the mechanics (the value of an interview with a servant rather than the official papers of a dignitary!), but also the moral purpose and importance of biography in human society.

Like Tolstoy's turnip, biography thus 'grew and grew' regardless, reflecting an ever-increasing appetite for lives great and small, from 'Lives and Letters' to brief dictionary* entries and obituaries.* By the late nineteenth century, however, the pressure to professionalize biography encouraged some practitioners to question and examine more closely what on earth they were doing – literally. Considerable, if fragmentary, thought was given to this; however, since biography was dismissed in the academy as a subsidiary of history, at best, or a lesser form of literature, no serious academic attention was paid to biographical theory. In the successive editions of *Theory of Literature* (1944) by René

Wellek and Austin Warren, which became a standard college textbook in successive editions, for example, the authors warned it was 'dangerous to ascribe to [biography] any real critical importance. No biographical evidence can change or influence critical evaluation.'

In the end, it was ironically left to a university professor of literature, in the mid-1980s, to protest. After forty years of disappointment, Professor David Novarr penned his treatise, *The Lines of Life* – a work he explained in his subtitle, *Theories of Biography, 1880-1970*. Over 192 pages, he highlighted the attempts of a succession of writers – from Sidney Lee and Leslie Stephen, Edmund Gosse and William Thayer, Lytton Strachey and Virginia Woolf, Harold Nicolson and André Maurois onwards – to direct more analytic attention to the business of recording real lives. He admitted that 'theory and criticism are about as important to writers of biography as ornithology is to birds,' yet felt it wrong that in the late twentieth century so little systematic thought had been paid to the genre and its role in human society, for good or ill. It was, he considered, a shame more than a scandal, for biography was an extraordinarily rich field for the cultural geographer and geologist: one that could be viewed through the lens of a multitude of aspects: human achievement, actions, aesthetics, ancestry, anecdotes, authorship, authorial romance, case history, character study, commemoration, literary criticism (despite Wellek and Warren!), debunking, definition, detachment, didacticism, discretion, documentation, drama, dual lives, ethics, evidence, excision, fiction, Freud, the graphic arts, group biography, hagiography, hero-worship – and so on, through the alphabet. Surely, given its burgeoning place in modern popular and intellectual culture in the West, Novarr reasoned, biography was on the cusp of serious systematic, academic and scholarly examination? He therefore applauded the biographer Leon Edel's 1981 reference to the 'Science of Man,' which offered, Edel maintained, 'a new role in literature and in history' – a genre that had lingered too long in the shadows of empiricism, and ought now 'to declare itself and its principles.'

Alas, instead of investigating principles, biographers watched as their two sister-genres, history and literature (belles lettres), were infected by the theoretical virus of poststructuralism and deconstruction – a disease which, as the philosopher Rebecca Goldstein later lamented, spawned a potentially fatal assault on the notion of 'truth' – the very lifeblood of biography and so many other scientific and cultural pursuits.

Postmodernists had taken 'relativism to its logical conclusion, asserting that the discourse of "truth" is a subterfuge concealing the structures of power,' Goldstein would note. 'For postmodernists, the relations of dominance and subordination constitute all that is human – not only our social and political milieus but also our various "discourses," including that of science. As they see it, the use by scientists of terms such as "evidence" and "scientific method" are mere bids for power.' The writings of such postmodernists, she snorted, were 'so opaque and filled with jargon that I've often wondered whether the authors themselves have any idea what they are trying to say.' And the victim, inadvertently or deliberately, had been 'truth' – which had become 'post-truth.'

Sadly, Leon Edel's own English department at the University of Hawaii, where he had hoped to launch the theorization of biography with a new journal dedicated to the study of biography, was the first to be infected – its editorial board and its contributors blinded by the new semiotic onslaught, and thus blind to its consequences. Though the journal was titled *Biography*, it no longer saw biography as the historical record of real lives, but only as a literary phenomenon. *Biography* thus withered on its once-pioneering vine – its pages devoted to the deconstruction of literature as text.

Mercifully, Hawaii was a long way from the mainland of the US, and though many English departments across the nation were submerged by the poststructuralist, literary-theoretical tide, historical biography was spared the full force of the virus. Abjuring 'deconstruction' and its associated ills, biographers had in fact revelled in the simultaneous artistic, creative and cultural interdisciplinarity ushered in by the late twentieth century.

Rather than taking their cue from – or umbrage at – postmodernist power-critiques directed their way, practising biographers ignored them. Or brushed them away. Where many historians were outraged at the assault on their citadel of truth-telling, biographers simply shrugged – aware that biography had *always* been as much an artistic challenge as an historical one, and was always open to be challenged or supplanted if deconstructionists had better ideas.

They did not: decades of postructuralists/deconstructionists/postmodernists had failed to produce a single biography considered worth reading, or even readable. Biographers, by contrast, happily absorbed new narrative influences from film, journalism, television, fiction and the Internet, but refused to bend to the postmodernist attack on truth and truth-gathering. Instead, they widened the aperture and sharpened their lenses to include a diversity of subjects and approaches that would previously have been unthinkable. Theory was not eschewed, but not permitted, either, to maul the output. The fresh, late twentieth and early twenty-first century approaches to biography – anaulytically highlighted in *The Biographical Turn*, an edited collection published in 2017 – were accompanied by the founding in 2004 of the Biography Institute in the Netherlands, with a special focus on the theory of biography, and also *La Société de Biographie*, or The Biography Society, in 2016: a 'scholarly society of research, international and interdisciplinary,' that was to be 'devoted to the development and the valorization of the theory and the practice of biography.'

For those interested in the systematic study of real lives both in their historical and literary expressions ('Biography Studies'), this was a landmark moment. Theory, in the academy, was finally catching up with practice – suggesting, moreover, that a better understanding of biography in modern society might not only contribute to higher education and knowledge, but might even contribute, modestly yet significantly, to better biographies. For although there is no such thing as *the* theory of biography, there are certainly a number of underlying principles, as well as a strong foundation for the genre in methods that deserve examination, identification and evaluation. The biographer who has some larger theoretical understanding of the genre will not necessarily produce a better biography, whether in print, on air, or on the screen, since narrative is an art rather than a science. *He will, however, begin with a better theoretical starting point in embarking on his project.*

Take, for example, the matter of aspect or perspective – two lenses addressed by David Novarr. The life of President Lyndon Johnson may be magnificently covered in Robert Caro's ongoing multi-volume (four out of a projected five tomes), for example. But his aim, Caro explained, was never to encompass every experience or aspect of Johnson's life, but rather to re-examine how Johnson came to operate *as a politician*: the 'Power Broker,' as Caro called his first volume. Different biographers have pursued different avenues of approach or interest. *No More Champagne*, an innovative new biography of Winston Churchill by David Lough, examines Churchill's life as a financial, often reckless *gambler* – not only throwing fresh light on the politician's finances, but by implication a new perspective on his political life and character, too. Likewise, a new biography of Vladimir Putin, *The New Tsar*, examines the former KGB officer's life from the perspective of Russian bureaucracy, just as the first volume of Volker Ullrich's new biography, *Adolf Hitler: Jahre des Aufsteigs, 1889-1939*, reconsiders the dictator's life from the perspective of how he interacted with his classmates and immediate family, as well as his obsession with vegetarianism. Niall Ferguson's recent first volume of a biography of Henry Kissinger sets the notorious national security adviser and secretary of state firmly in his formative Harvard years to help explain Kissinger's intellectual, political and power-dynamic development...

The author's chosen *perspective*, in other words, is key to biographical theory – for wittingly or unwittingly, every biographer has to make a preliminary (or belated!) decision as to the perspective he must adopt if his biography is to break fresh ground. Which, after all, is the goal of most, though not all, practising biographers. Fresh perspective does not guarantee a good or great biography, which is something that depends on a raft of other qualities, but it does give the biographer a Launchpad; and – if it succeeds – a distinctive value to society beyond its narrative and factual worth.

Similarly, the initial framing of the biographical portrait affects its outcome, as we have indicated in Composition.* The field of microhistory has expanded in line with modern biography, and large numbers of biographies in recent years have either zeroed in on 'small' communities or less distinctive people in history, using the individuals or groups as illustrative – generally speaking – of larger social units (families, tribes, institutions of 'pillarization', groups, cultures, genders, societies, etc.); a sort of reversal of Dilthey's famous notion that 'understanding of the particular depends on knowledge of the general.' Slice of Life, or the choice of a particular period, singular event or specific development in a chosen individual's life history, has equally grown in popularity as a framing device. Depth of focus, too, is seen by theorists of biography as a seminal aspect of modern biography: namely, the way deeply-researched, forensic investigation can change the way a society thinks about a person, an event, a time – even a creation, as in the history behind a painting, a play, a novel or a film: Biography as Corrective.

Just as memory is by nature selective, so too in biography turning-points allow the modern biographer – and thus the reader – to focus on the nature of agency and change in the life-course of an individual. The Dutch historian Ernst Kossmann once wrote that history especially focuses on change in the past, and the same could be said to apply to biography, where the emphasis is also on change –- and change in interpretation. A biographer must and does thus thus come to terms with the ephemeral nature of his work, and with humility: the certainty that sooner or later a subsequent biographer will be writing about 'his' subject, hero or villain; – part of an unending biographical process of recording and interpreting the past as truthfully as possible, and those real-life individuals who lived in it. For what the biographer is doing is the very opposite of what the sociologist or anthropologist is doing: the biographer is aiming to identify where the individual human being *departs from* the general pattern of human behaviour; a pattern the biographer still needs to see, however, to recognize the individuality of the individual. In short *individuality*, we may say, is the very essence of biography, while *pattern* is the essence of sociology – both depending, however, on an appreciation of the other.

Theories do not, then, offer biographers a template, as in 'How to Do Biography.' They can, however, offer the would-be biographer the chance to think more deeply about what he and his colleagues are doing: whether it is worth doing; where and why it is different from other genres and pursuits; and *what, today, are the various possibilities inherent in the doing.* Theories 'unify a range of apparently disparate, unconnected phenomena by postulating an underlying principle that these phenomena have put into common and that can explain their nature or behavior,' was a description of 'Theory' by Ludwig Wittgenstein – almost a definition. 'The common underlying principle, postulated by the theory – whether it takes the form of an entity, process, force, concept, or something else – is at least hidden from view,' Wittgenstein wrote – theory being 'the kind of understanding that consists in seeing connections.'

Theory thus takes us behind the scenes – in biography, as in everything else. According to Karl Popper, no theory can actually or definitively be proven; all you can do, rather, is to keep checking a theory to test its validity; searching for reliable observations which either accord with, or contradict, a certain theory. In other words, in the end, theories amount to assertions on which there is general agreement from verifiable observation – something which might also be said of facts and truth, the cornerstones of biography.

This, surely, is the crux of 'theory' as it pertains to biography today. In the current crisis of civilization, biographers – as well as students of biography – have a more crucial role to play in modern society than was perhaps recognized until recently. By questioning the nature and value of truth in history, politics and journalism, deconstructors and postmodernists saw themselves as a kind of intellectual elite: linguistic, social, psychological, ethnographic gurus, from Derrida to Lacan, proclaiming a new intellectual universe stretching from the Death of the Author to *Posthistoire*. Large swathes of academia were won over. By the time the virus had worked its way out of academia, it had, unfortunately, left many ordinary people outside academia perplexed as to the reliability of the once sacred tenets of scientific investigation and methodological enquiry. Creationism returned to America with new vengeance – its supporters demanding 'equal' time, equal coverage, equal print and equal museums to those who claimed Darwinian theory and evolution to be verifiable in nature. From global warming to epidemiology, the 'truth project' of Western man became tainted by a sort of flight from evidence-based science and discourse. The validity of research, solid science and the humble search for truth could increasingly be ignored in the public arena by those with radical political agendas – and why not, since those approaches had been discredited by an elite of intellectuals, linguistic philosophers, social scientists and theorists?

The upshot was a new political administration in the US in 2017, centred on the White House but supported by Congress, that to the consternation of scientists and educated citizens began to use terms such as 'alternative facts' to describe those things that the newly-elected and their appointees did not like. The term 'fake news' was applied to accurate press reports, together with a shameless assault on standards of verification in education, the environment, health, the arts and science that had never been seen before in US history.

In this context, the valorizing and theorizing of biography as the search for verifiable facts and truth in recording real lives is perhaps more important than any other aspect of biographical studies today – including the study of biography as a literary endeavour.

Biography is not, and has never been, hagiography or PR; one of its many roles since Suetonius has been to 'speak truth to power.' In societies today where that is impermissible, on pain of assassination – as in the Russian Federation, say, or fundamentalist religious societies – the future of civilized society is imperilled, placing a responsibility on the truthful biographer quite different, say, from that of the novelist, or even the memoirist who fudges truth in the pursuit of emotional power, catharsis and entertainment.

Ensuring biography's valorization in the academy and in public discourse is a vital educational charge, in our view – a lynchpin in the defence of civilized society. By spotlighting, examining, observing and debating how truthful biography works – and conversely, how untruthful biography does not – especially in co-existence with imaginative fiction, the work which David Novarr began in 1986 is being affirmed and renewed today.

Novarr died the year after his treatise was published, but one last *aperçu* still moves us. In the Conclusion to *The Lines of Life,* he wrote: 'Every life, however, prosaic, differs in its details; every interesting life has a new plot if the biographer is perceptive enough to find it. A biographer may feel shackled by facts, but he is apt to be more shackled by the limitations of his own vision and insight.'

Facts are the bedrock of biographical investigation, Novarr accepted, but it was biographical and artistic form or structure that gave 'coherence to the facts of a life lived.' The biographer is, in effect, the member of society designated by tradition, for thousands of years, to collect the evidence and give it coherence: a distinctive mantle no other member of our society wears, and which the biographer is still proud, in our society, to bear.

Sources: David Novarr, *The Lines of Life: Theories of Biography, 1880-1970* (West Lafayette, Indiana: Perdue University Press, 1986); Wilhelm Dilthey, *Der Aufbau der geschichtlichen Welt in den Geisteswissenschaften* (1910), in: Bernard Groethuysen (ed.), *Gesammelte Schriften* (Teubner/Vandenhoeck & Ruprecht, 1927), vol. VII; Nigel Hamilton, 'Biography as corrective', in: *The Biographical Turn. Lives in History*

(London: Routledge, 2017), 15-30; Sigurður Gylfi Magnússon, 'The Life Is Never Over: Biography as a Microhistorical Approach', in: *The Biographical Turn: Lives in History* (London: Routledge, 2017), 42-52; Hans Renders, 'Did Pearl Harbor Change Everything? The Deadly Sins of Biographers', in: *Journal of Historical Biography* 1 (2008) 3, 98-123; Hans Renders and Binne de Haan, 'Introduction: The Challenges of Biography Studies', in: Hans Renders and Binne de Haan (eds), *Theoretical Discussions of Biography: Approaches from History, Microhistory, and Life Writing* (Leiden: Brill, 2014), 1-8.

 **is for U-turn**

A human life can take a radically different turn following a radical event. Such an event can be your own decision (emigration, say, or terminating your job), but it can also involve an unsolicited turn in your life (the death of a loved one or being rejected by a loved one).

In the world of biography, we call such an important event a Turning Point. The condition in Biography Studies is that a Turning Point in a personal life must have consequences for the person's actions in public life. The concept of such a U-turn can – and should – be seen as a good argument for partial biography; a moment or an event in a person's life that influences the person's subsequent public deeds or actions, for it offers the biographer an important methodological *raison d'enquête*. And readers love investigations!

But what *is* a Turning Point? In reviewing the life of Adolf Hitler, one can regard his appointment as *Reichskanzler* in January 1933 as such an event, or his decision to start a world war on 1 September 1939. For Marcel Proust, the decisive moment came, he wrote, when he ate a madeleine. It seems simple; nevertheless, we have already mentioned two different kinds of Turning Points. Historians identify what they regard as the Turning Points of Hitler's public life via history; biographers, for their part, pinpoint different moments through the close investigation of someone's personal life. Take, for instance, Hitler's rejection by the art academy in Vienna. Was this the source of his lifelong dislike of modern art? That is quite plausible, because when he took the entrance exam in 1907, the Viennese art world was engulfed in the emerging era of modernist painting. And no matter how great or small Hitler's talents as a painter might have been, he wanted nothing to do with modernist painting. He became a soldier and a politician. And Proust's consumption of the madeleine? Is that a Turning Point? It was a very small personal experience, but it inspired him to start writing *À la recherche du temps perdu*, one of the great novels of his time.

Although biographers recognize Turning Points, they are seldom employed as an instrument to construct a question-driven, problem-based, thesis-producing perspective, sadly. This is a pity, because the relevance of detailed historical investigations for interpretative frameworks has been recognized in historiography since the rise of microhistory* in the 1970s. Microhistory has since yielded substantial results based on research that investigates specific occasions, themes, episodes, clues and persons. Integrating the microhistorical approach into biographies, by focusing on the turning points in the lives under scrutiny, could well add a new dimension to the concept of the critical 'interpretative biography'. By addressing turning points, decisive episodes or events in a life, as points of departure, the biographer can interpret grand narratives in new ways. Moreover, this fresh interpretation of an individual life can then serve to improve the understanding of history that goes beyond the limits of that life story. In this way, biography can function not merely as an illustration of a well-known story, but as a means to multiply the interpretations of historical events and structures.

Let us take an example, by going back a century ago. When the First World War broke out in the summer of 1914, many influential members of the community of European writers and artists could not wait to go to war. Concerned about the rapid industrialization of cities and the degradation of their societies, they were, in a time of crisis, enthusiastic about the prospect of national reconciliation and rejuvenation. The Austrian playwright Hugo von Hofmannsthal experienced the mobilization of 28 July with a joy that he had 'never experienced before, and never thought possible'. Even after serving at the front for a month, von Hofmannsthal remained enraptured: 'One has the uplifting knowledge that this Country and Nation stand at the beginning of a great development and must and will obtain hegemony over Europe.' Across Europe, artists were enthralled with the idea of a rebirth and a liberation from the spirit of materialism and rationalism. The French *libertin* and writer André Gide wrote how he and his friends had been hoping for months that the war would start. On 1 August 1914, the day before France mobilized its army, he impatiently wrote in his journal: 'A day of painful waiting. Why don't we mobilize? Every moment we delay is that much more advantage for Germany. Perhaps we owe it to the Socialist Party to let ourselves be attacked. This morning's paper tells about the absurd assassination of Jaurès.'

In general, it was not only nationalistic or political views that made European minds ready for a war, but rather an almost religious fervour to replace the old with something new. Or, as the painter Franz Marc said at the end of 1914: soldiers were dying for a new, chastened Europe, just as Jesus had died on the cross to make possible a better world. He was convinced that 'the people first had to go through the Great War before they could form a new life and new ideals'. And this was a desire that had a direct relation to the arts: 'Through this great war, with so many other things that have so unjustly managed to survive in our twentieth century, the pseudo-art with which the German good-naturedly contented himself will finally come to an end.'

Marc's statements feed discussions to this day. How should they be interpreted? The art historian Annegret Hoberg argues that these statements should be read in conjunction with the letters Marc sent his wife from the front: biographical information helps put the grandiose pronouncements of the war volunteer in a rather different perspective; as does his death. Marc was put on the *Liste der bedeutendsten Künstler Deutschlands* (List of Germany's Most Important Artists) by the German government, and as a result was about to be released from military service in 1916. But on the last day of his military career, on 4 March at the Battle of Verdun, he was killed by a grenade, ending his attempt to end 'pseudo-art.'

The British were initially not very keen to take part in a large war in Europe. Great Britain was the only great power that did not have obligatory military service and was therefore dependent on men voluntarily joining its army. But in only a few days' time, public opinion was reversed, again with an appeal to solidarity; in this case, volunteers gathered to support Belgium against an invasion by German forces. On 4 August 1914, Germany was handed an ultimatum to retreat, which expired at eleven o'clock at night (midnight in Berlin). Great excitement took hold of the British people, and when Big Ben struck eleven there was a level of enthusiasm for war that no one had ever thought possible. According to the then-Chancellor of the Exchequer, David Lloyd George, 95% of the British on 1 August 1914 would have opposed their country's involvement in the war; three days later, 99% would have supported it. Just as an event can serve as a turning point for a civilization, a specific moment, occurrence, or episode can change the course of an individual's life.

An excellent example of how the political, military and artistic background of a life can be mapped in a biography to detect a turning point, and thus to do justice to the biographical subject, can be found in the latest biography of Tristan Tzara. The author, Marius Henta, describes how in 1912 and 1913, the seventeen-year-old Tzara was influenced by the Balkan wars and the romance of military life. While studying philosophy in Bucharest, Tzara became enthralled with a teacher who saw the war as a contest between the masses and individuality. But when Romania declared itself neutral at the outbreak of the Great War, a turning point in Tzara's reasoning occurred. In 1915, he wrote the poem 'Song of War.' It was not a song of praise to higher goals such as nationalism, nor was it a lament for the damage inflicted on his culture by the enemy. Rather, it was the recounting of the sad personal experience of a soldier who loses his individuality, and of a ravishingly beautiful girl whom war has transformed into a pile of bones and guts. Tzara would thereafter remain a committed opponent of the war, just like many of his later fellow

Dadaists. For Tzara and many of the avant-garde artists, the U-turn was thus not the outbreak of the Great War, which they initially glorified, but their confrontation, through their own experiences or through the testimony of others, with the raw reality of the trenches, the machine gun fire, mustard gas and other terrors on the front.

Describing in detail the run-up to and course of the First World War in a biography is to usurp the job of the historian, while ignoring the task of the biographer; it is not very useful. Finding out whether the biographical subject's experience of and reaction to the war concurred with the commonly held narrative, or whether the individual's reaction was rather exceptional, is what counts in a biography – thereby enriching and complementing, even correcting, our knowledge of that period. In this sense, biography and history work in opposite ways. Classically, historians first consulted handbooks and then did supplementary archival research to fill in the historical picture. The biographer works the other way around: he first collects and studies material and research materials associated with an individual, then proceeds to investigate how unique or representative that individual was in the context and history of his time.

To pursue our World War I example: in 1914, Guillaume Apollinaire was enthused about the upcoming war, because he was convinced the world could become a better place if the ideas that he had fostered for a long time were finally put into practice. As a child of a Polish mother and an Italian father, Apollinaire voluntarily enlisted as a soldier in an eager attempt to show his loyalty to France, as his biographer Francis Steegmuller convincingly explains. There was more to it than that, however – for traces of his enthusiasm for war and violence itself can also be found in his work. The poem 'Zône' from his collection of poems *Alcools*, published in 1914, suggests a more plausible explanation of his embrace of war: namely, his praise of speed, technology and action. In a similar way, Max Jacob, Jean Cocteau and the Paris-based Italian artist Gino Severini were captivated by the war.

Many of the Dadaists escaped military service by travelling to neutral Switzerland on false passports. Famous Dadaists like Tzara and Hugo Ball, as well as Hans Arp and Marcel Janco, moved to Zurich to develop their anti-art. Richard Huelsenbeck was a conscientious objector. Thus, these artists are often lumped together in historiography. 'Dada believed that the Great War was an unprecedented process of converting Europeans into animals', writes Josepha Laroche in the online Dada-encyclopaedia. But in the case of Ball, the great initiator of Dada, a different story can be told, namely about the glorification of war.

In every biographical work about figures in the Dada movement, the claim is made that, disillusioned by the First World War, Ball fled to neutral Switzerland with his future wife, the artist Emmy Hennings, to open the Cabaret Voltaire in Zurich in 1916. And, moreover, that even before the outbreak of the war, 'Ball arrived at a comprehensive theory of progressive theatre'. Biographical reality, however, is rather different. A week after the declaration of war, Ball volunteered for the German army (as he told his sister), but he was in fact rejected (he applied three times, in vain), because of his weak heart. Eager to participate in the war, he went to the Belgian front on his own, as a citizen. He was not inspired by political considerations, but made the journey because he wanted finally to experience something real. Only after he was confronted with the horrors of the war did he move to Switzerland in May 1915, to take on the role of the anti-war artist. His anti-war identity was thus nowhere as clear and convincing as has been suggested. Even after his experience at the Belgian front, Ball remained very bellicose. Instead of wanting to continue to fight for the Germans, however, he now hoped that his homeland would lose the war, so that the Russian Revolution would erupt and bring the international proletariat to power. Ball thus made a political U-turn during the first year of the war – which in turn suggests that those writers, like Erdmute Wenzel White, who class 'Totentanz 1916', Ball's first real success at the Cabaret Voltaire, as an anti-war poem, are oversimplifying literary history. White calls it a *Zeitgedicht*, written in July and August 1915 and composed as a parody of the Prussian military march 'Dessauer'; and indeed there were ironic and cynical texts being written about dying during the war. But the poem ends with a longing for the Last Judgement and the Day of Reckoning. Thus, based on closer biographical investigation, 'Totentanz' might well be interpreted not as an anti-war poem, but as the ideologically-inspired text of a politically conscious poet hoping for a revolution – even a violent one – that would lead to a communist utopia.

This change formed a turning point in Ball's life. It represented a radically different perspective on participation in world events – but not the one most anthologists take it to be.

In other words, thinking more generally, a responsible mix of personal life and history does not necessarily mean more historical context. Rather, it suggests that the biographer needs to watch for how and where historical developments exerted a major impact on the subject's personal life. Were we to explore the first months of World War I as it affected individual lives, it would become clear that the general narrative of early-war Dadaism is in need of correction. By exploring, close up, the U-turn many Dadaist artists made, instead of accepting the grand but simplistic narrative of their lives, we can not only cast a spotlight on their individual lives and the true development of their work, but we can also enrich our knowledge of the First World War and the beginnings of the Dadaist Movement. And this is the reason why the question-based approach to biography – especially when focused on turning points in an individual's life – is, we think, destined to become a distinguishing feature of the modern genre.

Sources: Jean Bruneau (ed.), *Correspondance Flaubert; III: Janvier 1859 – Décembre 1868* (Paris: Gallimard, 1991); Marius Hentea, *TaTa Dada, The Real Life and Celestial Adventures of Tristan Tzara* (Cambridge, MA: MIT Press, 2014); Ewoud Kieft, *Oorlogsenthousiasme: Europa 1900-1918* (Amsterdam: De Bezige Bij, 2015); *Hugo von Hofmannsthal, Ottonie Gräfin Degenfeld, Briefwechsel* (Frankfurt am Main: S. Fischer, 1986); Hans Renders and Sjoerd van Faassen, 'The biographical turn in the field of knowledge', in: Hans Renders, Binne de Haan and Jonne Harmsma (eds), *The Biographical Turn. Lives in History* (London: Routledge, 2017); Hans Renders,

'The limits of representativeness: Biography, life writing and microhistory', in: Hans Renders and Binne de Haan (eds), *Theoretical Discussion of Biography: Approaches from History, Microhistory, and Life Writing* (Leiden: Brill, 2014), 129-138; Willi Schud (ed.), *Richard Strauss – Hugo von Hofmannsthal. Briefwechsel* (Atlantis Musikbuch-Verlag, 1952; 5th ed. 1978).

 **is for the Visual Arts**

Some biographers, it is true, seem so tied to the idea of the medium as solely one of print that they may be said to be visually impaired. The truth is, however, that since the dawn of civilization there have been efforts to portray real human individuals visually. No-one visiting a museum's collection of classical art today can fail to be awed by the busts, bas reliefs, paintings, coins, medallions and other visual images created of real persons in antiquity, however idealized. Many of their names fortunately passed from memory into script, but they live on in image, too – often unforgettably.

With the invention of the printing press, it became possible to illustrate book biographies with engravings and half-tone plates, so that both visual and written depictions could proceed in tandem, so to speak: the one aiding the other. The visuals were limited by their immobility: frozen at a moment in time, as it were. By contrast, a written account could record the course and development of a whole life, from birth to death – a largess that undoubtedly spurred portrait artists to even greater accomplishment, not only in producing a life-likeness, but imbuing their works with individual character and context.

Portraiture certainly became a major feature of the visual arts in the Renaissance. Since critical representation of the sitter had to be compressed into a single picture or work of art, every feature, every piece of clothing, every stance or glance had to tell the story of the subject's individuality, symbolically – leading to real-life portraits every bit as admirable as fictive, non-biographical painting. By the sixteenth century, every prince and every burgher seemed to want to be pictured for posterity. Portrait commissions, money, vanity and artistry were mixed together to be turned into paint, bronze, stone and other materials: collectively providing portraits of an age and society, as well as of individuals. By the nineteenth century, national museums of such art were called for, and established. The National Portrait Gallery of Sweden was founded in 1822 with more than 4,000 works; not to be outdone, the National Portrait Gallery was opened in London in 1856, followed by the National Portrait Collection of Ireland in 1872, the Scottish National Portrait Gallery in 1889, and a succession of such art galleries across the world thereafter.

The proud display in public of such portraits did not avoid, however, the problematic distinction among critics between art – i.e., 'pure' art, as a manifestation of beauty – and art that held, so to speak, a real individual's life story. Depictions of Jesus with or without an umbilical cord (deemed unnecessary in divine birth) had consumed art critics and historians in the Middle Ages, and continued to do so as similar disputes arose over representations of battles, biblical scenes, and real people through the centuries, without resolve. John Singer Sargent's painting of Virginie Gautreau in 1884, entitled *Portrait of Madame X*, had to be taken down from exhibition in Paris when it showed Madame Gautreau with the narrow brassiere-like strap of her already low décolleté-dress hanging suggestively off her upper arm. As a non-biographical work, in the tradition of the Nude, or as the depiction of a notional figure from the Bible or ancient mythology, it could have passed as 'art.' As the portrait of a well-known recognizable member of French bourgeois society, a conspicuous beauty to be sure, but also a banker's wife, it was considered *de trop*. The portrait was denounced as scandalous, and though Sargent repainted it with the strap more demurely replaced on her shoulder, it was never shown again in France, and now hangs in New York.

Many a portrait was declined or even destroyed, such as Graham Sutherland's famous portrait of Winston Churchill, owing to the vanity of the sitter or descendant – much as many book biographies that impugned the honour or reputation of the subject were contested or subjected to legal restraint at the whim of relatives, as described in Ian Hamilton's history, *Keepers of the Flame*.

It was in this ongoing and sometimes uneasy interdependence between the artist and the real individual as subject or sitter that the world of the visual arts was upended by moving photographs or pictures of people. Enter stage left: film.

Photography had been invented in the early nineteenth century, adding a further medium to the art and craft of portraiture: a visual record that became enormously popular during the American Civil War, for example, when every family commissioned a visual record of their son or relative before he went into battle on behalf of the Union. (Confederate families had to rely on drawings and paintings, since the essential chemicals for developing photographs had been denied the Confederacy by the northern blockade.)

Then came moving pictures – film. Initially, it was assumed the new medium would be documentary: recording real life, in motion, as had never been possible before. Many of the first names for recording companies, manufacturers and exhibition facilities therefore used the prefix *bio* or *vita* for life or lifelike – *Biograaf*, Vitagraph, Vitascope, for example. Film's value in newsgathering and visual tourism, on a global scale, could be seen right from the start – a typical programme shown at Proctor's Palace in New York in March 1897 included a carriage race from Paris to Bordeaux; a gondola scene in Venice; a charge by the Austrian Lancers; a fish market in Marseilles; German dragoons leaping hurdles; black ('Negro') minstrels dancing in the streets of London; and the Bath of Minerva in Milan. The distribution of these moving pictures – movies – went global, too, with 'operators' showing the new films across the world.

Slapstick dominated, initially, since it required less captioning than complicated storytelling. As audiences became conversant with the new medium, however, more challenging stories were requested by viewers – as well as non-fiction film, shot and fashioned *into* stories. Among these, *Nanook of the North* made by the explorer Robert Flaherty in 1924, was hailed as the first documentary film masterpiece – a biographical one, since it revolved around a real-life Eskimo, Nanook.

What quickly overshadowed documentary film, however, as far as visual biography was concerned, was the 'biopic,' or dramatized real life, on the screen: a genre created largely in Hollywood. *The Execution of Mary Queen of Scots* in 1895, or *Queen Elizabeth* in 1912, or *Madame De Barry* in 1919, *Danton* in 1920 and *Anne Boleyn* in 1920, gradually gave way to more ambitious biopics.

As the first major historian of the genre, George Custen, would later write, dramatized life stories literally made history, for 'the biopic provided many viewers with the version of a life that they held to be truth.' Movie-going required neither literacy nor education; thus from the 1920s to the 1950s, when the biopic reached its peak, the 'truth' of biopics would go largely uncontested, and continued until the 1970s, when public education and a new culture of protest caused viewers to become more sceptical of the film-fare that was being served.

Abel Gance's *Napoleon* remains the creation that is probably most celebrated by film historians and *aficionados* – one that epitomized the new genre, from the search for the right actor (Albert Dieudonné), the right camera (André Debrie's Parvo), the right cameraman (Jean-Paul Mundviller, who had filmed in Russia, then Jules Kruger), the right lenses (a Brachyscope, made by Société Optis, and a Wollensak soft-focus *objectif flou*), the right outdoor locations (Corsica and Toulon), the right number of distinct films intended for the biopic (six, similar to a multi-volume book biography), the right studio/distributor (Pathé), and the necessary funding (Europe 25.9 million francs, USA 20 million francs, rest of the world 29.7 million francs. 'Money? What's money!' was Gance's attitude, 'until it failed to arrive').

Filmed in black-and-white, but with a final triptych in colour and in 3D, *Napoleon* was scheduled to be shown in Paris for the first time on 7 April 1927, with an orchestral accompaniment composed by Arthur Honegger. Showing the silent rough-cut to a close friend, Gance was mortified to be told: 'There are some great bits in it, but I think if you cut three-quarters of it, you might avoid having the audience leave in the middle to catch the last métro.'

At nearly four hours, *Napoleon* – the first of the six proposed films, depicting Napoleon Bonaparte's whole life – was not a disaster, exactly, but it required drastic cutting to make it commercial. Even with sound added, however, biopics failed commercially – unable to match the glamour and pizzazz of the *Jazz Singer* and other fictional films, from romances to thrillers. And then, after World War II, came television, which offered a new biographical medium.

At first, television studios avoided dramatization by actors, in the manner of biopics, deeming them too expensive. Instead they commissioned 'documentaries' – films made for television that were modelled on past documentary films sponsored by governments, institutions or commercial companies in the 1930s and during the war. This, however, was a double-edged sword, for there was a ghost in the closet – most famously that of Leni Riefenstahl.

When making *Triumph des Willens* (*Triumph of the Will*), her biographical record of Hitler's self-glorification as Nazi Führer in Nuremberg in 1934, Riefenstahl had recognized the mesmerizing quality of well-made documentary film, especially when applied to real people, with music and speech. Such film could be used by governments as propaganda – and in a darkening age of dictators, it was. Riefenstahl was showered with prizes for her *Triumph*, and with Hitler's personal blessing, she had won a further major commission: her homage to male and female athletic beauty, *Olympia* (1938). When she saw innocent Jews being murdered by German officers as a volunteer film-reporter in Poland in 1939, she began to re-think her documentary profession, however, and switched to feature filmmaking, or plain drama, for the rest of the war.

As the reach of television and TV programming expanded exponentially in the 1960s, however, and with biopics fading in competitive popularity on the big screen, demand for more biographical programmes grew on the small screen. It was a screen, after all, that offered a growing international audience. Moreover, it was one that was sitting in the home rather than in a darkened cinema and – as in the early years of film – people were beginning to see television as a primary source of news, such as the assassination of President John F. Kennedy on 22 November 1963.

For TV producers and directors in the 1960s and 1970s, television thus offered big audiences – with many viewers more rational, critical, thoughtful and educated than in cinemas. Such directors proceeded much as did print biographers of the time, but with the luxury of research teams. Visual quotation* became key, using archival film, filmed documents, and filmed or videorecorded interviews: fresh ingredients that offered a treasure trove of biographical materials with which to help bring a life to life, in full sound and colour.

Certainly, there were many first-class documentary biographies produced for television and shown in Europe and the United States, especially those produced under the aegis of the BBC in London, which had a Documentary Television Department with its own modest but adequate budget taken from the annual license fee, paid by all owners of television sets in the country. Award-winning documentary profiles of Hadrian, Genghis Khan, King Alfred, the Life of Muhammad, Charles Dickens, Lawrence of Arabia, Churchill, Field Marshal Montgomery and many others were produced and broadcast, while in the United States, David Wolper's *Biography* series of the early 1960s was revived by A&E Television in 1987, and even spun off a separate network, The Biography Channel, in 1998 – screening documentary lives of popular celebrity figures and 'newsmakers,' from Marilyn Monroe to Queen Elizabeth II. Where good archival footage was lacking, new production techniques were invented, such as filmed re-enactments of key episodes by paid actors, thus mimicking something of the 'emotional' quality of film biopics.

In the United States, the Biography Channel was rebranded as BIO in 2007. Even this did not staunch the falling number of viewers, however, like grains cascading in a timer. In 2013, A&E

pulled the proverbial plug, rebranding the Biography Channel in 2013 as FYI – a channel tasked with focusing on reality shows, culinary programmes, and home renovation and makeover advice ('Epic Meal Empire,' 'World Food Championships,' 'Black Love' and 'Married at First Sight: First Year,' etc.), rather than biographies.

Not all hope for small-screen biography was lost, however. Made-for-television biopics presented an improbable yet welcome resurrection, aimed at the growing viewership of cable television; a new market where network providers provided the money, not advertisers directly, or unwilling license-payers. Thus, the new 'long-form' television biopic was born. It featured long, multi-part episodes of biographical drama, broadcast over weeks and months: *John Adams*, *Versailles*, *Genius*, *Medici: Masters of Florence*, *Da Vinci's Demons*, *The Young Victoria*, *The Virgin Queen*, *Freud*, *Borgia*, *Bonnie and Clyde*, *The Crown*, *A Very English Scandal*, *Ekaterina*...

These new, extended television epics initially suggested – as in the 1920s, when Abel Gance began work on his own multi-film extravaganza, *Napoleon* – a greater attention to factual accuracy and historical judgement, thanks to their longer running time. In the end, however, entertainment won out. Or perhaps it was simply that biographical 'docudramas,' as they were now called, were like 'creative non-fiction': fiction by another name.

'Never let the facts get in the way of a good story' was a saying misattributed to Mark Twain; it certainly epitomized the new age's almost wilful ignorance when creating and watching dramatized biography-based entertainment. The fact that *Darkest Hour*, a new biopic of Winston Churchill at the crossroads of history in May 1940, got almost all of its facts wrong, was perhaps inevitable, yet the film's poetic evocation (in 2017) of a lonely political leader attempting to prevail against the right-wing cowards in his own party (Neville Chamberlain, Lord Halifax, et al.) was certainly moving, indeed heroic: a moral truth. What if the facts were twisted, however, to produce, with all the visual power of film, the opposite: an immoral portrait?

One biographer of the late Senator Edward Kennedy, Neal Gabler, for example, spoke for many when he protested, in an Op-ed in *The New York Times* in April 2018, the arrival of a new biographical drama film, *Chappaquiddick*. 'Fake history is no better than fake news; it's maybe worse,' Gabler wrote. The Massachusetts senator, who had devoted his life to major social causes after a fatal car accident in Martha's Vineyard, was depicted as despicable. 'A more callow, cunning, cowardly and self-interested yet moronic figure you couldn't find,' Graber objected. 'His first words after the accident' — which took the life of a young, female campaign worker, Mary Jo Kopechne — 'are: "I'm not going to be president."' Words the senator had never spoken, so far as any biographer knew.

As the book-biographer noted: 'Obviously an artist isn't saddled with the same obligations to fact that a biographer or historian is. We accept artists appropriating lives and altering them. But we also expect an artistically valid justification for bending the truth, and sensationalism isn't one of them.' For Gabler, as someone who cared about truth, the cultural outlook was bleak if such distortion were to go unchallenged by serious biographers. As he warned, 'It is very possible that over time, through the osmosis of social media, the despicable Kennedy of this movie will eradicate the honorable if flawed real one.'

Biography as Corrective: Gabler's warning reminds us of the importance of serious, ethical book biography in the modern world: as corrective in relation to the visual arts as it is to the dangers of poor history and 'creative non-fiction' in print.

Sources: Neal Gabler, '"Chappaquiddick" is Bad History,' *New York Times*, April 7, 2018; Alan Rosenthal (ed.), *Why Docudrama? Fact-Fiction on Film and TV* (Carbodale: Southern Illinois University Press, 1999); Carl Rollyson, *Documentary Film: A Primer* (New York: iUniverse, 2004); Jack Ellis and Betsy McLane, *A New History of Documentary Film* (New York: Continuum, 2005); Richard Wendorf, *The Elements of Life: Biography and Portrait-Painting in Stuart and Georgian England* (Oxford: Clarendon Press, 1990); Kevin Brownlow: *Napoleon, Abel Gance's Classic Film* (New York: Knopf, 1983); George Custen, *Bio/Pics: How Hollywood Constructed Public History* (New Brunswick, NJ: Rutgers University Press, 1992).

 # is for War

War, sadly, has been the most prominent – and repeated – event in human history. For that reason it has dominated historiography, ever since Herodotus wrote his great history of the Greek and Persian Wars, and Thucydides recounted his *History of the Peloponnesian War*. Both works became classics – for violence, as is said, begets not only violence, it also begets readers.

Biography, in any event, was not far behind. Beginning with the *Anabasis*, Xenophon's autobiographical account of the retreat of the Ten Thousand mercenaries from Persia, 401-399 BC, war has been a primary feature of autobiography and biography, at every level and from every angle – from great leadership to disastrous decisions, from heroism to cowardice. In other words, while historians have tried to recount the causes, conduct, conclusions and consequences of wars, biographers have kept their focus on the persons who actually fought them and were impacted by them. In this respect, Plutarch, the Roman writer (though writing in Greek), expressed the difference between the historian's job and the biographer's very well in relation to war. Plutarch was, he explained, 'writing lives, not history,' since 'the truth is that the most brilliant exploits often tell us nothing of the virtues or vices of the men who performed them, while on the other hand a chance remark or a joke may reveal far more of a man's character than the mere feat of winning battles in which thousands fall, or marshaling great armies, or laying siege to cities.'

The moral, human dimension, as it relates to the individual, was the one which haunted Plutarch in studying history, and the tension between the two approaches – feat versus character – remains as true today as it was for Plutarch. Moreover, since war is probably the ultimate test of character – and will probably always remain so – it is in the arena of war that the biographer is himself most tested. Will he exult in great leadership, as, say, in a study of Napoleon? Or will he be interested in the damage wreaked by war on the individual? Would Hitler have become such a ruthless warmonger (and mass murderer) if he had not been dehumanized by combat in the trenches of World War I? It is a question for the biographer, who charts personality and character, but it affects, in turn, history – and not in any pro forma way, since the bloodletting of World War I affected different individuals in different ways. The up-front hatred of militarism expressed by conscientious objectors such as Lytton Strachey, D.H. Lawrence, Heinrich Mann and many others was duly confirmed by the catastrophic casualties of war. But those writers did not serve in combat: a much more wrenching experience, as memorialized in the poetry of World War I (Owen, Thomas, Sassoon, Graves and others) and art (Beckman, Dix, Grosz, Sargent and others). Investigating the effect of war on the psyche of real individuals – 'shell shock' for officers, exemplary execution for the common ranks – eventually gave rise to psychiatric care, akin to nursing, in the military. In biography, likewise, it compelled biographers and autobiographers in the aftermath to stop glorifying battles, as historians were wont to do, and start telling the truth.

It was not easy; patriotism and national pride, even loyalty to comrades, are powerful concoctions. As the military biographer Carlo D'Este recounted in *Patton: A Genius for War* (1995), the American tank commander might have won fame for his army's success in battle, but he horrified US army doctors in Sicily in the summer of 1943 by slapping and threatening to shoot 'malingerers' in a field hospital: soldiers who had simply 'lost it,' and could not continue licensed killing. Biographers like D'Este, when dealing with war, may thus be seen, in some ways, as retrospective doctors not only of letters but of the soul: practising their forensic skills against a natural tribal tendency to glorify courage and conquest.

One of the first authors to take on that task, after World War I, was the Welsh poet Robert Graves, who had served as an infantry captain in the trenches in Flanders. By 1929 he was in London and in dire financial and personal straits – the latter including a *ménage à quatre* conducted in a house in Hammersmith, and a nearby houseboat, moored on the river Thames. His mistress, the beautiful American poet Laura Riding, née Reichenthal, had just thrown herself out of a fourth-floor window crying 'Goodbye, chaps,' and, as Graves's biographer Richard Perceval Graves later chronicled, Graves had followed her, throwing himself out from the third floor. Miraculously they both survived. In post-traumatic zeal, as Laura recovered in hospital, Graves decided to dictate an autobiography of his life up to that point (aged only 33), focusing on the recent world war. As he subsequently admitted, following the autobiography's phenomenal success (it became a classic and has never gone out of print), he had 'put into the book all the frank answers to all the inquisitive questions that people like to ask about other people's lives' in biography – especially war. He had therefore 'mixed in all the ingredients that I know are mixed into other popular books,' including 'food and drink,' 'murders,' 'Ghosts,' 'kings … People also like reading about other people's mothers. I put in mine.' There were names of celebrities, too, that he'd inserted, such as Lawrence of Arabia and the Prince of Wales. There were 'racing motorists and millionaires,' also 'pedlars and tramps and adopted children and Arctic explorers,' he added, mischievously, tongue-in-cheek. 'People like reading about poets. I put in a lot of poets. I have met most of the best-known ones in England.' Also prime ministers, and foreign countries, sport, commerce, and 'school episodes, love affairs (regular and irregular), wounds, weddings, religious doubts, methods of bringing up children, severe illnesses, suicides. But the best bet of all is battles, and I had been in a few good ones.'

War, in other words, trumped all in biography – and Graves's account, *Goodbye to All That*, electrified a nation. There had been, and would be, fictional narratives, such as Hasek's *The Good Soldier Schweik*, or Remarque's *All Quiet On the Western Front*, but Graves's record of his life in the cauldron of the Great War was undeniably *real*: irreverent, written with black humour and a kind of flat, relentless, journalistic, devil-may-care urgency that was bewitching – a manner and tone that eschewed 'heroics, respect, "rights," honour and nobility,' as Graves' friend and biographer, Martin Seymour-Smith, would write. In sum, a searing 'contempt for all conventional values' – especially the myth of war as something to be proud of.

Others had tried to write truthfully in autobiographical accounts of the war, but Graves was different in that he was the first to go for *absolute* truth: hitching personal candour to a vast and destructive war in which he'd willingly volunteered for service, fought in battles, risked his life, been badly wounded, and given up for dead.

Composed in a mere four weeks of nightly dictation, Graves's 'goodbye' was in fact a farewell to his crazed life of adultery and what he saw as a dead society – but it also cleared the path ahead not only for his subsequent, post-traumatic life with Laura, abroad, but also for modern memoir* – seen through the lens of modern war as the most violent of man's pursuits. And in doing so, reversing many of the shibboleths, deceits and airbrushings of the past.

Novels, for their part, had traditionally allowed a reading audience to embrace what non-fiction writers could not, or would not, say, being constrained by decorum, laws of libel, familial ties and public propriety. After 1918, however, the sheer obscenity of a world war in which eighteen million people had lost their lives was simply too great to park off-site in fiction. The biographical taboo against absolute truth had been broken, thanks to war – and it has never mended.

In its quality as the 'brief biography of the self' – or selfie – memoir would, of course, always be a *mischling*, since total honesty about ourselves and our actions is a losing battle. When errors of fact and understanding in *Goodbye to All That* were pointed out to him, Graves defended himself, writing that the 'memoirs of a man who went through some of the worst experiences of trench-warfare are not truthful if they do not contain a high proportion of falsities.

High-explosive barrages will make a temporary liar or visionary of anyone.' However, the determination to *try* to tell the truth about the reality of war, rather than its glory, was genuine – and would have a major impact on biographies subsequently written which addressed war. Survival in the face of industrial slaughter, not glorification, became the new lens of serious biography, in that respect: deliberately contesting the notion of heroes in war, however much politicians and generals, from Winston Churchill (*The World Crisis* – five volumes) to Maréchal Ferdinand Foch (*Mémoires pour servir à l'historie de la guerre de 1914-1918*) might extol themselves in its wake.

A decade later, in another war, the floodgates of biography opened for another reason. With the German bombing of Rotterdam World War II, civilians – in the wake of Guernica – now became 'legitimate' targets of war operations – and genocide. Afterwards, refugees, victims of bombing, and above all Holocaust survivors such as Primo Levi became determined to tell their personal stories. Levi's memoir *If This is a Man* (1947) would be but one of many hundreds of testaments to evil deliberately committed on a scale never seen in human history before: one that no Holocaust 'denier,' such as the right-wing historian David Irving, could dismiss. So potent did war-memoir become, in fact, that there were even cases of fake Holocaust memoirs, such as those by Binjamin Wilkomirski (pseudonym of Bruno Dössekker, born Bruno Grosjean), whose *Fragments: Memories of a Wartime Childhood* (1996) was entirely imaginary. Such exceptions, however, merely proved the rule: namely that war memoirs had become a vital part of modern literature and memory – spawning myriad subsequent, similar attempts to reveal the truth of real lives in peacetime struggles, too – ranging from rape and incest to drug addiction and depression.

What, then, of war biographies? These, too, had an uphill battle against the power of myth. On the victors' side, the war and its leaders were seen as heroes, while on the side of the defeated there was a collective effort to conceal knowledge, let alone guilt for the Holocaust. Hitler could be criticized, post-mortem – and was, in critical biographies by the likes of Joachim Fest. But the autobiographies of Hitler's surviving subordinates – for example, by Keitel, Kesselring, Guderian, Warlimont and Speer – held to a consistent line of self-exonerating amnesia and innocence (the so-called 'clean' record of the Wehrmacht, as Peter Fritzsche would call it) of the mass murder of Soviet, Jewish and Gypsy civilians: a guilt-free card that went largely uncontested by biographers for many decades, since British and American readers, especially, remained bewitched by the professional battlefield prowess of German generals, from Rommel to Rundstedt; they preferred not to see them as guilty of war crimes, or crimes against humanity. (Field Marshal Kesselring, for example, was spared the hangman's noose owing to appeals for clemency by British generals.)

The problem went back to Napoleon and beyond. Maréchal Pétain, like Kesselring, was also spared execution at the behest of admirers, despite being convicted of treason – not to speak of his complicity in the arrest and mass murder of hundreds of thousands of French Jews.

Since biographers are as prone to hero worship as anybody – in fact more so, thanks to the years they spend in the service, so to speak, of their subject – the head of the Vichy government would be given pretty much a free pass by chroniclers of his life, such as Charles Williams in *Pétain*, in 2005. Gitta Sereny's 1995 book, *Albert Speer: His Battle With Truth*, (later made into a theatre play by the British National Theatre in 2000) proved in this respect a landmark in modern war biography, however – for Sereny saw that the question of German war guilt and genuine remorse ultimately went down to the individual, and she was determined, as a biographer, not to let Speer evade her microscopic, X-ray lens, as she recorded how, at the end of his life, Speer was flattered by his English mistress to see himself as a great man. (Ugh!) Likewise, the historian Ian Kershaw abandoned history and turned his own lens onto Speer's beloved führer, in what became a two-volume biography: *Hitler*: *Hubris* and *Hitler: Nemesis* (1998 and 2000). In both cases the platitudes of historians, in relation to individuals, were finally addressed by the forensic work of modern biographers – many of who began to accept not only the challenge of telling the truth about the war, but also the challenge of who, traditionally, had been included by historians in such accounts. The very field of vision of biography, so to speak, expanded as a result of World War II, as biographers addressed the exclusion, for example, of women – from transport pilots to cryptologists. African-Americans had finally been armed and committed to combat in the US Army and Army Air Forces (Tuskegee squadrons); in the aftermath, their individual stories, recorded in memoirs and autobiographies, diversified and literally coloured a record that had hitherto been monochrome and anonymous; a pattern that spilled over into other exclusionary areas of post-war life.

War, in short, helped to transform modern biography. And since war did not end – even if it was smaller in scale than World War II had been – it remained a primary feature of biography as the twentieth century approached its end and, against the background of smoking towers in Manhattan and major subsequent wars in Afghanistan and Iraq, began a new century. These, in turn, presented an increasingly familiar challenge to biographers: how to navigate the tension between socially and politically palatable platitudes, on the one hand, and truth-telling on the other.

After the two world wars, there was no possibility, however, of going back – indeed the biographical response to war today is almost unrecognizable from that of a century ago. In terms of modern media – print, radio, film, television and the Internet – biography has moved to the very forefront of truthful reportage, documentation and respect for personal, individual experience and responsibility. Winston Churchill's self-lauding memoirs, *The Second World War*, had helped the prime minister win the Nobel Prize for Literature in 1953; 62 years later, however, Svetlana Alexievich would be awarded the same prize, for (in part) her biographical *Zinky Boys: Soviet Voices from the Afghanistan War*, in 2015. The sufferings of war, in other words, were no longer going to be overshadowed by the accounts of generals or politicians.

Vietnam, for Americans, was the same as Afghanistan for Russians. Pivoting on the testimonies of Vietnamese and American survivors, Ken Burns's epic seventeen-hour PBS television documentary and book in 2017, *The Vietnam War*, testified not only to how the war is now remembered by individuals, but also to how the war itself remains a major trauma in the American soul.

Plutarch, the biographer who ended his days in Delphi contemplating the morality and character of those who had gone to war, would doubtless feel, were he alive today, 2,000 years later, his work had not been in vain.

Sources: Plutarch, *The Age of Alexander: ten Greek lives: Artaxerxes, Pelopidas, Dion, Timoleon, Demosthenes, Phocion, Alexander, Eumenes, Demetrius, Pyrrhus* (London: Penguin, 2011); Richard Perceval Graves, *The Years With Laura (1926-40)* (London: Weidenfeld and Nicolson, 1990); Martin Seymour-Smith, *Robert Graves: His Life and Work* (London: Bloomsbury, 1995); Hans Renders, 'Biography in Academia and the Critical Frontier in Life Writing: Where Biography Shifts into Life Writing', in: Hans Renders and Binne de Haan (eds), *Theoretical Discussions of Biography. Approaches from History, Microhistory, and Life Writing* (Leiden: Brill, 2014); Peter Fritzsche, Preface to Wolfram Wette, *The Wehrmacht* (Cambridge, MA: Harvard University Press, 2006); Gitta Sereny, *Albert Speer: His Battle with Truth* (New York: Random House, 1995); Nigel Hamilton, 'Biography as Corrective', in: Hans Renders et al. (eds), *The Biographical Turn: Lives in History* (London: Routledge, 2017), 15-30; David Reynolds, *In Command of History: Churchill Fighting and Writing the Second World War* (New York: Random House, 2005).

is for Xanadu

X marks the spot of... Xanadu, for example.

Xanadu enjoys a very special place in literary and film biography studies. It was the site of a vision (or fragment of one) seen by the great English Romantic poet Samuel Taylor Coleridge, recorded in his mystic ode, *Kubla Khan* (1816). And it was the location for a cinematic vision by one of the greatest filmmakers of the twentieth century, Orson Welles, in his masterpiece *Citizen Kane*, the following century (1940).

Between those two creations, Xanadu came to stand for the triumph of the exotic, wayward imagination: a 'stately pleasure-dome,' as Coleridge described it in his poem; 'the costliest monument a man has built to himself,' as Welles pictured the place on celluloid. Strange to say there was (and still is, in ruins) a real Xanadu: Shangdu in Chinese, Zanadu in Dutch, situated 220 miles north of Beijing. In its time, it was as famous as Nineveh, Troy or Knossos: the summer palace of Kublai Khan, the grandson of Genghis Khan and Emperor of Mongolia, as well as the first Emperor of the Yan Dynasty of China, who lived from 1215 to 1294 AD.

Before his death Xanadu was visited by the Venetian explorer, Marco Polo, who described the emperor's summer residence in 1275.

> There is at this place a very fine marble palace, the rooms of which are all gilt and painted with figures of men and beasts and birds, and with a variety of trees and flowers, all executed with such exquisite art that you regard them with delight and astonishment. Round this Palace a wall is built, inclosing a compass of 16 miles, and inside the Park there are fountains

and rivers and brooks, and beautiful meadows, with all kinds of wild animals (excluding such as are of ferocious nature), which the Emperor has procured and placed there to supply food for his gerfalcons and hawks, which he keeps there in mew. Of these there are more than 200 gerfalcons alone, without reckoning the other hawks. The Khan himself goes every week to see his birds sitting in mew, and sometimes he rides through the park with a leopard behind him on his horse's croup; and then if he sees any animal that takes his fancy, he slips his leopard at it, and the game when taken is made over to feed the hawks in mew. This he does for diversion.

Three centuries later, an English clergyman, Samuel Purchas, quoted Marco Polo's description in a collection of travellers' tales, *Purchas his Pilgrimes – or Relations of the world and the Religions observed in all ages and places discovered, from the Creation unto this Present*, published in 1614 – the same year Sir Walter Raleigh published his *Historie of the World*,

How Coleridge, in the dying years of the eighteenth century, came across Purchas's 1,200-page compilation, no-one really knows. Supposedly reading it while sitting in his chair, resting sick at a lonely farm on his own travels on foot across Exmoor in Southwest England, Coleridge later claimed to have fallen into a 'profound sleep, at least of the external senses,' as he himself later described. This apparently induced a three-hour dream or reverie,

during which time he has the most vivid confidence, that he could not have composed less than from two to three hundred lines; if that indeed can be called composition in which all the images rose up before him as things, with a parallel production of the correspondent expressions, without any sensation or consciousness of effort. On awakening he appeared to himself to have a distinct recollection of the whole, and taking his pen, ink, and paper, instantly and eagerly wrote down the lines that are here preserved. At this moment he was unfortunately called out by a person on business from Porlock, and detained by him above an hour, and on his return to his room, found, to his no small surprise and mortification, that though he still retained some vague and dim recollection of the general purport of the vision, yet, with the exception of some eight or ten scattered lines and images, all the rest had passed away like the images on the surface of a stream into which a stone had been cast, but, alas! without the after restoration of the latter.

In truth, Coleridge was an opium addict, having first been prescribed the drug Laudanum (tincture of opium) for various ailments, including an attack of dysentery. The poem he composed certainly showed signs of having been drug-induced, but whether in sleep or delusion, its truncated residue was enough to go down in the history of Romantic literature; *Kubla Khan; or, a Vision in a Dream: A Fragment*, beginning:

> In Xanadu did Kubla Khan
> A stately pleasure-dome decree:
> Where Alph, the sacred river, ran
> Through caverns measureless to man
> Down to a sunless sea.
> So twice five miles of fertile ground
> With walls and towers were girdled round:
> And there were gardens bright with sinuous rills,
> Where blossomed many an incense-bearing tree;
> And here were forests ancient as the hills,
> Enfolding sunny spots of greenery.
>
> But oh! that deep romantic chasm which slanted
> Down the green hill athwart a cedarn cover!
> A savage place! as holy and enchanted
> As e'er beneath a waning moon was haunted
> By woman wailing for her demon lover!...

Fearing to publish this strange, 54-line 'vision' (though Wordsworth's sister Dorothy mentioned its existence in her diary in

October 1798), Coleridge was only persuaded to do so by Lord Byron in April 1816, almost two decades later. Coleridge's wife thought publication of such a clearly drug-inspired dream a great mistake ('Oh! when will he ever give his friends anything but pain?' she wrote to a friend), but the publisher's payment of 80 pounds was duly accepted, and helped fund his continuing opium addiction.

Disparaged by many literary critics, the story of its genesis was also widely disbelieved. Purchas's huge book of narratives was unlikely to have been at the lonely Exmoor farm. Moreover, the arrival of a visitor from Porlock, interrupting the unconscious yet complete composition, seemed equally unlikely in that context. Nevertheless, the poem slowly became a favourite – even gaining special status as an early poetic description of the drug experience. By the end of the century, *Kubla Khan* was much anthologized; indeed, it was considered a work of genius.

As such, Kubla Khan duly inspired another work of genius, of great interest to biographers: that of a young student of English literature and rising radio and stage drama director, as well as aspiring American filmmaker, Orson Welles. Welles was fascinated both by the story of Emperor Kubla Khan, ruler of lands extending from Afghanistan to the Pacific, and his summer palace, Xanadu.

With a huge budget and full control of a still-undetermined new movie project commissioned by RKO studios in 1940, the 24-year-old Welles, along with his hugely experienced screenwriting assistant, Joseph Mankiewicz, decided that in creating a Kubla Khan-like emperor as a fictional character in modern-day America, 'Xanadu' would be the perfect name for the quasi-emperor's vast palace and grounds. The film would therefore begin with views of Xanadu. Moreover, the movie would be a pioneering, challenging, faux-biography, with even a faux-movie newsreel within the movie, to mimic the authenticity of a film biography. In the manner of the regular *March of Time* newsreels of the day, this faux-newsreel would have an unseen voiceover narrator, reporting in a deep voice the death of a major figure in American life – and where precisely he had died: Xanadu.

Here, on the deserts of the Gulf Coast, a private mountain was commissioned and successfully built. One hundred thousand trees, twenty thousand tons of marble are the ingredients of Xanadu's mountain. Contents of Xanadu's palace pictures, statues, the very stones of many another palace — a collection of everything so big it can never be catalogued or appraised; enough for ten museums; the loot of the world. Xanadu's livestock: the fowl of the air, the fish of the sea, the beast of the field and jungle. Two of each; the biggest private zoo since Noah. Like the Pharaohs, Xanadu's landlord leaves many stones to mark his grave. Since the Pyramids, Xanadu is the costliest monument a man has built to himself.

The technical feats that Welles – a neophyte in filmmaking – introduced in *Citizen Kane* were prodigious, including scratching the film negative of the faux-Xanadu newsreel to appear real. As the famous film critic Pauline Kael would later write, there was little doubt the 24-year-old was creatively talented, a genius, really – nor that, in making a movie about the life of a larger-than-life fictional American figure, Welles was indulging in a kind of autobiographical fantasy: achieving power and success. Joseph Mankiewicz's suggestion they base the film on the real-life career and sex-life of an actual American power player, the press magnate William Randolph Hearst (who also had three names, like Kane), was, however, inadvisable. It was, after all, a time when defamation of character – libel – was a criminal offence. Hearst, as a multi-millionaire with better things to do, would be unlikely to sue, and he did not – knowing, though, that he could use other, better means to nip the biographical film in the bud. Using proxies, he therefore offered RKO $800,000 to destroy it.

Unfortunately for Hearst, this only made Welles more anxious to finish and disseminate the potential libel. The very fact that William Randolph Hearst, the muckraking, amoral, 'yellow journalist' in America, would pay so much money (substantially exceeding the costs of making the movie) indicated to Welles that he had hit paydirt – for the commercial prospects of a biopic that was not even a real biopic were in truth limited. Hollywood never really made money on biopics; a fictional biopic would not make much, either. Controversy, by contrast, garners attention – and can sell. The likeness of Kane to Hearst as a well-known, controversial press magnate, famous for his 'yellow journalism,' could be played up, publicized and used to create a scandal – one that would match or even exceed the radio waves Welles had made with his Mercury Theater on the Air adaptation of H.G. Wells's *The War of the Worlds*, in 1938; a broadcast which had supposedly produced near-national panic in America by its evocation of reports of a Martian landing.

Welles, who had practised magic since childhood, had a haunting ability to mimic and mock reality. He insisted on the inviolability of his contract with RKO, and the tragi-comedy thereafter unfolded as Welles did his best to sensationalize his faux-biopic, while Hearst did everything he could to spoil Welles's projected triumph – even persuading major cinema chains to decline to show *Citizen Kane* in their cinemas when it was released in 1941, the summer before Pearl Harbor.

Thus, savaged but still reeling, so to speak, the thinly-veiled fictional biopic *à clef* hit at least some of America's screens, starring Welles himself as the Hearst-like central figure, John Foster Kane. Even the title, *Citizen Kane*, was a mockery of the way Hearst had posed as man of the people, while rich as Croesus.

As Kael later pointed out, the portrait of Kane bore little resemblance to Hearst in terms of Hearst's personality or character – which was far smaller, nastier and more loathsome than Welles' creation. But the resemblances to Hearst's lifestory were shockingly close – beginning with Xanadu, a spoof on Hearst Castle. For Hearst was famous for having built, in 1919, his own vast palace on a mountaintop in San Simeon, Southern California, boasting 56 bedrooms, 61 bathrooms, 19 sitting rooms, an airfield and a zoo, on a 240,000-acre ranch inherited from his father. Many famous folk were invitees there, from Charlie Chaplin and Greta Garbo to Franklin Roosevelt and Winston Churchill. Xanadu was, in short, an unmistakable allusion, despite being fictionally transposed to a faux-mountain location in Florida.

The fate of the film is well-known – a commercial flop, it was quickly dismissed in the incoming tide of World War II, when Americans looked to the enemy for examples of megalomania, not to their own leading figures. Over time, however, it gradually became recognized as a masterpiece by cinéastes and film critics in the 1960s such as André Bazin; indeed, by the end of the century it was repeatedly voted by critics the greatest film of all time.

Among faux-biographies, too, *Citizen Kane* of Xanadu was acknowledged as a masterpiece. Biographers cherished it as the most memorable visual paradigm for the biographical quest ever made; it became a key text for the teaching the art of biography itself – the film's storytelling skills and structure a model for aspiring biographers in any medium..

Ironically, though Welles and Mankiewicz were not actually sued for libel by Hearst, they were sued for copyright infringement and theft by Hearst's 1936 biographer, Ferdinand Lundberg. Though they defended and won the lawsuit, Welles later admitted the biographical information for Kane was stolen (i.e., taken without acknowledgement) from Lundberg's *Imperial Hearst*. He also confided that the haunting image of Xanadu owed its snarky contempt to 'Manky's' visits with his wife to Hearst Castle, and his abiding animus towards Hearst as a muckraker-in-chief. The portrait of John Foster Kane, himself, however was a combination of Mankiewicz's hostility and Welles's more playful fascination with power as it shapes personality. 'It was a kind of controlled, cheerful virulence,' Welles later described Mankiewicz's approach:

> I personally liked Kane, but I went with that. And that probably gave the picture a certain tension, the fact that one of the authors hated Kane and one loved him. But in his hatred

of Hearst, or whoever Kane was, Mank didn't have a clear enough image of who the *man* was. Mank saw him simply as an egomaniac monster with all these people around him.

It was Welles who had invested the character with a fearful charm – or, as the film and English literature professor, Robert Carringer, put it: 'Welles added the narrative brilliance — the visual and verbal wit, the stylistic fluidity, and such stunningly original strokes as the newspaper montages and the breakfast table sequence. He also transformed Kane from a cardboard fictionalization of Hearst into a figure of mystery and epic magnificence.'

From the opening sequence – the camera panning over the Xanadu estate, with its 'No Trespassing' sign and large 'K' welded on the gate – *Citizen Kane* is a kind of homage to the art and *process* of biography, biographers today recognize, as editors in a smoky projection room watch a newsreel summary of Kane's life and are told by their boss, Mr. Rawlston, they need to dig deeper than the myth; not only to decipher the potential meaning of Kane's last word, but to fill in his 'character.' And 'motivation':

> RAWLSTON: That's it – motivation. What made Kane what he was? And for that matter, what was he? What we've just seen are the outlines of a career – what's behind the career? What's the man? Was he good or bad? Strong or foolish? Tragic or silly? Why did he do all those things? What was he after?

And, Rawlston adds: even if Thompson, the investigative reporter, fails to discover the meaning of 'Rosebud,' he must 'Ask the question anyway, Thompson! Build the picture around the question, even if you can't answer it… Here's a man who might have been President. He's been loved and hated and talked about as much as any man in our time – but when he comes to die, he's got something on his mind called "Rosebud." What does that mean?'

Citizen Kane zigzags its way through Kane's life not as a chronology, in other words, but as an investigation of Kane's life, beginning at its end. It progresses with interviews with those who knew him best: his second wife, Susan Alexander; his banker-guardian, Mr. Thatcher; his friends; his employees; his butler – and their memories, shown in vivid flashbacks. There is also archival research; Thompson is permitted to read portions of Walter P. Thatcher's unpublished memoirs in the 'Thatcher Memorial Library,' under the watchful eye of spinster Bertha Anderson, the archivist:

> As we dissolve in, the door opens in and we see past Thompson's shoulders the length of the room. Everything very plain, very much made out of marble and very gloomy. Illumination from a skylight above adds to the general air of expensive and classical despair. The floor is marble, and there is a gigantic, mahogany table in the center of everything. Beyond this is to be seen, sunk in the marble wall at the far end of the room, the safe from which a guard, in a khaki uniform, with a revolver holster at his hip, is extracting the journal of Walter P. Thatcher. He brings it to Bertha as if he were the guardian of a bullion shipment.

For biographers, this archival scene and the investigative structuring of the whole black-and-white film is eye-candy of a special kind: a kind such as only biographers can perhaps truly relish. For them, the word 'Xanadu' does not mean a fragmentary, drug-induced vision or even a castle in Southern California. Rather, it is the visual key to their own profession: modern explorers of real lives, told with style.

Sources: Richard Holmes, *Coleridge: Early Visions, 1772-1804* (New York: Pantheon, 1999); Robert Carringer, *The Making of Citizen Kane* (Berkeley: California University Press, 1985); Pauline Kael, Orson Welles and Herman Mankiewicz, *Raising Kane* (Boston: Little, Brown, 1971); Nigel Hamilton, *Biography: A Brief History* (Cambridge, MA: Harvard University Press, 2007).

 # is for Youth

Of all aspects of modern biography, the matter of youth is arguably the most distinctive, perhaps even unique. Though other media address 'youth' in great detail in certain ways – say, for example, Young Adult novels – no other area of modern art or literature incorporates the developmental transition between adolescence and responsible adulthood as biography does; an aspect that goes to the heart of the genre as detective non-fiction.

How exactly an individual grows from youth to become an adult member of society: that is the question that haunts the modern biographer's quest. Was the character of the adult discernible in his youth? How did the years between 15 and 24, or even 30 (the UN's two official definitions of 'youth') help establish the character and even the later achievements – or lack of achievements – of the biographee? What do we *know* of those years in the case of the individual? And what can we discover?

Youth – the period of an individual's early years – has fascinated biographers since Greek and Roman times; in fact, it goes back to one of the first masterpieces of biography, Xenophon's *The Education of Cyrus*, written around 370 BC.

Xenophon had fought as a volunteer in the ill-fated mercenary Greek army, fighting on behalf of King Cyrus the Younger when attempting to take the throne from Cyrus's older brother, in Persia. It is believed Xenophon collected the information necessary for his biography of Cyrus during his military service there. In any event, his *Cyropedia* or *Education of Cyrus* broke entirely new literary ground, since Xenophon – a student of Socrates, and successor historian to Herodotus – never intended his biography to be history. Rather, he aimed to tell the story of *how* Cyrus became

Cyrus the Great, ruler of the largest empire of its time – and to do so, he set about recounting the development of Cyrus's character in his formative years. So powerful a work did the biography become that, over time, it became a kind of textbook in the study of leadership qualities, extolled by political thinkers from Cicero to Machiavelli, and from Machiavelli to John Adams. In this sense, Xenophon may even be said to have invented biography two centuries before Plutarch's famous claim to be writing 'not history, but lives.' Lives, though, that began with the search for evidentiary material in the *youth* of an individual, rather than relying only on the testimony and evidence of the subject's later years.

Xenophon, of course, idealized his chosen subject – an aspect of biography commonly considered under the rubric of excess enthusiasm or zeal, even if falling short of hagiography or religious ideology. The focus on Cyrus's youth – his adolescent impetuousness, his touching relationship with his grandfather, his willingness to contradict others, and his burning, teenage desire not to be restricted or imprisoned within the confines of the king's court for his own 'safety,' presented a wonderfully compelling account; one that helped explain Cyrus's extraordinary success in forming alliances or coalitions with other nations, and his ultimate victory over the armies of the Babylonian empire. Ultimately, he became King of Persia, King of Ashan, King of Media, King of Babylon, King of Sumer and Akkad, and King of the Four Corners of the World; even an 'anointed one' of the Jews, in *Isaiah* – the only non-Jew in the Bible to be so called, which was no mean feat.

All biographers in the almost 2,400 years since Xenophon's biography have therefore paid due attention to the youth or 'formative years' of their biographee, from Suetonius to Samuel Johnson, thus helping to make biography a wholly different, distinctive enterprise from history. What changed in the late eighteenth century, however, was the posthumous publication in 1782 of Jean Jacques Rousseau's *Les Confessions*: a work that transformed autobiography from self-adulation to self-examination, or memoir.*

Rousseau's self-appointed task was to be honest to the point where he could say to his Maker, on the Day of Judgement, 'This is what I have done, what I have thought, what I was.' And on that day Rousseau wanted not only his Maker but also his 'fellow-men' to hear his confessions: his 'lament for my unworthiness.' For them to witness him 'blush for my imperfections' – yet for each man to be forced to compare himself to Jean-Jacques 'with the same frankness, the secrets of his heart at the foot of the Throne, and say, if he dare, "*I was better than that man!*"' In other words, Rousseau was not, like St Augustine, merely appealing for God's forgiveness and mercy, but was making a statement of defiance: that he was no worse than any other mortal, nor needed any human being's forgiveness. And with that preface, Rousseau had set about telling the story of his youth, his travels, his romances, his religious training, his fellow men – and his women. It was not, like his contemporary Giacomo Casanova's memoirs, *The Story of My Life*, a self-lauding history of his sexual conquests, but a determined effort to examine his memories of youth and adulthood in order to find his inner identity as a person, behind the many books and articles he had written, and going back to his early years.

'I should have been quite happy to have Mademoiselle de Graffenried as a mistress,' Rousseau commented on the memory of the 'twelve hours' he had spent with her as a young man, for example; 'but, if it had depended entirely upon myself, I think I should have preferred her for an intimate friend.' And addressing not God, like Augustine, but his posthumous audience, Rousseau wrote:

> My readers will not fail to laugh at my love adventures, and to remark that, after lengthy preliminaries, even those which made the most progress, end in a kiss of the hand. O, my readers, do not be mistaken! I have, perhaps, had greater enjoyment in my amours which have ended in a simple kiss of the hand, than you will ever have in yours, which, at least, have begun with that!

Eschewing shame or embarrassment, Rousseau thus recorded his youth with unique, indeed revolutionary introspective candour, in literary terms – which in turn helps the reader to understand his revolutionary ideas as a social and political philosopher. Introspection thus became a modern phenomenon – but a problem, too for biographers. For whereas a man or woman might reveal in complete candour their *own* formative years in memoir, since there was no law of self-libel, it was another matter where biographies of other people were concerned. Recounting the story of someone else's formative (and later) years with similar frankness ran up against laws of libel, obscenity, copyright infringement, family objections, public hostility and social decorum.

Into the introspective gap between memoir and biography, therefore, stepped *The Sorrows of Young Werther* – an epistolatory, autobiographical ('fed with the blood of my heart') novel, written and published anonymously by Johann Wolfgang von Goethe in 1774, when he was only 24. It recorded (like Rousseau) a chaste love for a young woman, Charlotte – who was, however, engaged to an older man; and it results in Werther's broken-hearted suicide.

Sturm und Drang writers, followed by the Romantics and Victorian novelists, thereafter thrust themselves into Goethe's wake: male and female writers who admired the biographical trope in which youth is examined as an explicator of subsequent 'mature' life, but who, as writers of fiction, were unrestricted by the legal, social and cultural restrictions that shackled biographers. Thereby leaving biographers, as Virginia Woolf would later mock in her spoof biography *Orlando*, to 'plod' along behind.

The twentieth century, however, was to see a major change in the way real-life youth could be depicted and examined in biography. *The Education of Henry Adams*, written and privately printed for his friends by Henry Adams, in 1907 (but only published in 1918, after his death), reprised Rousseau's autobiographical introspection in the third person, namely as a biography of Adams by himself. The proud grandson of President John Quincy Adams, Adams-*grandfils* denounced his Victorian education and his stultifying upbringing in the classics, history and literature, which he considered unsatisfactory preparation for a new age of scientific advance and technological progress – and ever-more restrictive decorum. The book – which recorded Adams's Brahmin, Puritan WASP youth in Boston – a youth in which, he claimed, 'sex was a species of crime,' and where 'the monthly-magazine-made American female' possessed no feature 'that would have been recognized by Adam' – won him the posthumous Pulitzer Prize. Like Rousseau's *Confessions,* it swiftly became a classic; protected, still, by its legal status of autobiography. Once the legal and social conventions shackling biography were removed, however, it would be the biographers' turn – which came, decades later, after World War II.

Unshackled both by Freudian discourse and major post-war economic and cultural changes in the West, the legal restraints on biographers' rights to examine in depth the formative years of a biographee with the same candour as novelists were gradually lifted. By the 1960s and 1970s, 'youth' became synonymous with a cultural revolution as, in conservatives' eyes, 'morality, authority and discipline disintegrated' in the West (as the social historian Arthur Marwick put it). And, in that era of 'counter-culture,' a renewed field of biographical enquiry began, as biographers sought to explore and discover the mysteries of psychological, social and sexual character-development, as demonstrated in specific real-life individuals. Coinciding with an explosion of new pedagogy and youth-protest, the new focus served to make biography a core aspect of modern culture, since few people were now satisfied with traditional stories of achievement per se; readers wished to know the inner developmental story of that achievement. Youth, in short, became the new *anvil* of biography. So much so that, by the late 1980s and early 1990s, no serious life of a major historical figure, whether in art, literature, music, science or politics, could be undertaken without forensic, candid study of the biographee's early years.

Richard Perceval Graves's *Robert Graves: The Assault Heroic 1895-1926* pointed the way in 1986; the first volume of a trilogy in which he unabashedly recorded Graves's early years, experience of war,* and tumultuous, adulterous affair that gave rise to *Goodbye to All That*.

The publishers of the *Cambridge Biography of D.H. Lawrence*, for their part, also commissioned three volumes – each one to be written by a different biographer. The first of these, John Worthen's *D.H. Lawrence: The Early Years*, appeared in 1991 and chronicled the first 27 years of the novelist's life. In a 626-page account, Worthen left no stone unturned in his search to record the writer's formative experiences, culminating in Lawrence's masterpiece, *Sons and Lovers*. As the three biographers noted in a collective preface to the trilogy, 'to have three people write his life is an explicit (even dramatic) acknowledgement that, however important the continuities, the Lawrence of the last years (for example) is so different from the nineteen-year-old who visited the Haggs Farm' in his youth that at times it seemed 'only by accident that they share the same name.' The development was extraordinary – yet Lawrence was also a man who had also remained, at a deeper level, the same: 'somewhere still the same Bert who rushed with such joy to the Haggs,' as Lawrence himself observed when later recalling, at the age of 43, he had not even dared hold hands with his longtime early girlfriend, Jessie Chambers. Between his exclusively 'non-physical,' 'spiritual' relationship with Chambers and his profoundly sexual relationship with Mrs. Frieda Weekley, *née* von Richthofen, at the age of 26, however, a convulsive, life-changing drama had taken place – one that Worthen charted with profound empathy and strikingly fresh, forensic literary scholarship.

Freud had been at pains to locate the deepest and most formative psychological and sexual experience in the early childhood or infancy of his patients. While not entirely dismissing such notions of nursery sexuality, biographers in the late twentieth century found their supposedly Freudian impact hard to substantiate. They thus preferred to highlight the experiences of adolescence and early adulthood, instead, as the key to understanding the formation of individual character, and the clue to later achievement. In a rapidly technologically accelerating world in which attention spans were reducing, this put forensically-detailed biography somewhat at odds with the approaching twenty-first century – a new century which undoubtedly spurred the trend towards 'partial' biography, in which only a very limited, dramatic period of a real life could be addressed in great detail. Yet Worthen's study of Lawrence's youth became a classic, indispensable to any reader of Lawrence's later work and his place in English literature. Moreover it was joined by a veritable cohort of similar 'doorstop-sized' works addressing the youth of the biographee, whether in literature, art, politics or science; works such as Martin Stannard's *Evelyn Waugh: the Early Years, 1903-1939* (1986), John Richardson's *A Life of Picasso, Volume 1: 1881-1906* (1991), Nigel Hamilton's *JFK: Reckless Youth* (1992), Blanche Wiesen Cook's *Eleanor Roosevelt, Volume One, 1884-1933* (1992), Peter Guralnick's *Last Train to Memphis: The Rise of Elvis Presley* (1994), Hilary Spurling's *The Unknown Matisse: A Life of Henri Matisse: The Early Years, 1869-1908* (1998), and onwards to Ilan Stavans's *Gabriel García Márquez: The Early Years* (2010) and Reiner Stach's *Kafka: Die frühen Jahre* (2013, English edition: *Kafka: The Early Years*, 2017).

In each case, the biographer achieved something *no historian had ever done*, or could do without becoming a biographer: namely, to research into the biographee's youth in unmatchable depth, detail, candour and context. This provided the reader not only with a rich portrait of an individual's early years, but also, in doing so, offered revelatory insights into the individual's later life and career – often focusing on 'turning-points' or breakthrough moments in the individual's coming-of-age, either as a person or in their achievements – or both.

Worthen's painstaking reconstruction of Lawrence's life in Nottinghamshire, for example, offered new depth and colour to a reader's appreciation of the genesis of *Sons and Lovers* – especially in its record of Lawrence's relationship with his mother, Lydia Lawrence. The eventual novel – which began in manuscript as 'Paul Morel' – might well have been called 'Sons and Mothers.' But Worthen, recording in new detail the story of Lawrence's infatuation with the sensual German wife of a modern languages professor at Nottingham University College, invested Mrs. Frieda Weekley – through quotation from her contemporary letters – with a powerful, engaging personality, sufficient to jolt Lawrence finally out of his mother-obsessed, class-conscious and depressed world. *'Was hier so uneträglich ist: es giebt keine lebendigen Menschen,'* Frieda had written to a friend, depicting the people of Nottingham as *'Dickhäuter, Schlafhauben, Gänse Enten'* – dinosaurs, retards, fat and waddling ducks. What Frau Weekley really wanted to do was give them all *'ein gewaltiger Fusstritt'* – a huge kick up the backside. She had already enjoyed a passionate affair with the Austrian psychoanalyst Otto Gross in 1907 in Munich, among other lovers she had taken 'on the side' to assuage her boredom and dissatisfaction with her marriage (at the age of 20), and escape from English decorum. Gross – a brilliant disciple of Freud, and neo-pagan drug-addict – had declared Frieda to be 'a woman of the future': one who had managed to slough off 'two thousand bleak years of spells and filth' to overcome 'Christianity, Democracy, and chaste morality and all that heap of shit.' Five years later, aged 32 and six years older than Lawrence, Frieda had therefore cast a distinctly post-Victorian, pagan spell on the working-class, struggling, would-be novelist – prompting Worthen to ask rhetorically, in the context of the lovers' virtually penniless getaway to Germany and Italy in 1912, 'how much Frieda influenced Lawrence' in the writing of his pre-Frieda portrait of his mother in *Sons and Lovers.*

It is in the question that Worthen posed – and the answer he gave – that lies the great benefaction of biography in addressing the early years of a real individual's life. For what Worthen did was not only to record for posterity the formative years of a great English twentieth-century novelist, but he was able to locate and narrate the turning-point in Lawrence's path from son to man, and from aspiring artist to great writer – 'the greatest imaginative novelist of our generation,' as E.M. Forster later called Lawrence. Worthen's narrative account was – and remains – a phenomenal biographical achievement; one that put on virtuoso display the new skills and fresh contribution of the biographer to modern letters. Not because the biography was itself a work of art – which Worthen's work was never intended to be – in terms of architecture, language and style, but because, in its patient, relentless narrative quest to reach the 'heart of darkness,' it was storytelling that penetrated to the very kernel of human character and its development to maturity.

Stannard's insights into the shocking impact in 1929 of his first wife Evelyn's sexual betrayal (as Waugh saw it) upon the later Waugh novels; Richardson's insights into the crucial importance to Picasso of his early female models and muses upon his art; Hamilton's insights into JFK's youthful efforts to forge independence from his ogre-like father, and the impact it would have on the fate of Lend-Lease in World War II, as well as JFK's subsequent political trajectory; Wiesen Cook's insights into Eleanor Roosevelt's early years, and her 'outing' as a woman's woman, following her husband's tempestuous affair with Lucy Mercer, with major consequences, once her husband became US President: these and other insights could only have been made – and have been acknowledged by readers as unimpeachable – by biographers willing to do the years of research, forensic investigation and revelation of their subjects' early years: the anvils of their subsequent lives.

Other writers would harness those skills and incorporate them in full, single-volume biographies, such as Ron Chernow's *Alexander Hamilton* (2004), Kai Bird and Martin Sherwin's *American Prometheus: The Triumph and Tragedy of J. Robert Oppenheimer* (2005), or Hermione Lee's *Edith Wharton* (2007). But by then, the central role of the individual biographer in modern letters as the interpreter and storyteller of historical lives, from early years to the later ones, had been incontestably established. The biographer – not only the biographee – finally counted.

Sources: John Dillery, *Xenophon and the History of his Times* (London: Routledge, 1995); Arthur Marwick, *The Sixties* (Oxford: Oxford University Press, 1998); Nigel Hamilton, *Biography: A Brief History* (Cambridge, MA: Harvard University Press, 2007); Hermione Lee, *Biography: A Very Short Introduction* (Oxford: Oxford University Press, 2009); Hans Renders, Binne de Haan and Jonne Harmsma (eds), *The Biographical Turn: Lives in History* (London: Routledge, 2017).

 **is for Zigzagging to the End**

With the letter Z, we come to the end of our alphabetical journey through biography. And since the end in a biography is death, let us look squarely at the Grim Reaper.

It is remarkable that among the books that have been written about biography so few have addressed death. Yet of all the events that go into a life – from birth to love, marriage, children, a house ('the full catastrophe,' as Kazantzakis' hero, Zorba, put it) – death is probably its most distinctive and certainly inevitable feature.

For a start, death comes in many forms, from old age to assassination, and from disease to murder. Or suicide. The details of such endings are of scant intrinsic interest to historians or sociologists, since they are primarily interested in discovering or establishing patterns of behaviour and society. The biographer, by contrast, is interested in how an actual individual's life came to an end, *as closure* – indeed it is remarkable how, for psychological reasons, the relatives of a deceased individual often find it difficult to come to terms with the person's death if there is no body to bury, or cremate. And so it is in biography; death brings closure to the life, whether it is a noble departure or an unworthy one.

Suicide notes, famous last words, Last Will and Testaments – these, like popular quotations – are a kind of coda to this part of the biographical undertaking. Supposedly famous last words, however, are usually unsubstantiated. Did Frank Sinatra really say, 'I'm losing it,' before expiring? Did Marie-Antoinette really step on the executioner's toe before laying her head beneath the guillotine and apologize to him, saying 'Pardonnez-moi'? There are whole compendia of such purported sayings, but we read them tongue-in-cheek, as a kind of mockery of the end – 'O death where is thy sting?' – since few of us are unafraid of death, or rather: how we shall meet it on the day.

Thus we turn, for real sustenance, to serious biography, where we have some hope of learning the truth: the verification of the end; the last recorded words, the last rites, the last tears, which bring closure to an individual's actual life, compelling us to consider the course and meaning of that life, and reflect on our own. In this respect, it is where biography first began: with the encomium, or eulogy. James Agee's *Let Us Now Praise Famous Men*, published in 1941, became an instant classic for recording – and praising – the lives of 'ordinary' impoverished tenant farmers and sharecroppers in the American South during the Great Depression – drawing its title from the Book of Ecclesiasticus, or Ben Sira. Agee's book reminds us that, in the Darwinian sense, life is a struggle for survival – one which biographers record, but which will end inevitably with death, whether or not one believes in an afterlife. The inevitability of death, as a contrast to life, thus gives life its quality of vividness, however grotesque. Without the death of the subject, it follows, a biography is like an unfinished work of art or music. Death completes the life, for good or ill.

To some extent, of course, death has lost its sting, since we do not die so young, are less religious, and are helped on our way out with drugs. The Victorians, by contrast, paid great attention to the end, both in life and in biography. With the decline in religious fervour in the twentieth century (save for fundamentalist and evangelical sects), their attention to death gave way to a different, more nuanced, ironic lens. Thomas Mann's great novella, *Death in Venice*, published in 1911, portrayed an ageing writer's homoerotic fascination with a Polish boy, Tadzio, leading the hero to ignore warnings of cholera in the watery city and to find death on the beach – a sort of precursor to the AIDS epidemic seventy years later. Biographers like Lytton Strachey certainly took note of Mann's stance: death as a corruption not only of the body, but of life and love. Strachey's account of the passing of Cardinal Manning (1807-1892), in *Eminent Victorians* (1917), became a new model: perhaps the most perfectly paced, devastatingly cruel account of personal ambition masquerading as spiritual quest in a real individual ever composed by a biographer. By the end of Strachey's detailed account of how Manning converted to Roman Catholicism, then sought to deny cardinal status to his elderly mentor, Henry Newman, the reader is longing for Manning's come-uppance; which Strachey provided. 'So, though Death came slowly, struggling step by step with that bold and tenacious spirit,' Strachey recounted, 'when he did come at last the Cardinal was ready. Robed in his archipiscopal vestments, his rochet, his girdle, and his mozzetta, with the scarlet biretta on his head, and the pectoral cross upon his breast,' the former Episcopalian

> made his solemn Profession of Faith in the Holy Roman Church. A crowd of lesser dignitaries, each in the garments of his office, attended the ceremonial. The Bishop of Salford held up the Pontificale and the Bishop of Amycla bore the wax taper. The provost of Westminster, on his knees, read aloud the Profession of Faith, surrounded by the Canons of the Diocese. Towards those who gathered about him, the dying man was still able to show some signs of recognition, and even, perhaps, of affection; yet it seemed that his chief preoccupation, up to the very end, was with his obedience to the rules prescribed by the Divine Authority. 'I am glad to have been able to do everything in due order,' were among his last words.

Which led Strachey, in turn, to quote Dostoevsky's novel *The Adolescent*, regarding men of such overweaning pride that they cannot be humble before others: "'Si fort qu'on soit," says one of the profoundest of the observers of the human heart, "on peut éprouver le besoin de s'incliner devant quelqu'un ou quelque chose. S'incliner devant Dieu, c'est toujours le moins humiliant."'

This did not end Strachey's sarcastic description, however. 'The funeral was the occasion of a popular demonstration such as has rarely been witnessed in the streets of London,' he continued.

> The route of the procession was lined by vast crowds of working people, whose imaginations, in some instinctive manner, had been touched. Many who had hardly seen him declared that in Cardinal Manning they had lost their best friend. Was it the magnetic vigour of the dead man's spirit that moved them? Or was it his valiant disregard of common custom and those conventional reserves and poor punctilios which are wont to hem about the great? Or was it something untameable in his glances and in his gestures? Or was it, perhaps, the mysterious glamour lingering about him, of the antique organisation of Rome? For whatever cause, the mind of the people had been impressed; and yet, after all, the impression was more acute than lasting.

'The Cardinal's memory is a dim thing today,' Strachey ended his account.

> And he who descends into the crypt of that Cathedral which Manning never lived to see, will observe, in the quiet niche with the sepulchral monument, that the dust lies thick on the strange, the incongruous, the almost impossible object which, with its elaborations of dependent tassels, hangs down from the dim vault like some forlorn and forgotten trophy – the Hat.

The biographer, in other words, was claiming the right, in chronicling death, to use death as his authorial right to review the life – and to find it wanting. Ever since Strachey, the death scene as both as the end of a life and as the pivot for an author to reconstruct and re-assess an individual's real life has only grown in importance. Today, the biographer who downplays death is in grave danger of failing in his task – one which Hermione Lee, in her *Biography: A Very Short Introduction* (2009) likened to that of an autopsy, or the 'process of posthumous scrutiny.'

Such scrutiny can be sad, but it can also be wickedly suggestive – or both. Oleg Chlevnjoek's biography of Joseph Stalin begins, for example, with the report of the death of the Soviet leader, written on the basis of several eyewitness accounts. On 2 March 1953, after a day of anxious hesitation, a bodyguard walked into Stalin's office uninvited and found the almost 75-year-old dictator lying on the floor. The floor beneath Stalin, however, was damp. Problem. In fact, a big one. The bodyguard was one of 408 servants charged with looking after, and guarding, the Secretary-General of the Communist Party in the Kremlin, and in his various dachas. Would the bodyguard survive if it was heard he had found Stalin lying in his own urine? There were feverish discussions throughout the day between political leaders, the security service and the house staff on how to act; the great leader had not asked for food in the morning, and no one was allowed to enter the room without being summoned by Stalin. Even his private doctors did not dare to enter his room without permission, let alone touch him. Thanks to his own dictatorial rules, then, the man who had so much blood on his hands died, lying unfed and in his own waste matter...

Strachey would certainly have approved of this reversal – for death certainly concentrates the mind of the biographer. Death is the end, but also the beginning of biographical enquiry. Death defines biography as a genre, and though it raises questions, the biographer is usually humble enough to know he will not necessarily be able to answer them. The biography of Jan Campert, the Dutch poet, for example, ends with the simple sentence: 'In the hierarchy of known facts about Jan Campert, one thing is clear: that on 12 January 1943, the poet died in a concentration camp.'

Requiescat in pace.

Sources: Jacqueline Bel, *Bloed en Rozen* (Amsterdam: Prometheus/Bert Bakker, 2015); Oleg Chlevnjoek, *Stalin. De Biografie* (Amsterdam: Nieuw Amsterdam, 2015; Helge Hesse, *Dan liever de lucht in! De wereldgescchiedenis in 75 beroemde uitspraken* (Amsterdam: De Arbeiderspers, 2008); Hans Renders, *Wie weet slaag ik in de dood. Biografie van Jan Campert* (Amsterdam: De Bezige Bij, 2004); Hermione Lee, *Biography: A Very Short Introduction* (Oxford: Oxford University Press, 2009).

Bibliography

Allen, Richard and Malcolm Turvey, 'Introduction', Ludwig Wittgenstein, *Philosophical Investigations* (Oxford: Basil Blackwell, 1967).
Andersen, Kurt, *Fantasyland: How America Went Haywire: A 500-Year History* (New York: Random House, 2017).
Appleby, Joyce, Lynn Hunt and Margaret Jacob, *Telling the Truth about History* (New York: Norton, 1994).
Augustine, Saint, *Confessions*, tr. R.S. Pine-Coffin (London: Penguin, 1961).
Baar, Mirjam de, Yme Kuiper and Hans Renders, *Biografie en religie. De religieuze factor in de biografie* (Amsterdam: Boom, 2011).
Backscheider, Paula, *Reflections on Biography* (Oxford: Oxford University Press, 1999).
Baets, Antoon De, 'Postume Privacy en reputatie', in: Hans Renders and Gerrit Voerman, *Privé in de politieke biografie* (Amsterdam: Boom/Biografie Instituut, 2007), 108-123.
Bakewell, Sarah, *At the Existentialist Café* (New York: Other Press, 2016).
Barbey d'Aurevilly, J., *Les Ridicules du temps* (Paris: Éd. Rouveyre et G. Blond, 1883).
Barthes, Roland, 'The Death of the Author', in: *Aspen* (1967), 5–6.
Batchelor, John (ed.), *The Art of Literary Biography* (Oxford: Oxford University Press, 1995).
Bel, Jacqueline, *Bloed en Rozen* (Amsterdam: Prometheus/Bert Bakker, 2015).
Boorstin, Daniel, *Image: A Guide to Pseudo-Events in America* (New York: Harper, 1961).
Boswell, James, *The Life of Samuel Johnson LL.D.*, 1791.
Boucharenc, Myriam, *L'Écrivain-reporter au coeur des années trente* (Villeneuve d'asq Cédex: Presses Universitaires du Septentrion, 2004).
Boynton, Robert, 'Till Press Do Us Part: The trial of Janet Malcolm and Jeffrey Masson,' *The Village Voice*, November 28, 1994.
Briggs, Julia, *Virginia Woolf: An Inner Life* (London: Allen Lane, 2005).
Brockmeier, Jens, 'Identity', in: Margaretta Jolly (ed.), *Encyclopedia of Life Writing* (London: Fitzroy Dearborn, 2001).
Brownlow, Kevin, *Napoleon, Abel Gance's Classic Film* (New York: Knopf, 1983).
Bruneau, Jean (ed.), *Correspondance Flaubert; III: Janvier 1859 – Décembre 1868* (Paris: Gallimard, 1991).
Brusse, Peter, 'Celebration of life', in: Hans Renders (ed.), *Het leven van een doodsbericht. Necrologie en Biografie* (Amsterdam: De Bezige Bij, 2005), 75-88.
Burridge, Richard A., *What are the Gospels? A Comparison with Graeco-Roman Biography* (Michigan/Cambridge: Wm. B. Eerdmans Publishing Co, 2004).
Carringer, Robert, *The Making of Citizen Kane* (Berkeley: California University Press, 1985).
Cheney, Theodore, *Writing Creative Nonfiction: Fiction Techniques for Crafting Great Nonfiction* (Berkeley, CA: Ten Speed Press, 2001).
Chlevnjoek, Oleg, *Stalin. De Biografie* (Amsterdam: Nieuw Amsterdam, 2015).

Coates, Ta-Nehisi, 'The First White President', *The Atlantic*, October 2017.
Crews, Frederick, *Freud: The Making of an Illusion* (New York: Henry Holt, 2017).
Custen, George, *Bio/Pics: How Hollywood Constructed Public History* (New Brunswick, NJ: Rutgers University Press, 1992).
Dekker, Peter, blog 16 October 2010.
Dillery, John, *Xenophon and the History of his Times* (London: Routledge, 1995).
Dilthey, Wilhelm, *Der Aufbau der geschichtlichen Welt in den Geisteswissenschaften* (1910), in: Bernard Groethuysen (ed.), *Gesammelte Schriften* (Teubner/Vandenhoeck & Ruprecht, 1927), vol. VII.
Eaton, Arthur, *History Telling: The Rise and Fall of Psychohistory* (Leiden: Brill, 2018).
Edel, Leon, *Literary Biography* (London: Rupert Hart-Davis, 1957).
Edel, Leon, *Writing Lives: Principia Biographia* (New York/London: W.W. Norton & Company, 1984).
Ellis, Jack and Betsy McLane, *A New History of Documentary Film* (New York: Continuum, 2005).
Elms, Alan, *Uncovering Lives: The Uneasy Alliance of Biography and Psychology* (Oxford: Oxford University Press, 1994).
Etty, Elsbeth, 'Doden hebben geen privacy. Het persoonlijke in de politieke biografie', in: Hans Renders and Gerrit Voerman (eds), *Privé in de politieke biografie* (Amsterdam: Boom, 2007), 97-107.
Evans, Richard J., *In Defence of History* (New York: Norton, 1999).
Fellman, Susanna and Marjatta Rahikainen (eds), *Historical Knowledge in Quest of Theory, Method and Evidence* (Cambridge: Cambridge Scholars Publishing, 2012).
Ferrer, Sean, *Audrey Hepburn, An Elegant Spirit: A Son Remembers* (New York: Atria Books, 2005).
Folkenflik, Robert (ed.), *The Culture of Autobiography: Constructions of Self-Representation* (Stanford, CA: Stanford University Press, 1993).
Furia, Philip, 'As Time Goes By,' in: Carolyn Forché and Philip Gerard (eds), *Writing Creative Nonfiction* (Cincinatti: Story Press, 2001).
Gabler, Neal, '"Chappaquiddick" is Bad History,' *New York Times*, April 7, 2018.
Gay, Peter, *Freud: A life For Our Time* (New York: Norton, 1988).
Gaddis, John Lewis, *The Landscape of History* (Oxford: Oxford University Press, 2002).
Gelder, Roelof van, *Naporra's omweg. Het leven van een VOC-matroos (1731-1793)* (Amsterdam: Atlas, 2003).
Goodwin, James, *Autobiography: The Self Made Text* (New York: Twayne Publishers, 1993).
Hamilton, Nigel, *JFK: Reckless Youth* (New York: Random House, 1992).
Hamilton, Nigel, *Biography: A Brief History* (Cambridge, MA: Harvard University Press, 2007).
Hamilton, Nigel, *How To Do Biography: A Primer* (Cambridge, MA: Harvard University Press, 2008).
Hamilton, Nigel, 'Biography as corrective', in: Hans Renders et al. (eds), *The Biographical Turn: Lives in History* (London: Routledge, 2017).

Harrison, Brian, 'A Slice of Their Lives: Editing the DNB, 1882-1999', in: *English Historical Review* 119 (2004), 484, 1179-1201.

Hawthorne, Julian, 'Journalism the Destroyer of Literature' in: *The Critic* 48 (1906) February, 166-177.

Hentea, Marius, *TaTa Dada, The Real Life and Celestial Adventures of Tristan Tzara* (Cambridge, MA: MIT Press, 2014).

Hesse, Helge, *Dan liever de lucht in! De wereldgeschiedenis in 75 beroemde uitspraken* (Amsterdam: De Arbeiderspers, 2008).

Hitchens, Christopher, *God is Not Great: How Religion Poisons Everything* (New York: Grand Central Publishing, 2007).

Hofmannsthal, Hugo von and Ottonie Grafin Degenfeld, *Briefwechsel* (Frankfurt am Main: S. Fischer, 1986).

Holmes, Richard, *Coleridge: Early Visions, 1772-1804* (New York: Pantheon, 1999).

Homberger, Eric and John Charmley, *The Troubled Face of Biography* (New York: St Martin's Press, 1998).

Houghton, Walter E., *The Victorian Frame of Mind, 1830-1870* (New Haven/London: Yale University Press, 1957), 110-180.

Howes, Craig, 'Collective Biography', in: Margaretta Jolly (ed.), *Encyclopedia of Life Writing* (London: Fitzroy Dearborn, 2001).

Hume, Janice, *Obituaries in American Culture* (Jackson: University Press of Mississippi, 2000).

Jefferson, Ann, *Biography and the Question of Literature in France* (Oxford: Oxford University Press, 2007).

Johnson, E.W. and Tom Wolfe (eds), *The New Journalism* (New York: Harper & Row, 1973).

Johnson, Marilyn, *The Dead Beat* (New York: HarperCollins, 2006).

Johnson, Samuel, *Life of Savage*, ed. Clarence Tracy (Oxford: The Clarendon Press, 1971, original 1744).

Kael, Pauline, Orson Welles and Herman Mankiewicz, *Raising Kane* (Boston: Little, Brown, 1971).

Kelley, Kitty, *The Royals* (New York: Grand Central, 1997).

Kelley, Kitty, 'Unauthorized, But Not Untrue. The real story of a biographer in a celebrity culture of public denials, media timidity, and legal threats', in: *The American Scholar*, December 1, 2010.

Kendrick, Walter, *The Secret Museum: Pornography in Modern Culture* (Berkeley: University of California, 1987).

Kieft, Ewoud, *Oorlogsenthousiasme: Europa 1900-1918* (Amsterdam: De Bezige Bij, 2015).

Kuitert, Lisa, '"Reading the Body": Authors' Portraits and their Significance fot the Nineteenth-Century Reading Public', in: J. Arianne Baggerman et al. (eds), *Controlling Time and Shaping the Self. Developments in Autobiographical Writing since the Sixteenth Century* (Leiden/Boston: Brill, 2011).

Lahr, John, *Tennessee Williams: Mad Pilgrimage of the Flesh* (New York: Norton, 2014).

Lancaster, Jordan, 'Royal Biography', in: Margaretta Jolly, ed., *Encyclopedia of Life Writing: Autobiographical and Biographical Forms* (London: Fitzroy Dearborn, 2001).

Larkin, Philip, *High Windows* (New York: Farrar, Strauss and Giroux, 1974).

Lee, Hermione, *Biography: A Very Short Introduction* (Oxford: Oxford University Press, 2009).

Lee, Sidney, *Principles of Biography* (Cambridge: Cambridge University Press, 1911).

Lehman, Daniel, *Matters of Fact: Reading Nonfiction over the Edge* (Columbus: Ohio State University, 1997).

Lepore, Jill, 'After the Fact. In the history of truth, a new chapter begins', in: *The New Yorker*, March 21, 2016.

Magnússon. Sigurður Gylfi, 'The Life Is Never Over: Biography as a Microhistorical Approach', in: Hans Renders et al. (eds), *The Biographical Turn: Lives in History* (London: Routledge, 2017), 42-52.

Makari, George, *Revolution in Mind: The Creation of Psychoanalysis* (New York: HarperCollins, 2008).

Makarova, Arina, 'Necrologieën in de Franse pers 1800-2000', in: Hans Renders (ed.), *Het leven van een doodsbericht. Necrologie en Biografie* (Amsterdam: De Bezige Bij, 2005), 43-59.

Malcolm, Janet, *The Silent Woman* (New York: Knopf, 1994).

Malcolm, Janet, *Two Lives: Gertrude and Alice* (New Haven: Yale UP, 2007).

Marnham, Patrick, *The Man Who Wasn't Maigret* (New York: Farrar, Straus & Giroux, 1993).

Marwick, Arthur, *The Sixties* (Oxford: Oxford University Press, 1998).

Maychick, Diana, *Audrey Hepburn: An Intimate Portrait* (New York: Birch lane, 1993).

McCullough, Jeanne, interview with Leon Edel, 'The Art of Biography', *Paris Review* (1985) 98.

Munslow, Alun, *Deconstructing History* (London: Routledge, 1997).

Myers, Stephen Lee, *The New Tsar: The Rise and The Reign of Vladimir Putin* (New York: Alfred A. Knopf, 2015).

Nadel, Ira Bruce, *Fiction, Fact and Form* (New York: St Martin's, 1984).

Nadel, Ira Bruce, 'Fingerprint or Photograph?', in: *Cercle*, (2015) 35.

Nicolson, Nigel, *Portrait of a Marriage* (London: Weidenfeld and Nicolson, 1973).

Novarr, David, *The Lines of Life: Theories of Biography, 1880-1970* (West Lafayette, Indiana: Perdue University Press, 1986).

Plutarch, *Fall of the Roman Republic*, tr. Rex Warner (London: Penguin, 1958).

Plutarch, *Vitae parallellae*, numerous editions.

Power, Tristan and Roy Gibson, *Suetonius the Biographer: Studies in Roman Lives* (Oxford: Oxford University Press, 2014).

Rainer, Tristine, *Your Life as Story: Discovering the 'New Autobiography' and Writing Memoir as Literature* (New York: Putnam, 1997).

Renders, Hans and Sjoerd van, 'The Biograhpical Turn in the Field of Knowledge', in: Hans Renders, Binne de Haan en Jonne Harmsma (red.), The Biographical Turn. Lives in History, Routledge, (Londen/New York: Routledge, 2017), 91-103.

Renders, Hans, *Wie weet slaag ik in de dood. Biografie van Jan Campert* (Amsterdam: De Bezige Bij, 2004).

Renders, Hans, 'Did Pearl Harbor Change Everything? The Deadly Sins of Biographers', in: *Journal of Historical Biography* 1 (2008) 3, 98-123.

Renders, Hans, 'The limits of representativeness: Biography, life writing and microhistory', in: Hans Renders and Binne de Haan (eds), *Theoretical Discussions of Biography: Approaches from History, Microhistory, and Life Writing* (Leiden/Boston: Brill, 2014), 129-138.

Renders, Hans, 'Contemporary values of life. Biographical Dictionaries', in: Hans Renders and Binne de Haan (eds), *Theoretical Discussions of Biography. Approaches from History, Microhistory, and Life Writing* (Leiden/Boston: Brill, 2014), 94-101.

Renders, Hans, 'Roots of Biography. From Journalism to Pulp to Scholarly Based Non-Fiction', in: Hans Renders and Binne de Haan (eds), *Theoretical Discussions of Biography. Approaches from History, Microhistory, and Life Writing* (Leiden/Boston: Brill, 2014), 24-42.

Renders, Hans, 'Biography is not a Selfie: Authorisation as the Creeping Transition from Autobiography to Biography', in: Hans Renders et al. (eds), *The Biographical Turn. Lives in History* (London: Routledge, 2017), 159-164.

Renders, Hans and Binne de Haan, 'Introduction: The Challenges of Biography Studies', in: *Theoretical Discussions of Biography: Approaches from History, Microhistory, and Life Writing* (Leiden/Boston: Brill, 2014), 1-8.

Renders, Hans and Binne de Haan, 'Roots of Biography. From Journalism to Pulp to Scholarly Based Non-Fiction', in: Hans Renders and Binne de Haan (eds), *Theoretical Discussions of Biography: Approaches from History, Microhistory, and Life Writing* (Boston/Leiden: Brill, 2014), 24-42.

Renders, Hans and Binne de Haan (eds), *Theoretical Discussions of Biography. Approaches from History, Microhistory, and Life Writing* (Leiden/Boston: Brill, 2014).

Renders, Hans, Binne de Haan and Jonne Harmsma (eds), *The Biographical Turn: Lives in History* (London: Routledge, 2017).

Revel, Jacques, *Jeux d'Echelles. La micro-analyse à l'expérience* (Paris: Gallimard/Le Seuil, 1996).

Reynolds, David, *In Command of History: Churchill Fighting and Writing the Second World War* (New York: Random House, 2005).

Rhiel, Mary and David Suchoff (eds), *The Seductions of Biography* (New York: Routledge, 1996).

Riblet Gabriel, *Ces chers disparus. Essai sur les annonces nécrologiques dans la presse francophone* (Paris: Éditions Albin Michel, 1992).

Roberts, Brian, *Biographical Research* (Buckingham: Open University Press, 2002).

Rollyson, Carl, *Documentary Film: A Primer* (New York: iUniverse, 2004).

Rollyson, Carl, *A Higher Form of Cannibalism? Adventures in the Art and Politics of Biography* (Chicago: Ivan R. Dee, 2005).

Rollyson, Carl, 'Authorized Biography', in: Carl Rollyson, *Biography: A User's Guide* (Chicago: Ivan R. Dee, 2008), 10-17.

Rose, Jacqueline, *The Case of Peter Pan or The Impossibility of Children's Fiction* (London/Basingstoke: Macmillan, 1984).

Rosenthal, Alan (ed.), *Why Docudrama? Fact-Fiction on Film and TV* (Carbodale: Southern Illinois University Press, 1999).

Runyan, W.M., *Life Histories and Psychobiography: Explorations in Theory and Method* (Oxford: Oxford University Press, 1982).

Rutherford, Adam, *A Brief History of Everyone Who Ever Lived* (New York: Experiment, 2017).

Santora, Marc, 'Holocaust Law in Poland Chips at Shared Pain', *The New York Times*, February 7, 2018.

Schud, Willi (ed.), *Richard Strauss – Hugo von Hofmannsthal. Briefwechsel* (Zürich/Freiburg i. Br.: Atlantis Musikbuch-Verlag, 1952, 5th ed. 1978).

Seghal, Parul, 'A Writer Aware of Her Contradictions', *New York Times*, October 11, 2017.

Sereny, Gitta, *Albert Speer: His Battle with Truth* (New York: Random House, 1995).

Shribman, David, 'Yes, the Truth Still Matters,' *New York Times*, December 12, 2017.

Sisman, Adam, *Boswell's Presumptuous Task: The Making of the Life of Dr. Johnson* (New York: Farrar Strauss, 2001).

Southgate, Beverley, *History Meets Fiction* (Harlow: Longman, 2009).

Stone, Lawrence, 'Prosopography' in: *Daedalus*, Winter 1971, 46-9.

Strachey, Lytton, *Eminent Victorians* (New York: Modern World Library, 1918).

Suetonius, *The Twelve Caesars*, tr. Robert Graves (London: Allen Lane, 1979).

Shapiro, Barbara J., *A Culture of Fact. England, 1550-1720* (Ithaca/London: Cornell University Press, 2000).

Starck, Nigel, *Life after the Death: The Art of the Obituary* (Melbourne: Melbourne University Press, 2006).

Stephen, Leslie, 'Emerson,' in: *Studies of a Biographer* (London: Duckworth, 1902).

The Epic of Gilgamesh, tr. N.K. Sandars (London: Penguin, 1972).

Thompson, Hunter S., *Fear and Loathing on the Campaign Trail '72* (New York: Simon & Schuster, 1971).

Turner, A. Richard, *Inventing Leonardo* (Berkeley: University of California, 1992).

Tosh, John, *The Pursuit of History* (New York: Longman, 1995).

Trela, D.J., 'Carlyle', in: Margaretta Jolly (ed.), *Encyclopedia of Life Writing* (London: Fitzroy Dearborn, 2001).

Tuchman, Gaye, 'Objectivity as Strategic Ritual: An Examination of Newsmen's Notions of Objectivity', in: *American Journal of Sociology* 77 (1972) 4, 660-679.

Wendorf, Richard, *The Elements of Life: Biography and Portrait-Painting in Stuart and Georgian England* (Oxford: Clarendon Press, 1990).

Winchester, Simon, *The Meaning of Everything. The Story of the Oxford English Dictionary* (Oxford: Oxford University Press, 2004).

Wiesenthal, Christine, 'Ethics and the Biographical Artifact: Doing Biography in the Academy Today,' in: ESC: *English Studies in Canada* 32 (2006) 2-3, 63-81.

Wood, Gordon S., *The Purpose of the Past* (New York: Penguin, 2008).

Woodward, K., *Questioning Identity: Gender, Class, Ethnicity* (London: Routledge, 2004).
Young, James, *Cultural Appropriation and the Arts* (Oxford: Blackwell, 2015).
Young, Kevin, *Bunk: The Rise of Hoaxes, Humbug, Plagiarists, Phonies, Post-Facts, and Fake News* (Minneapolis: Graywolf Press, 2017).
Zinsser, William (ed.), *Inventing the Truth: The Art and Craft of Memoir* (Boston: Houghton Mifflin, 1998).
Zomerdijk, Marije, 'Een ideaal lijk. Necrologieën in de Nederlandse krant', in: Hans Renders (ed.), *Het leven van een doodsbericht. Necrologie en Biografie.* (Amsterdam: De Bezige Bij, 2005), 140-155.

Index

Abele, Robert 11
Ackroyd, Peter 21
Adams, Henry 29, 222-223
Adams, Herbert Baxter 69
Adams, John 7, 200, 220, 222
Adenauer, Konrad 117
Agee, James 230
Agrippina, Vipsania 167
Ailes, Roger 105-106
Alcibiades (warlord) 77
Alexander the Great 172, 209
Alexander, Susan 218
Alexandra Feodorovna 96
Alexievich, Svetlana 208
Alfred (king) 199
Ali, Mohammed (pseudonym of Cassius Marcellus Clay) 164
Allen, Richard 58
Andersen, Kurt 24, 92, 98, 101, 110
Anderson, Bertha (Georgia Backus) 218
Apollinaire, Guillaume 190
Appleby, Joyce 76
Aristotle (philosopher) 43
Arnold, Thomas 60
Arp, Hans 191
Artaxerxes (king) 209
Asdrubal (Barca) 77
Assurbanipal (ruler of Assyria) 120
Atwood, Margaret 21
Auden, W.H. 61, 173
Augustine (from Hippo) 113-114, 172-173, 221
Augustus (emperor) 151-152, 167, 173
Aulus Hirtius 151
Aurelius, Marcus 30, 94

Baar, Mirjam de 166
Backscheider, Paula 128
Baets, Antoon De 44, 50
Baggerman, J.A. 40
Bair, Deidre 125
Bakewell, Sarah 63-64, 67
Ball, Hugo 191-192
Balzac, Honoré de 161, 173
Barbey d'Aurevilly, Jules 35-36, 86-87, 92
Barnes, Julian 21, 30, 57, 161
Barnum, P.T. 116
Barrus, Tim *see* Nasdijj

Barry, du Madame (Jeanne Bécu) 197
Barthes, Roland 20, 24
Batchelor, John 32
Bate, Jonathan 48-49
Bateman, Mary 49-50
Baudelaire, Charles 173
Bauer, Carlene 21
Bax, Maarten 11
Bazin, André 216
Beardsley, Aubrey 173
Beauvoir, Simone de 174
Beckman, Max 203
Bel, Jacqueline 233
Ben Sira 230
Bentham, Jeremy 130
Berenson, Bernard 142
Berkeley, George 16, 157
Bernays, Minna 144
Bernhardt, Sarah 173
Bernstein, Leonard 173
Beschloss, Michael 126
Beyle, Marie-Henri *see* Stendhal
Bird, Kai 227
Blair, Eric *see* Orwell, George
Blake, Hohn Lauris 38, 173
Bloch, Robert 146
Boccacio, Giovanni 173
Boer, Frank de 11
Boer, Ronald de 11
Boleyn, Anne 173, 197
Bonnie Parker 200
Boorstin, Daniel 55, 58
Borgia, Cesare 77, 200
Borgia, Lucrezia 173
Boswell, James 17, 86, 149-150, 153, 157, 173
Boswell, Tetty 150
Boucharenc, Myriam 89, 92
Boyle, T.C. 21
Boynton, Robert 154-157
Brady, Matthew 36
Brando, Marlon 131
Brands, H.W. 74
Brecht, Bertolt 173
Briggs, Julia 32
Brockmeier, Jens 84
Brontë, Charlotte 116
Brontë, Emily 116
Brown, Daniel 124

Browne, Thomas 32
Browning, Robert 32
Brownlow, Kevin 201
Bruneau, Jean 192
Buff, Charlotte 222
Bullock, Alan 83
Burns, Ken 209
Burns, Robert 173
Burridge, Richard A. 166
Burton, Richard 170
Bury, J.B. 69
Bush, George W. 56, 105
Byatt, A.S. (pseudonym of Antonia Susan Drabble) 130
Byron, G.G. 173, 213

Callas, Maria (pseudonym of M.A.S.C. Kalogeropoulos) 173
Campert, Jan 233
Camus, Albert 173
Capote, Truman (pseudonym of Truman Streckfus Persons) 22, 123-124
Caravaggio, M.M. Da 173
Carlyle, Thomas 78, 84
Carmiggelt, Simon 133
Caro, Robert 20, 28, 31, 47, 90, 125-127, 162, 180
Carpenter, Humphrey 61-62
Carringer, Robert 217-218
Carroll, Lewis (pseudonym of C.L. Dodgson) 23
Carter, Jimmy 92
Casanova, Giacomo 115, 174, 221
Catiline, L.S. 77
Cellini, Benvenuto 115
Cervantes, Miguel de 79
Chadeau, Emmanuel 45
Chalmers, Robert 130
Chamberlain, Neville 200
Chambers, Jessie 224
Chaplin, Charlie 216
Charcot, Jean-Martin 112, 146
Charmley, John 24, 128
Chateaubriand, F.R. de 114
Cheney, Theodore 128
Chernow, Ron 57, 62, 125, 227
Chesterfield, lord (P.D. Stanhope) 39
Chlevnjoek, Oleg 232-233
Chomsky, Noam 20
Churchill, Clementine 47
Churchill, Randolph 174
Churchill, Winston 47, 117, 174, 180, 195, 199-200, 206, 208-209, 216

Cicero, Marcus Tullius 220
Clark, Leon Pierce 143
Clark, Mark 117
Cleopatra (queen) 94, 152, 170
Clinch, Nancy Gager 143
Clinton, William J. [Bill] 55-56
Clyde Barrow 200
Coates, Ta-Nehisi 101
Cocteau, Jean 190
Colbert, Stephen 56-57
Coleridge, Herbert 38
Coleridge, Samuel Taylor 210-213, 218
Communes, Philippe de 114
Comte, Auguste 37
Congreve, William 32
Conrad, Joseph [born Joseph Korzeniowski] 111
Conway, Kellyanne 109
Cook, Blance Wiesen 20, 74, 225, 227
Corneille, Pierre 79
Crews, Frederick 144, 148
Cromwell, Thomas 97
Cryer, Jon 11
Custen, George 197, 201
Cyrus the Great (Cyrus the Elder) 220
Cyrus the Younger (king) 219

Daguerre, Louis 36
Dallek, Robert 74
Danton, Georges 197
Debrie, André 197
Defonseca, Misha 80
Degenfeld, Ottonie von 192
Dekker, Peter 166
Demetrius (Poliorketes) 209
Demosthenes (statesman) 209
Derks, Thea 13-14
Derrida, Jacques 19-20, 71-72, 161, 183
Diana (princess) [born Spencer] 131
DiCaprio, Leonardo 145
Dickens, Charles 111, 116, 154, 161, 199
Diderot, Denis 39
Didion, Joan 91
Dietrich, Marlene 134
Dieudonné, Albert 197
Dillery, John 228
Dilthey, Wilhelm 181, 184
Dion (of Syracuse) 209
Dix, Otto 203
Dodge Mary Abigail *see* Hamilton, Gail
Donaldson, Frances 96
Donaldson, William 133
Donne, John 32

Dössekker, Bruno *see* Wilkomirski, Binjamin
Dostoejevsky, Fyodor 161, 231
Douglass, Frederick 116
DuBarry, Jeanne 197
Duchamp, Marcel 143
Dumas, Alexandre 116

Eaton, Arthur 148
Edel, Leon 27, 32, 58, 73, 177-178
Edward VIII 96-97
Einstein, Albert 163
Eliot, George 111, 162
Elizabeth I 124, 197
Elizabeth II 97, 199
Ellis, Jack 201
Ellmann, Richard 146
Elms, Alan 148
Elton, Geoffrey 70
Emerson, Ralph Waldo 77-79, 84
Erikson, Erik 143
Este, Carlo D' 203
Etty, Elsbeth 43, 50
Eumenes (of Cardia) 209
Evans, Richard J. 69, 71, 76

Faassen, Sjoerd van 192
Farrell, James J. 135
Farrell, Nicholas 28
Fellman, Susanna 110
Ferguson, Niall 74, 180
Fest, Joachim 83, 207
Fitzgerald, Zelda 163
Flaherty, Robert 196
Flaubert, Gustave 30, 57, 161, 168, 192
Flemings, Thomas 62
Fliess, Wilhelm 144
Foch, Ferdinand 206
Folkenflik, Robert 119
Forché, Carolyn 128
Forster, E.M. 79, 227
Foucault, Michel 75
Fourier, Charles 105
Frank, Anne 19
Franklin, Benjamin 116
Fraser, Antonia 96, 127
Freud, Sigmund 26-27, 43, 139-147, 156, 200, 224, 226
Frey, James 109
Fricker, Sara 213
Fritzsche, Peter 207, 209
Fry, Roger 25, 80, 122
Furia, Philip 127-128

Gaal, Louis van 12
Gabler, Neal 201
Gaddis, John Lewis 76
Gance, Abel 1 97, 200-201
Gandhi, Mahatma 143
Gans, Evelien 22
Garbo, Greta (pseudonym of Greta Lovisa Gustafsson) 216
Gasteren, Joséphine van 55
Gasteren, Louis van 55
Gaulle, Charles de 117
Gautreau, Virginie (Madame X) 195
Gay, Peter 146, 148
Geminius, Gaius 172
Gerard, Philip 128
Gershwin, Ira 127-128
Ghandi, Mahatma 143
Gibson, Roy 157
Gide, André 188
Gilbert, Martin 74
Gilgamesh (king) 120-121, 128
Gladstone, William 121-122
Gleick, James 34
Glendenning, Victoria 125
Goethe, Johann Wolfgang von 222
Goldstein, Rebecca 178
Goodwin, Doris Kearns 49, 74, 126
Goodwin, James 119
Gordon, C.G. 60
Gordon, Lyndall 20
Gordon-Reed, Annette 56, 66, 74
Gosse, Edmund 32, 177
Gosse, Philip Henry 32, 163
Gould, Vanessa 136
Grant, Ulysses S. 115
Graves, Richard Perceval 204, 209, 224
Graves, Robert 175, 203-205, 209, 224
Gray, Thomas 32
Greene, Graham 164
Greer, Germaine 45
Groethuysen, Bernard 184
Gropius, Walter 105
Gross, Otto 226
Grosz, George 203
Guderian, Heinz 207
Guralnick, Peter 225
Gussows, Mel 133

Haan, Binne de 15, 24, 32, 40, 92, 110, 185, 192-193, 209, 228
Hadrian (emperor) 150, 199
Halifax (lord) E.F.L. Wood 200
Hamilton, Alexander 57, 62, 99, 163, 227

243

Hamilton, Gail (pseudonym of Mary Abigail Dodge) 87-89
Hamilton, Ian 45-46, 91, 132, 196
Hamilton, Nigel 8, 24, 32, 40, 50, 67, 84, 92, 101, 110, 148, 175, 184, 209, 225, 227-228
Hanlo, Jan 49
Hardy, Thomas 111, 116, 162
Hari, Badr 11
Harmsma, Jonne 192, 228
Harrison, Brian 40
Hasdrubal (Barca) 77
Hašek, Jaroslav 204
Hawkins, John 153
Hearst, William Randolph 214-217
Heidegger, Martin 63-64
Hemings, Sarah (Sally) 56, 66
Hemingway, Ernest 163
Hennings, Emmy 191
Henry VIII 97
Henta, Marius 189, 192
Hepburn Ferrer, Sean 14-15
Hepburn, Audrey (pseudonym of Audrey Ruston) 14-15, 131
Herodotus (historian) 202, 219
Hesse, Helge 233
Hillenbrand, Laura 124
Hippocrates (physician) 41
Hirohito (emperor) 78
Hitchens, Christopher 158, 166
Hitler, Adolf 30, 43, 69-70, 78, 80-81, 83-84, 88, 134, 143-144, 147, 180, 185-186, 198, 203, 206-207
Hoberg, Annegret 188
Hofmannsthal, Hugo von 187, 192-193
Holinshed, Raphael 95
Holmes, Richard 30-31, 125, 218
Holroyd, Michael 104, 106-108, 146
Homberger, Eric 24, 128
Homer (poet) 120
Honegger, Arthur 197
Houten, Carice van 11
Howes, Craig 60, 67
Huelsenbeck, Richard 191
Hughes, Ted 46, 48-49, 175
Hughes-Orchard, Carol 48
Hugo, Victor 36
Hume, Janice 134, 138
Hunt, Lynn 76
Husserl, Edmund 20

Ibsen, Henrik 32
Irving, David 44, 206

Isaacson, Walter 31, 62, 90, 145

Jacob, Margaret 76
Jacob, Max 190
James, Henry 48, 73
Janco, Marcel 191
Jaurès, Jean 188
Jefferson, Ann 40
Jefferson, Thomas 56, 134
Jobs, Steve 62
Johnson, C.A. (Lady Bird) 47
Johnson, E.W. 92
Johnson, Lyndon 28, 47, 90, 162, 180
Johnson, Marilyn 131-132, 138
Johnson, Samuel 16-17, 39, 85-86, 92, 119, 145, 149-150, 153, 157, 174, 176, 220
Jolly, Margaretta 84, 101
Jones, Ernest 144
Jones, Margaret B. *see* Seltzer, Margaret
Julia (daughter of Augustus) 167
Julius Caesar 29, 94, 151
Jung, C.G. 26, 43, 139, 141-142, 145

Kael, Pauline 214-215, 218
Kafka, Franz 225
Kazantzakis, Nicos 229
Keitel, Wilhelm 207
Kelley, Kitty 12, 14-15, 97, 101
Kendrick, Walter 175
Keneally, Thomas 124
Kennedy, Edward 201
Kennedy, Jacqueline 100, 131
Kennedy, John F. 47, 100, 136, 152, 165, 172, 199, 225, 227
Kennedy, Ludovik 96
Kershaw, Ian 74, 83-84, 207
Kesselring, Albert 207
Keynes, John Maynard 19
Khan, Genghis 199, 210
Kieft, Ewoud 192
Kiernan, Denise 66
King, Larry 12
King, Martin Luther 164
Kinsey, Alfred 79
Kissinger, Henry 180
Knox, Ronald 26, 164
Kopechne, Mary Jo 201
Kossman, Ernst 181
Krafft-Ebing, Richard 145
Kruger, Jules (also Jean-Paul Mundviller) 197
Kruseman, A.C. 34, 38
Kuiper, Yme 166

Kuitert, Lisa 40

Lacan, Jacques 20, 161, 183
Lages, Willy 55
Lahr, John 163, 166
Lamar, Hedy 127
Lancaster, Jordan 101
Langer, Walter 143
Lanjuinais, Victor 135
Larkin, Philip 168-169, 175
Laroche, Josepha 191
Larson, Erik 124
Lawrence, D.H. 168, 203, 224-227
Lawrence, Lydia 226
Lawrence, Thomas Edward (Lawrence of Arabia) 199, 204
Layard, A.H. 120
Lazarus, Emma 105
Lee, Hermione 31, 91, 125, 227-228, 232-233
Lee, Sydney 17, 38, 40, 177
Leeuw, Reinbert de 13-14
Lehman, Daniel 156-157
Leonardo da Vinci 26, 43, 90, 139-145, 200
Lepore, Jill 58
Levi, Primo 22, 206
Lewis, C.S. 61
Limbaugh, Rush 105-106
Lin, Maya 18
Lincoln, Abraham 99
Lipstadt, Deborah 44
Livia 151-152
Lough, David 180
Louis XIV 97
Lovell, Mary 65
Loyd George, David 189
Lucius Antonius 151
Lundberg, Ferdinand 216
Luther, Martin 29, 143, 164

MacArthur, Douglas 28, 117
Machiavelli, Niccolò 220
MacLaine, Shirley (pseudonym of Shirley MacLean Beaty) 136-137
Maechler, Stefan 22
Magnússon, Sigurdur Gylfi 185
Makari, George 148
Makarova, Arina 138
Malcolm X (pseudonym of Malcolm Little) 164
Malcolm, Janet 48-49, 90, 125, 154-157, 162

Mankiewicz, Joseph (Mank) 213-214, 216-218
Mann, Heinrich 203
Mann, Thomas 88, 230
Manning, H.E. 60, 230-232
Manstein, Erich 117
Mantel, Hilary 97
Marc, Franz 188
Marco, Enric 22
Marie-Antoinette (queen) 229
Mark Antony (general) 151
Marlowe, Christopher 95
Marnham, Patrick 175
Márquez, Gabriel García 225
Marwick, Arthur 175, 223, 228
Marx, Karl 69, 105
Mary Stuart 96, 197
Massie, Robert 96
Masson, Jeffrey 154-155, 157
Matisse, Henri 225
Maugham, William Somerset 166
Maurois, André (pseudonym of E.S.W. Herzog) 177
Maychick, Diana 14-15
Mazlish, Bruce 143
McCourt, Frank 126
McCullough, David 28, 31-32, 127
McGinniss, Joe 155
McKinley, William 100
McLane, Betsy 201
Meijer, Jaap 22
Mercer, Johnny 128
Mercer, Lucy 227
Merleau-Ponty, Maurice 63
Messinger, Philip 51
Michaud, Louis-Gabriel 37
Mill, James 143
Mill, John Stuart 143
Miller, Arthur 134
Miller, Henry 117, 146
Milton, John 127
Miranda, Lin-Manuel 57
Mondrian, Piet 17
Monk, Ray 58
Monroe, Marilyn (pseudonym of Norma Jeane Mortenson) 134, 199
Montaigne, Michel de 63, 113
Montgomery, Bernard 117, 199
Morel, Paul 226
Moreri, Louis 33
Morris, Edmund 20, 31, 125, 127
Morris, Roger 100
Moses, Robert 90

245

Muhammad (prophet) 199
Mulisch, Harry 13
Mundviller, Jean-Paul (*see* Kruger, Jules)
Munslow, Alun 72, 76
Murdoch, Iris 64
Murdoch, Rupert 81, 106
Mussolini, Benito 28, 78
Myers, Stephen Lee 92

Nadel, Ira Bruce 58, 122, 128
Nanook (eskimo) 197
Napoleon Bonaparte 164, 197-198, 200-201, 203, 207
Nasaw, David 74
Nasdijj (pseudonym of Tim Barrus) 109
Newman, Henry 231
Nicolas II 95-96
Nicolson, Harold 169, 177
Nicolson, Nigel 169, 175
Nightingale, Florence 60
Nixon, Richard 100-101, 105, 136, 143, 154
North, Thomas 95
Novarr, David 177, 180, 184

Onassis, Jackie *see* Kennedy, Jacqueline
Oppenheimer, J. Robert 227
Orwell, George (pseudonym of Eric Arthur Blair) 51
Owen, Robert 105, 203

Pater, Walter 140
Pathé, Charles 197
Pathé, Émile 197
Patton, George 203
Paulinius (alleged lover of Theodocia) 51
Pelopidas (general) 209
Pétain, Philippe 207
Phocion (statesman) 209
Piaf, Édith (pseudonym of Édith Giovanna Gassion) 134
Picasso, Pablo 163, 225, 227
Pimlott, Ben 74
Pine-Coffin, R.S. 175
Piozzi (Hester Lynch Thrale) 153
Plath, Sylvia 46, 48-49, 175
Pliny (the Elder) 35
Plotina (Hadrian's wife) 150
Plutarch (L. Mestrius) 7, 18, 31, 35, 59-61, 64-65, 67, 74, 94-95, 101, 171-172, 175-176, 202, 209, 220
Polo, Marco 210-211
Pompey the Great 172

Porter, Cole 127
Pound, Ezra 127
Power, Tristan 157
Presley, Elvis 132, 225
Presser, Jacques 103
Proust, Marcel 186-187
Pulitzer, Joseph 87
Purchas, Samuel 211, 213
Putin, Vladimir 92, 180
Pyrrhus of Epirus 209

Rahikainen, Marjatta 110
Rainer, Tristine 119
Raleigh, Walter 41, 94-95, 211
Ranke, Leopold von 69
Rasmussen, Dennis 66
Rasson, Hormuzd 120
Rawlinson, Henry 120
Rawlston (Philip Van Zandt) 217
Reagan, Ronald 105
Reichenthal, Laura *see* Riding, Laura
Remarque, Erich Maria 204
Renders, Hans 8, 15, 24, 32, 40, 50, 84, 92, 110, 138, 166, 185, 192-193, 209, 228, 233
Reynolds, David 209
Rhiel, Mary 32
Riblet, Gabriel 138
Richard II 95
Richard III 95
Richardson, John 225, 227
Richthofen, F.F. *see* Weekley, Frieda
Riding, Laura (pseudonym of Laura Reichenthal) 203
Riefenstahl, Leni 198
Roberts, Andrew 74
Roberts, Brian 152, 157
Rochefoucauld, duke of (François VI) 114
Rohe, Mies van der 105
Rollyson, Carl 15, 24, 201
Rommel, Erwin 207
Roosevelt, Eleanor 163, 225, 227
Roosevelt, Franklin 99, 147, 154, 216
Roosevelt, Theodore 99
Root, Henry (pseudonym of Charles William Donaldson) 133-134
Rose, Jacqueline 58
Rosenthal, Alan 201
Rousseau, Jean-Jacques 114-115, 117-118, 220-223
Rufilla (alleged mistress of Mark Antony) 152
Rundstedt, Gerd von 207

Runyan, W.M. 148
Rutherford, Adam 67
Rutte, Mark 165

Sackville-West, Vita 169
Saint-Exupéry, Antoine de 45
Saint-Simon (Louis de Rouvroy) 114
Saint-Simon, Henri de 105
Salerno, Shane 91
Salinger, J.D. 45, 91, 132
Salvia Titisenia 152
Samuel, Raphael 71
Sand, George (pseudonym of A.L.A. Dudevant) 34
Sandars, N.K. 128
Santora, Marc 76
Sargent, John Singer 195
Sartre, Jean-Paul 63-64, 161
Sassoon, Siegfried 203
Saussure, Ferdinand de 71, 161
Savage, Richard 86
Schlegel, Friedrich 115
Schmid, Jeanette 134
Schmidt, Benito Bisso 50
Schnitzler, Arthur 146
Schrödinger, Erwin 72
Schud, Willi 193
Scott, C.P. 53
Seailles, Gabriel 140
Seghal, Parul 175
Seltzer, Margaret (pseudonym of Margaret B. Jones) 57, 80, 109
Sereny, Gitta 207, 209
Severini, Gino 190
Seymour-Smith, Martin 205, 209
Shakespeare, William 22, 26, 41, 69, 94-95, 100
Shapiro, Barbara J. 58
Sherman, Gabriel 106
Sherwin, Martin 74, 227
Shields, David 91
Shreve, Peter 130
Shribman, David 109-110
Simenon, Georges 174
Simpson, Wallis 96
Sinatra, Frank 12, 134, 229
Sisman, Adam 149, 153, 157
Sittenfeld, Curtis 21
Skidelsky, Robert 19, 80
Smith, Canon 131
Smith, George 120-121
Sobel, Dava 31
Socrates (philosopher) 219

Solzhenitsyn, Alexander 43
Speer, Albert 207, 209
Spengler, Oswald 69-70
Spurling, Hilary 225
Stach, Reiner 225
Stalin, Joseph 78, 159, 232-233
Stannard, Martin 225, 227
Starck, Nigel 138
Stavans, Ilan 225
Steegmuller, Francis 190
Stein, Gertrude 125, 128
Stendhal (pseudonym of Marie-Henri Beyle) 116
Stephen, Leslie 37-38, 84, 116, 177
Stevens, Cat, also Yusuf Islam (pseudonym of Stephen Demetre Georgiou) 164
Stone, Lawrence 59, 67, 71
Strachey, Lytton 42, 60-62, 67, 116, 122, 124-125, 128, 145-146, 177, 203, 230-233
Strauss, Richard 193
Suchoff, David 32
Suetonius, Gaius 18, 31, 41-42, 60-61, 64, 94, 101, 150, 152, 157, 167, 175, 184, 220
Sutherland, Graham 47, 195
Švejk, Josef 204

Talese, Gay 91
Taylor, Elizabeth 133, 170
Temple, William 53
Terentilla (alleged mistress of Mark Antony) 152
Tertulla (alleged mistress of Mark Antony) 152
Thackeray, W.M. 116, 162
Thatcher, Walter P. 218
Thayer, William 177
Theodisius II 51
Theodocia (wife of Theodisius II) 51
Thomas, Dylan 158
Thomas, Edward 203
Thompson, Hunter S. 91-92
Thucydides (historian) 29, 202
Tiberius (emperor) 167
Timoleon (of Corinth) 209
Titisenia, Salvia (alleged mistress of Mark Antony) 152
Tjeenk Willink, H.D. 34
Toklas, Alice 125, 128
Tolkien, J.R.R. 61
Tolstoy, Lev 52, 161, 168, 176
Tomalin, Claire 31, 125
Torianus (slave-dealer) 151

Tosh, John 76
Tracy, Clarence 92
Trajan (emperor) 150
Trefusis, Violet (pseudonym of Violet Keppel) 169
Treitschke, Heinrich von 69
Trela, D.J. 84
Trevor-Roper, Hugh 80-81
Trollope, Anthony 87
Truman, Harry 28
Trump, Donald 62, 98, 147
Tuchman, Gaye 165-166
Turner, A. Richard 148
Turvey, Malcolm 58
Twain, Mark (pseudonym of S.L. Clemens) 200
Tynan, Kenneth 133
Tzara, Tristan (pseudonym of Sami Rosenstock) 189-192

Ullrich, Volker 180

Valéry, Paul 140
Vasari, Giorgio 35
Veenstra, Piet 13
Veer, Paul van 't 133
Verne, Jules 36
Victoria (queen) 200
Vinci, Leonardo Da see Leonardo
Voerman, Gerrit 50

Wagner, Richard 83
Wallage, Christine 45
Walters, Barbara 12
Warhol, Andy 123
Warlimont, Walter 207
Warner, Rex 175
Warren, Austin 177
Washington, George 99
Watson, James 66
Watt, Richard 95
Waugh, Evelyn 25-27, 61, 164, 168, 225, 227
Weber, Bruce 136-137
Weekley, Frieda (pseudonym of F.F. Richthofen) 224, 226
Weir, Alison 74

Wellek, René 176-177
Welles, Orson 162, 210, 213-218
Wells, H.G. 215
Wendorf, Richard 201
Wette, Wolfram 209
Wevill, Assia 175
Wharton, Edith 227
White, Erdmute Wenzel 191
White, Hayden 70-71
Wiesenthal, Christine 50
Wilcox, Margaret 79
Wilde, Oscar 57, 146
Wilhelm II (emperor) 95
Wilkomirski, Binjamin [born Bruno Grosjean] (pseudonym of Bruno Dössekker) 22, 206
Williams, Charles 61, 207
Williams, Tennessee 163
Wills, Gary 100
Wilson, Angus 26
Wilson, William P. 136
Winchester, Simon 40
Winfrey, Oprah 12, 80
Wittgenstein, Ludwig 58, 182
Wolfe, Tom 90-92, 103, 105-106, 123
Wolpers, David 199
Wood, Gordon S. 76
Woodward, K. 84
Woolf, Virginia [born A.V. Stephen] 25, 32, 37, 42, 47, 57, 90, 116, 122-123, 125, 169, 177, 222
Wordsworth, Dorothy 212
Wordsworth, William 212
Worthen, John 224-227

Xenephon (of Athens) 18, 202, 219-220, 228

Young, James 84
Young, Kevin 109-110

Zagt, Ab 11
Zaslav, David 106
Ziegler, Philip 96
Zinsser, William 118-119
Zizka, Jan 7
Zomerdijk, Marije 135, 138

About the authors

Nigel Hamilton, former Professor of Biography at de Montfort University and currently Senior Fellow in the McCormack Graduate School, University of Massachusetts Boston, is the author of 27 works of biography and memoir, including the NYT bestselling *JFK: Reckless Youth* and *Biography: A Brief History*. Awarded the Whitbread Prize for Biography and the Templer Medal for Military History, his *Mantle of Command: FDR at War, 1941-1942* was longlisted for the National Book Award in 2014. He is currently completing his 'FDR at War' trilogy.

Hans Renders is Professor of the History and Theory of Biography and Director of the Biography Institute at the University of Groningen, the Netherlands. He has acted as a juror for many international literary prizes, including the Plutarch Award and Erik Hazelhoff Biography Prize. He has authored and co-authored many publications in the field of (literary) history and biography, including major biographies of the poets Jan Hanlo and Jan Campert. In cooperation with Sjoerd van Faassen, he is currently writing the life of the artist Theo van Doesburg, founder of *De Stijl*.

A true *Fundgrube* for both writers and readers of biographies. In 26 beautiful essays, Nigel Hamilton and Hans Renders – both impressive biographers – describe every conceivable aspect of biography. For everybody who wants to know why we should never read an authorized biography and is curious to learn why a new biography of John F. Kennedy comes out every month. Read and feast!
  Elsbeth Etty, biographer, critic and columnist

For students of biography, for experts, and for anybody who's just interested in how the lives of individuals tell the story of our time, this exquisite volume serves as a road map – and provocative spur.
  John A. Farrell, journalist and author of Richard Nixon: The Life, *and* Clarence Darrow: Attorney for the Damned, *winner of the Los Angeles Times Award for Best Biography of the Year*

Nigel Hamilton and Hans Renders' compact and companionable *ABC of Modern Biography* is an essential guide, certain to be cherished by both readers and writers. I learned and laughed, and lingered over many an entry. Take it along on your own journey through life!
  Megan Marshall, Pulitzer Prize-winning author of Margaret Fuller, The Peabody Sisters, *and* Elizabeth Bishop: A Miracle for Breakfast

An incisive yet remarkably comprehensive introduction to the controversies and complexities of biography by two of the world's leading authorities on the subject. Contemporary examples of biographical practice are put into the context of the history of biography, beginning with Plutarch. No scholar or student of biography can afford to ignore this indispensable volume about an indispensable genre. Bravo!
  Carl Rollyson, biographer of Susan Sontag, Rebecca West, Marilyn Monroe, Michael Foot and William Faulkner

The rise of biography is the literary event of our time; Hamilton and Renders are its pioneer scholars, and their compelling primer is a must-read.
  Joanny Moulin, President of the Biography Society, Institut Universitaire de France